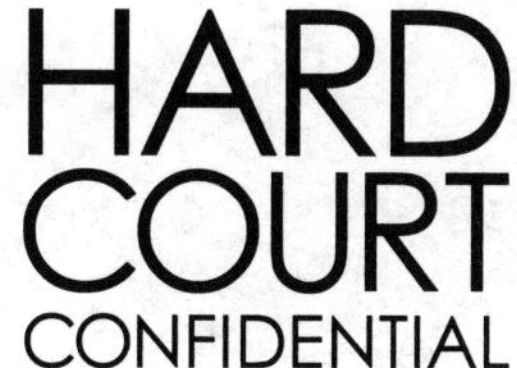
HARD
COURT
CONFIDENTIAL

HARD COURT CONFIDENTIAL

TALES FROM TWENTY YEARS IN THE PRO TENNIS TRENCHES

PATRICK McENROE

with Peter Bodo

HYPERION
NEW YORK

Library of Congress Cataloging-in-Publication Data has been applied for.
ISBN: 978-1-4013-2381-3

Hyperion books are available for special promotions and premiums. For details contact the HarperCollins Special Markets Department in the New York office at 212-207-7528, fax 212-207-7222, or e-mail spsales@harpercollins.com

Book design by Renato Stanisic

FIRST EDITION
10 9 8 7 6 5 4 3 2 1

THIS LABEL APPLIES TO TEXT STOCK

We try to produce the most beautiful books possible, and we are also extremely concerned about the impact of our manufacturing process on the forests of the world and the environment as a whole. Accordingly, we've made sure that all of the paper we use has been certified as coming from forests that are managed to ensure the protection of the people and wildlife dependent upon them.

For Melissa,

who surrounded my own small world
with so many new and shining ones, and gifted
me with our three beautiful daughters.

INTRODUCTION

The best reason to write a book is because you have a story to tell. In my case, I'll change that to the plural, *stories*. As a player, ESPN broadcaster, U.S. Davis Cup team captain, and head of player development for the United States Tennis Association, I've experienced, observed, and been an integral part of many events and incidents that helped transform tennis into the electric, global game it is today. Only soccer has expanded its franchise to transfix more of the world than tennis, but give us a little more time . . . After all, the "Open" game is just over forty years old.

In fact, the very process by which tennis went global played out in my time, and is a story unto itself. It's easy for someone like me, or even a fan who follows the game on a daily basis, to get lost in the funhouse, forgetting the details of how we got where we are today. Where we are today is a place where the traditional stranglehold the United States, Australia, and a few other select nations had on tennis is broken. Where stylistic variety has yielded to a kind of world game. Where surfaces have been altered, sometimes drastically, to help create a more interesting, athletic game. Where fitness and biomechanics have caught up with technique as critical factors in success.

Where we are today is also a place where international stars are more well-known and visible to the public than ever before, which makes their stories—or stories about them—that much more compelling. Still, I wasn't convinced I needed or wanted to write a book until someone pointed out that I ought to take all those stories I've told over a casual drink or dinner—stories that were often greeted with surprise, delight, shock, and even disbelief—and pull them together in one place. That's how the idea for this book was spawned.

I've been in the game for twenty-five years now, and I've traded forehands, talked strategy, and rubbed shoulders off the court with loads of players. I have a wealth of experiences at big events, and have witnessed historic matches as well as important changes driven by game-shaping issues and people. Twenty-five is a nice, resonant number. It's also a big enough number to have made me feel a little urgency to tell my stories while they are still fresh and relevant—while the people in them are still familiar. So I figured, what the hell—serve 'em up.

The most challenging part of collecting all these stories in one place was finding the right way to tell them—it's easier for someone who sets out to write a straight autobiography. My collaborator, Peter Bodo, and I decided to adopt a loose, calendar-based format of twelve chapters, corresponding to the events of the year, because tennis is, after all, an all-year sport. Each chapter handles themes appropriate to the month, or personalities who are linked to the events that take place that month.

We didn't want to force the issue, though. We just wanted to impose some direction on our kaleidoscopic journey through twenty-five years of tennis, covering all aspects of my experience—from growing up a McEnroe to trying to alter our nation's official approach to creating champions; from hitting with Roger Federer to navigating the conflicts inherent in having multiple roles in the game; from certain high (or low) moments of my career, to the transformation of the very way the game is played.

It would have been incomplete to tell my stories without trying to connect some dots and extract some meaning from the material. So I've been free in expressing my opinions and convictions. That's going to surprise some people, because I was always known as the mild McEnroe—in fact, when we were kids, my brothers teasingly called me "Perfect Pat." I was far from perfect then, and I'm far from perfect now, but I still felt an obligation to produce a book that's honest, colorful, and tackles issues head-on.

I hope that when you finish the last page and close this book, you'll feel like you know and understand more about the players, events, and trends that have shaped the past quarter-century in tennis. I hope it's as stimulating and entertaining a ride for you as it has been, and I hope continues to be, for me.

—Patrick McEnroe
New York, February 9, 2010

HARD
COURT
CONFIDENTIAL

THE AUSTRALIAN SEMIS: BECKER, EDBERG, LENDL, AND P. McENROE

The first round of the Australian Open, 1991: There I was, on a field court way out in the middle of nowhere, playing Sweden's Tomas Hogstedt. I was lucky to be there at all, despite the terrible beating Hogstedt was inflicting on me. With a ranking of no. 120, I was the last player accepted into the main draw. If I were ranked one measly spot lower, I wouldn't even have bothered to make the trip just to play qualifying.

Hogstedt had me by two sets, and I was serving, down a break already in the third, at love–30. With two swings of the racket, Tomas could deliver the equivalent of a knockout blow. As I hit my next serve, my baseball cap slipped on my head, covered my eyes, and I lost the point—and I felt utterly like a doofus. *Fucking hat*, I thought, ripping it off my head and casting it aside. *Fuck this hat!*

Here it was, triple break point for Hogstedt.

Somehow, though, I ended up holding the game and suddenly things started looking better. Tomas seemed to be tiring. And once I clawed my way back into that third set, I got a huge boost of energy and confidence. I took the set, and won the next two with authority.

After I beat Hogstedt, the draw opened up for me; that happens sometimes: a big upset here, a withdrawal there, and a guy with a bit of luck can go very deep in an event without having to play a legitimate contender or proven champion. As an unseeded player, I might have met a top seed—a Boris Becker or Ivan Lendl—in the first or second round. Instead, I got Hogstedt, followed by a low-ranked player who was in on a wild card and had won his first match.

After that, I had a tough match with one of the game's best competitors—and currently one of my top aides in USTA player development—Jay Berger. I won that one in straights. Then, I had a good win over the Aussie hope Mark Woodforde to make the quarters, where I met no. 101 Christiano Caratti. No offense to Caratti, but most guys would give their eye teeth to get a player of his caliber (or me, for that matter) in the quarters of a major.

I quickly went up two sets to love on Caratti, but then I hurt my back. I received treatment a few times in the fourth and fifth, but I was determined to tough it out. I rallied from losing the third and fourth sets to win in five, and earn a date with Boris Becker with a place in the final on the line.

An experienced tennis fan reviewing the facts could easily put my run down to the luck of the draw. I didn't entirely see it that way, because I knew how hard I had worked and how much I craved validation. At the time, I was already a very good doubles player, with a Grand Slam tour championship title to my name. Because of my quick success in doubles and maybe a little bit because of my family tree, I had assumed I was going to make it in singles. I thought I was good enough.

But I realized after about a year and a half of trying: *I'm not gonna make it.* Not unless I did something differently. So in 1991, I trained for the upcoming Australian Open like never before, although the process actually began a full year earlier, at the end of 1989, back at our family compound in the Long Island, New York, town of Cove Neck.

I stayed out at the house for a month, and I ran every morning for ninety minutes, trained on court for a few hours, then went running again for another ninety minutes in the afternoon. (Incidentally, I wouldn't dream of recommending that amount of jogging for any aspiring player.) I didn't know what I was doing, but I was doing it hard, and I did know one thing: I needed to lose weight. I had to shed some of those pounds I'd gained at Stanford, where eating an entire pizza and drinking a few bottles of Coke were a standard pre-bedtime snack. I ran fifteen miles a day, in addition to working on the court for three, four hours a day.

My ranking crept up through 1990, and I worked my tail off in the short off-season around the holidays. When John heard that I'd made the cutoff for direct entry into the first Grand Slam of the year he invited me to stop in Hawaii on my way Down Under for some last-minute prep. He had rented a place there with his wife at the time, Tatum O'Neal, and his old buddy from Stanford, the great Olympic games speed skater Eric Heiden.

Eric, who's now a prominent physician and the U.S. Olympic skating team's official doctor based in California, was a real stud. I found out that he had to have his slacks custom made, because of the size of his quads (I kiddingly called him "Quadzilla"). I trained with Eric for a week. We went on long runs in the mountains, and he showed me all kinds of power exercises for my legs. The workouts would have killed me, had I not been in pretty good shape. We did a lot of side-to-side stuff, and worked out with these big beanbags full of rice on our shoulders. Eric never touched regular weights.

Then I left for New Zealand and Australia. I had no coach, no nothing. In Wellington, New Zealand, and elsewhere, I would go to a gym and repeat the drills Eric had taught me. I ran on indoor tracks. Initially, I shared an apartment with two other guys trying to make it on the tour, Kelly Jones and Robbie Weiss. We stayed in the cheapest place we could find, on Darling Street; the place backed onto a rail yard, so I heard the commuter trains pulling in and out at all hours. But at least we had three bedrooms, and our own kitchen and laundry room. When Kelly and Robbie lost their first-round matches, I suddenly had the place to myself, just three days into the event. I slipped into an ultracalm, focused mood.

I had a few places where I would get my take-out food; then I would go back to the flat and sequester myself. So much for the glamorous life of a tennis player. I had my drinks—mostly water—and I would just pound them, whenever I was awake, trying to stay hydrated because of the heat down there. I was up three, four times a night just to pee. The one guy I talked to was Paul Palandjian, an old friend who had played tennis at Harvard and was the best man at my wedding. We talked every day. He's a nutcase, but in a good way, like a coach. He filled my head with all this stuff—*Stick it to this guy tomorrow. You're gonna do it, just go out and kick some ass. . . .*

Just over a week later, I had my win over Caratti and my place in the Australian semifinals. When I walked into the crowded press interview room after that quarterfinal win, the first question was the obvious one: "Are you surprised to be in the semis?"

I smiled slightly and said, with a straight face, "Hey, it was just like you guys all predicted in the semis: Becker, Edberg, Lendl, and McEnroe."

Tennis Without Borders

The tennis year is basically an endless summer that begins immediately in the New Year in Australia and doesn't end until around the first week in December, when the Davis Cup finals are played . . . who knows where? I used to travel to Australia as a player, just days after celebrating Christmas and New Year's at home. Now, more than a decade since I played my last singles match in the land called "Oz," I squeeze out an extra week or two at home before I head for Melbourne and the first Grand Slam of the year as an on-air analyst/color commentator for the sports network ESPN.

In Australia, I'm one of a U.S.-based ESPN crew of about forty, with close to double that number of Australians joining us to help bring the first Grand Slam event of the year to—we hope—millions of viewers.

The four Grand Slam tournaments are the crown jewels of the game, although for the longest time Australia was the lump of coal among the diamonds. Even though the nation has a great tennis tradition, it was too far-flung from the largely North American and European capitals of the game. The great Aussie champs, like Rod Laver, were real road warriors, earning their fame largely at the other three Grand Slam events, or "majors": The French Open (Roland Garros), Wimbledon, and the US Open.

Until 1988, the Australian Open was often played at Kooyong, a Melbourne tennis club. If Monty Python wanted to do a skit about Anglophile Australians, the troupe might have chosen Kooyong as a stage set. Kooyong had plenty of shortcomings. For one thing, the stadium-court turf from the baseline to the net was noticeably pitched (for drainage purposes), so the players often complained about having to run "uphill" when charging the net. The stadium has a modest capacity of 8,500, so it was always overcrowded during the tournament, especially after the advent of "Open" tennis in 1968. This new era began when the Lords of Tennis finally gave up their stubborn campaign to keep tennis "pure" and allowed pros to compete alongside amateurs at the prestigious majors. That launched the worldwide tennis boom of the 1970s and '80s, and the rest, as they say, is history.

For a variety of reasons, from about 1975 on, many of the top players didn't even bother playing in the Australian Open. It didn't help that the tournament was the last Grand Slam event of the year, played right around Christmas. What if they gave a Grand Slam and no one came? That was the story of the Australian Open.

The Aussies finally got up to speed in 1988, emulating the highly successful US Open, by moving to a new facility featuring hard courts in a public park, a stone's throw from downtown Melbourne. It was another blow aimed at the elitist, club-based history of the game. You have to give the Aussies credit for going big—the Australian Open was the first major sports stadium to feature a retractable roof. (By 2011, they will have three convertible arenas.) The French and US Opens still don't have one.

The history of the Australian Open can be read as the story of the explosive, tennis-without-borders growth of the game. And the way promoters now position it as "the Grand Slam of Asia-Pacific" is telling. The Australians have been carving out a new national identity, and having a Grand Slam event that seems like a Wimbledon wannabe no longer fits their vision of themselves. The only downside is that while Australian tennis officials have produced a real Grand Slam extravaganza, they've had trouble developing new champions to advance their grand tradition.

John Never Got the Memo . . .

The Australian Open has special significance for me for a diversity of reasons. By the time I made my first trip Down Under, in 1991, the tournament was already situated in Melbourne Park and regaining its lost luster. I tacked up my best-ever Grand Slam singles result that year and it's the one major where I can say my brother John never did better. And just one year earlier, it was also the scene of John's most memorable debacle.

January 21, 1990, was the day John became the first player defaulted from a major tournament since Willie Alvarez, a Colombian-born Spaniard, who was thrown out of the French Open in 1963. It's just one of the many singular distinctions that belong to John in the Open era.

That's a pretty good reason for having a sharp memory of the 1990 event. Unfortunately, I have another, dark reason why the memory of that year's tournament overshadows even that of my career-best performance as a player.

I'd done well in doubles in 1989 (among other things, I'd bagged the French Open doubles title with my partner, Jim Grabb), but deep down I had my heart and sights set on becoming a decent pro singles player. I still lacked experience, though, and my ranking wasn't quite high enough to get me straight into the main singles draw for the 1990 Australian Open.

The typical cutoff for automatic qualifiers for a Grand Slam event is technically no. 104, meaning anyone with that ranking or better is automatically entered in the 128-man field. The other twenty-four slots are set aside for qualifiers and wild cards. The former are players who fight through a qualifying tournament to earn a berth despite low rankings; the latter are places awarded at the discretion of the tournament. The wild cards are usually given to talented but untested juniors, homegrown journeymen, or name players coming back from injury or hoping to give it one more shot.

I fell into the category of "none of the above" in 1990, and I decided against making the long and costly trip to attempt to qualify. Instead, I stayed in New York and watched in semi-disbelief as John, who was playing commanding tennis, melted down while leading Mikael Pernfors by two sets to one in a fourth-round match.

The details aren't really important—a crying baby, a couple of close line calls, a few costly errors, and a few choice, vulgar words directed at tournament officials all played a role in John's expulsion. But the real reason John got thrown out was because he was unaware of a rule change that had reduced the process by which cumulative violations of the written code of conduct inexorably led to a default. The old system, built on a four-step sequence (a verbal warning, followed by a point penalty, a game penalty, and then the final, drastic step of a default) had been reduced that year to a three-step process (warning, point penalty, default). John never got the memo.

Even in the most blazing heat of anger, John always knew where he stood with the law. But in this instance he assumed that he had one more tantrum card to play. Knowing John as I do, I'm confident that if the old system were still in play, John would have settled down to take care of business after that costly third infraction. Arriving at the point of no return almost always had a way of calming him, and it led him to accept rather than buck his fate. And that's often when he re-focused and played his best. I'm not saying John would have beaten Pernfors, but . . . he probably would have beaten Pernfors. As he was just thirty at the time, and playing well, he would have been competitive at any stage of the event.

Just a few days after John was defaulted, he and Tatum were back at his beachfront pad in Malibu, California. I was out at a bar on New York City's Upper East Side, celebrating a friend's birthday with a couple of my longtime friends, including John Schmitt, a doubles partner with whom I'd won a few big junior doubles tournaments, including the prestigious Orange Bowl.

We were sitting at the bar with our dates when I saw a headline on television: *Plane Crash, Special Report.* The screen zoomed in on a map of nearby Long Island, closed in on the town of Oyster Bay, and settled on a neighborhood called Cove Neck, with a highlight on Tennis Court Road. "Holy shit," I said, "that's *our* road."

There was a delicious irony in the road's name. While many people assumed that John had thrown his weight around to have the byway named to somehow acknowledge him, Tennis Court Road was there long before John and my parents bought the Cove Neck estate. It was so named for the two indoor courts that stood at the foot of the road, an amenity for the residents of the patrician enclave. (President Teddy Roosevelt's historic, landmark home, Sagamore Hill, is in Cove Neck.) I got to play on one of those two perfect, indoor clay courts just once. We weren't really allowed, being low-born Irish Catholics and arrivistes in Cove Neck. I'm sure John's reputation factored into it, too.

Anyway, John and my other brother, Mark (he's the middle McEnroe; I'm the youngest), were nowhere near New York that night. And my parents, John and Kay, were off in Egypt on a Nile cruise. I realized that I'd better get out to the house; for all I knew the plane, en route to New York's JFK airport from Colombia, had crashed right on top of it.

We squeezed into the car, girls and all, and sped out there. The entire main road, for about the last two miles, was closed and lit by the harsh lights of police cruisers, EMS vehicles, and emergency flares. We had no option but to walk, and legions of people had decided to do the same. It was surreal, like a scene from a big-budget disaster movie.

Finally, we arrived at the foot of the hill below our house, near the forbidden tennis courts, which now appeared in an entirely different and almost sinister light. The area around the courts was crawling with cops. When we approached, one of them said, "Wait, boys, you don't want to go up there."

"I know," I said, his ominous warning making me that much more curious to see what lay up there. "We're not rubbernecking. I just want to go and check on my house."

"You don't want to go up there," the cop reiterated, firmly. "You don't want to see what's up at the top of that hill."

I wasn't going to get anywhere with him. The only solution was for us to take advantage of the chaos and sneak up, which is what all six of us did. We stole up to the modest entrance of the property we had moved to almost a decade earlier on a powerful wave of pride. My dad had always dreamed of having something like a McEnroe family compound; I guess it was the brick-and-mortar embodiment of his lifelong obsession with family life, a fixation that caused us plenty of headaches as well as comfort and joy. Dad had been an only child who had battled up the economic and academic ladders (his family at one point was on welfare) to make his mark as a lawyer, a partner in an international, New York–based law firm.

After we purchased the estate, the old stable was completely renovated into John's private home. Oddly, though, John never really warmed to the place, and you couldn't blame him. It was uncomfortably close to our parents. And unlike Dad, John wasn't obsessed with family relations. Having two brothers, a highly involved dad, and a smart, disciplinarian mom, he'd probably had it up to here with the glories of family life.

The Avianca plane, I learned later, came down because of a miscommunication between the Spanish-speaking pilot and the tower. He was running low on fuel, and he asked for landing "priority," instead of declaring that he had an emergency. Had he done the latter, all airport traffic would have come to a halt as they immediately cleared a runway. Instead, the tower instructed him to circle until they could accommodate him. The plane eventually ran out of fuel, and took out many trees in the surrounding woods as it fell and crashed just down the street from our home. It hit the ground, belly first, sliding up a hill until it finally came dangerously close to a neighboring home. The only factor that mitigated the disaster was that having run out of fuel, the plane didn't explode or burst into flames. About half of the passengers survived the flight.

But it would have been impossible for us to believe that when we saw the scene all around our house. Strange, dark lumps lay all over the lawn—there must have been thirty of them. They were some of the dead, already stuffed into body bags. Our home had become a triage center and a staging area for the rescue cleanup effort. Many of the surviving passengers were in severe distress. It was like a war zone.

When I went to check on the house, half the fence around the property was torn down. Emergency crews had started to rip it up in order to use the area as a helicopter landing pad, but they quickly found a more suitable, spacious area behind the house. Our buildings were untouched, and everything inside seemed okay. I ended up spending the night at my friend Schmitty's nearby home, and when we went back the next morning, the lawn was littered with bloody clothes and rags, hypodermic needles, and bandage wrappers. They were bringing in satellite dishes for the television trucks and Porta Pottis, because the ongoing cleanup and investigation would take a week.

Over the ensuing days, we learned that the flight, which had originated in the narco-haven of Colombia, had many drug "mules" on board. They had ingested condoms filled with cocaine. When they passed them and the hospital staff noticed what they were, some of the survivors were moved right from hospital beds to jail.

When I told John what had happened, he freaked out. If you read his best seller, *You Cannot Be Serious*, you may remember he only mentioned the incident in passing. But it was a depressing episode that really shook him to the core. As a result, our days in Cove Neck were numbered; John wanted to have nothing to do with the place anymore. By then, my parents already owned an apartment in New York City, and we all more or less drifted back to Gotham.

Oz: Wizards Wanted

Back when the Australian Open tournament was a backwater major, it was played—like Wimbledon and the US Open—on grass. And Australia led the world in churning out grass-court champions, including Rod Laver, Lew Hoad, Ken Rosewall, John Newcombe, Tony Roche, my frequent ESPN boothmate Fred Stolle, Margaret Court, Evonne Goolagong, and others. Those are legendary names, iconic names.

In Melbourne Park, the new facility featured a controversial surface, Rebound Ace (now it's a slightly different and more player-friendly hard court, Plexipave). Going with Rebound Ace seemed a shrewd choice, for the surface was in many ways suited to the emerging power baseline game. Unfortunately, it was also a significant break with the grand Australian grass-court tradition, and a game that Australians had no real idea how to play.

Almost to a man, the great Aussie players were aggressive serve-and-volley practitioners. They liked to rip the big serve and come barreling to the net to end points with the volley or overhead. Since typical grass courts back then were slick and fast, the style was extremely productive. Rod Laver, an icon of the grass-court game, is the only man in history to complete the singles Grand Slam—twice. Although most people use the terms "Grand Slam" or "Slam" as a synonym for any of the four majors, the term originally referred to the achievement of sweeping all four in the same year. (The ageless pundit Bud Collins, reveling in his erudition, never misses an opportunity to scold anyone who calls a major a "Slam." But common usage has drowned out his voice—no mean feat. . . .)

Don Budge was the first man to complete a Grand Slam (in 1938), and Laver did it twice. The first time was in 1962, when he was an amateur, and it earned him a lucrative contract as a pro. Laver missed Wimbledon (and the other majors) because of the ban on pros until the Open era began six years later, but he completed another Grand Slam in 1969, this time against all comers.

No Aussie man has even come close to achieving a Grand Slam since.

When the Australians abandoned grass, they were left without a stylistic tradition or developmental philosophy. For a while in the 1980s, they thought that a state-sponsored academy would get them up to speed. They turned to a public agency, the Australian Institute of Sport, but the wonks at the AIS decided all Australian kids ought to learn to hit the same sledgehammer forehand as four-time Aussie Open finalist Ivan Lendl. They even put it on videotape and broke it down into component parts. It didn't work. Episodes like that helped shape my own coaching; I believe you need an overarching philosophy toward development, but you need to treat each player as a unique individual and adjust accordingly.

Rebound Ace, the surface in those early years at Melbourne Park, created a different, more subtle problem for the Aussies. That surface was basically made of ground-up tires, and while it was bouncy and responded to spin beautifully, it got as hot as NASCAR racing slicks on a typically torrid Australian summer day. It was nearly unbearable for the players and, because the surface also became tacky in contact with rubber soles, it caused numerous ankle, knee, and foot injuries.

My fellow ESPN analyst Darren Cahill and other Australians also believe that Rebound Ace was terrible for player development. With the ball bouncing so much, it was hard for young players to get grooved and develop the proper technique—a process that takes endless repetition and develops "muscle memory." Andre Agassi, who's probably been the best player at the Australian Open in the present era, also developed his precise game on hard courts in Las Vegas and Florida. But those courts don't respond nearly as dramatically to different spins as Rebound Ace.

This was an unfortunate disadvantage for up-and-coming Aussie players because it kept them from developing the combination of power and consistency that the changing game would demand. This was a shame, as well as an awful irony because of the robust tradition and popularity of the game Down Under. Australia may be a nation even better suited to creating great players than the U.S. Okay, it has far fewer people—and that counts for a lot. But the country has as strong a tradition in the game as the U.S., slightly better weather, a comfortable standard of living, and a far less crowded sports stage. Aussies love their cricket, rugby, and "Aussie rules" football. They like golf, and swimming is pretty popular. But tennis stands tall alongside any of them.

Luckily, tennis has remained a major Aussie sport despite the nation's current dearth of top domestic stars. Tennis promoters in the U.S. and Europe can only gnash their teeth when they see the kind of hold the Australian Open has on the native population. For two glorious weeks, the tournament is pervasive in life on the island continent. Channel 7, the Australian national broadcasting network, is the official host. During the tournament, the network beams its national evening news from a stage at Melbourne Park. If you're an American, imagine Katie Couric hosting the CBS prime-time news from a set in the shadow of Arthur Ashe Stadium.

Australian newspapers in recent years were obsessed with Lleyton Hewitt, the best player Australia has produced since, well, Rod Laver. And it didn't hurt his cause that he married Bec Cartwright, a fellow Aussie and star of the popular television series *Home and Away*. She's kind of a Jennifer Aniston with an Aussie twang. During the Open, Hewitt is all over the tabloids: *Hewitt Out to Dinner—Chooses Chinese!* Even the staid broadsheets think nothing of putting a Hewitt match report on page one—above the fold. The highest rated television show in Australia for 2005 was the final of the tournament, pitting Marat Safin against Hewitt. The entire nation died a little as Hewitt came up short in that one. But the Aussies got over it; they're a fair-minded nation of good sports.

So there have been two conflicting things going on in Oz. Australia certainly embraces its heroes, but it has also undermined some of its younger players by trying to keep up with the Grand Slam Joneses. Eager to shed its provincial reputation, the tournament went out of its way to welcome and promote the very best players in the world, even though its own pool of domestic talent was contracting. It's the same challenge the U.S. faces these days.

The Aussies are walking a tennis tightrope, and staying upright—barely.

Pat Cash, an Aussie, won the Wimbledon title in 1987, the year before the change from grass at Kooyong to hard courts at Melbourne Park. But he never did capture the no. 1 ranking. Since then, only two Aussies have won majors and/or held the no. 1 ranking: Pat Rafter and Lleyton Hewitt.

I played Rafter a few times, and I can tell you that he was no typical old-school serve-and-volley Aussie, even though his aim in any given point was to get to the net. Unlike a John Newcombe, Pat didn't rely on serving aces; he used his kick serve—which travels through the air more slowly than a flat serve and then takes an exaggerated, high bounce—to get to the net, where he pressured you to make precise passing shots. As a returner, he got every single, blessed ball back into play. He forced you to run, and was willing to run as well.

Pat was a superb grinder, which is unusual for an attack-minded player. He made you work until eventually you would miss, or he would get to the net and end it, one way or another. I was 0–2 with Pat; he beat me in Tokyo once, 6–3, 6–2, a score that suggests a pretty ho-hum match. It didn't feel that way to me; by the time it was over, I felt like we'd gone to 7–6 in the third because of how hard both of us worked for every point. Rafter won the US Open twice (that was his total haul of majors) because the fast hard court in New York helped his game. But his style was self-punishing as well, and his body took such a beating that he retired relatively early.

If Rafter, with his daredevil diving and lunging for volleys, had one foot in the old Aussie tradition, Hewitt represented the new breed that Australia was hoping to develop. Hewitt came along after my time, but he won a Wimbledon and US Open title and held the no. 1 ranking, too. He was the first—and so far only—blue-chip Australian player who really understood the emerging power baseline game.

Hewitt, with his lightning reflexes, superb shot selection, and excellent placement, was like water—if there was a hole anywhere in your game, or on the court, he'd flow into it to good advantage. He didn't have much power, although his serve was better than it looked (which wasn't hard to achieve). Watching how steady and crafty he was from the baseline, you'd think of him as a player well designed for success on clay. But he never did as well at the French Open as at the majors that use a faster surface, because he liked to take the ball early. This in effect enabled him to make the court narrow. Hewitt could get enough pace to slip the ball through on faster courts, and he could outmaneuver most guys when it came to quick exchanges of low-bouncing balls. But on clay, he didn't have enough power, or generate enough heavy topspin, to get it through the court or make the most of the angles opened up by the wider court, and his opponents had just that little bit of extra time to deal with his tricks.

In the mid-1990s, the Aussies coughed up another player who

was dialed into the new international gestalt, Mark Philippoussis. I played doubles with Mark in 1995 in Kuala Lumpur. As the take-charge doubles veteran, I said to Mark: "Listen, just go out there and hit the crap out of every ball. Hit it as hard as you can."

He stared at me, his big, pale blue eyes growing wider and wider. "Are you serious, mate?"

Of course I was serious, but just as important, I knew that's what he most profoundly wished I'd say. And giving a young stud like Mark a vote of confidence in his preferred game could go a long way toward success. I said, "Yup. Just hit the crap out of the ball and leave the scurrying around and strategy stuff to me."

"I'm not used to that," he said, still with some disbelief. "Usually, my partners are always telling me to back off a little. . . . Thanks, mate!"

We went out and won the title.

Mark is a big, raw-boned kid who's on the short list for "Best Player Never to Win a Major." Like Pete Sampras, Mark was a Greek immigrant's kid, and he might have become an Australian Grand Slam champion a few times over. But Mark was as soft as his game was big and powerful. He was trained as well as stifled by his father, Nick, who was reluctant to trust him to "outsiders" (as in "a coach"). The role he played in his son's life was more along the lines of what you find on the WTA tour. Mark played two Grand Slam finals: losing at the US Open in 1998 to his countryman, Rafter, and falling at Wimbledon in 2003 to Roger Federer.

At Wimbledon in 1999, Mark took the first set from Pete Sampras in their quarterfinal, but blew out a knee and had to quit the match; in the ensuing years, injuries and surgeries hampered his efforts, but they may have been caused partly by poor training habits. Not long after Mark put up those big early results, he moved to an island just off Miami and became a regular on the South Beach scene. He indulged his love of wake boarding, motorcycles, and supermodels—which were plentiful on SoBe. He never stepped it up enough to build on his early success and faded from the game, a very sweet guy who just never understood how hard you had to work, and how much you had to think about and understand what you were doing in order to succeed. The last time he was on television, it wasn't on a tennis court but in a cheesy reality show where he had to choose a girlfriend from one of two groups: pretty young things or cougars.

Mark was atypical for the players Australia produced in my time, guys like Wally Masur, Darren Cahill, Brad Drewett, Scott Draper, Jason Stoltenberg, and even Pat Rafter. None of them was a big hitter like Mark. They were smart, versatile, crafty percentage players with an attacking bent, while Mark had a combination of raw power, size, and a solid baseline game that could have carried him far.

I guess he liked the scenery where he was.

Andre Agassi: A Las Vegas Yankee in Rod Laver's Court

One player who benefited enormously from the Australians' choice of surface was Andre Agassi, who won the Open in four of his nine trips Down Under. The most impressive aspect of his dazzling record may be that he beat his great career rival Pete Sampras the only two times they played in Melbourne, in a semi and a final. Pete won every other match they played at a Grand Slam.

Pete was a superb hardcourt player, and the Rebound Ace was friendly to his game. But he disliked the way the difference between day and night affected the Rebound Ace; he wasn't crazy about the heat (he took great pains through his career to disguise the fact that he suffered from thalassemia, a form of anemia common to men of Mediterranean descent), and he thought the change in the way the balls played from year to year was too pronounced.

Agassi probably enjoyed a slight advantage Down Under by virtue of his pure stroking talent; he's the best ball striker (off either wing) I've ever seen. I'm talking about the ability to hit the ball pure, clean, and with conviction. Even Roger Federer doesn't hit the ball as cleanly (especially off the backhand side), but Roger more than compensates for it with his other attributes, starting with his speed.

Andre's genius comes from being a control freak, a supreme irony when you consider how much he rebelled against the control exerted on his life by his father, Mike, and his early coach, Nick Bollettieri. I experienced Andre's controlling tendencies over the years as his friend, his Davis Cup captain, and his opponent. That streak was obvious in the precise, clean way he played the game in the last glorious half decade of his career. Put the ball almost anywhere near his strike zone and it was like clockwork: boom, boom, boom. He fired crisp, stinging, laserlike bullets.

Andre's talent as a hitter helped shape his game, which became surprisingly one-dimensional (if effective) in the second half of his career. To me, it bordered on boring, insofar as such precision and consistency could be called that. But his game plan was simple: I'm gonna go crosscourt, time and again, until I get my opening, then I'm going to go down the line for the winner or to force an error. It's a color-by-numbers formula, but don't underestimate the skill it takes to pull it off consistently. His results spoke for themselves.

One of the few guys good enough to keep Andre from imposing that killer template on a match most of the time was Pete. He knew he had to keep Andre contained. But Pete had some big advantages on any medium-to-fast surface, starting with the serve. Pete always felt confident he could hold because of his big serve, and while Andre served smart and picked his spots, Pete would usually find a way to get stick on the ball. Andre often kicked the serve to Pete's backhand, forcing Pete to chip the return. If the shot floated at all, Andre would pounce on it, setting up shop in the middle of the court and, as Pete put it, "It was time to put on the track shoes."

It's not as if Pete was averse to the athletic game. Paul Annacone, his coach through the glory years, always encouraged Pete to find a way to make athleticism a big factor in his matches against everyone, especially Andre. But Pete understood that you just couldn't allow Andre to play the role of the puppeteer. You had to impose the game on him, which is why Pete tended to play a lot of serve-and-volley tennis against Andre. One of Andre's few vulnerabilities was his defense; he didn't have the sheer athleticism to transition from defense to offense as quickly as a Pete Sampras or a Roger Federer.

Pete also staked a lot on his ability to make the most risky of groundstrokes, the backhand down the line, even though that shot flew to Andre's dangerous forehand. Pete risked that because he liked to set himself well over on the backhand side, literally daring Andre (and anyone else) to go for the big shot to the open (forehand) court. Unless the shot was of the highest quality, Pete would track and respond to it with his best and most dangerous shot—the running forehand.

One of the best performances by Pete, if not the most competitive Sampras-Agassi match, occurred in the Wimbledon final of 1999. Pete was striving to tie Roy Emerson's Grand Slam singles title record (twelve) that year, but Andre's astonishing late-career resurgence was just beginning. Just weeks earlier, Andre had stunned everyone by winning Roland Garros (aka the French Open), becoming only the fifth man in tennis history to post a career Grand Slam—meaning he'd won every major at least once. Now here he was, facing Pete in the Wimbledon final.

Pete's game rose to another level that day, and it wasn't just a matter of good luck. Pete, the athlete nonpareil, actually enjoyed running and trading blows. The guys who had the most success against him, and the ones he feared most, were the big, strapping players (Richard Krajicek, Goran Ivanisevic, Michael Stich) who hit huge serves and tried to aggressively finish points with two or three swings of the racket. In other words, guys who had power and service ability comparable to his own. But while Pete actually enjoyed playing the run-and-gun game that was Andre's specialty, those other thunder merchants did not; nor did they have the ability for it.

Andre and Pete held serve to 3–all in the first set of that match, and Andre had Pete down, love–40, in the seventh game. But Pete escaped with a hold. Andre served the next game with new balls (in a match the balls are changed after the first seven games, then every nine games thereafter; it's an advantage to serve with new balls), but he had a mild letdown after letting Pete off the hook; and on grass, service breaks are as rare as cold springs in a desert. Sensing Andre's disappointment, Pete pounced on Andre's serve, made a few good returns, and suddenly found himself serving for the set at 5–3. That was the nightmare scenario for Andre, given Pete's atomic serve.

Pete took the set, and in the next two his game hit heights it rarely did before or after. Feeling that he could hold his service games almost at will, thanks to his power, while Andre could not, put him in a mental comfort zone. Pete started to hit out—he hit his way into "the zone," that place where you can't seem to do anything wrong, you feel like you have all the time in the world, and the ball looks as big and easy to hit as one of those multicolored beach balls.

Pete grew so confident as the games rolled by that he was content to play Andre from the backcourt. This wasn't entirely inspiration; the properties of Wimbledon's grass at that time also worked in Pete's favor. Although grass plays fast (and back then, it played very fast), it also caused Andre's shots to sit up a bit.

On hard courts, Pete often felt pressed for time by Agassi's lasers. But on grass, Pete had that extra fraction of a second to draw a bead. The effect was also pronounced on Andre's kick serve. On hard courts, it bounced high enough to force Pete to chip it back or play it defensively. On grass, Pete was able to get up and over the ball, to drive the return back flat and hard. And when Pete could make a return that started the point on even terms, he was justifiably confident in his athletic ability. As he put it, "It was like, okay, here we go—let's see who moves better."

Andre didn't just make Pete play his best on that and a few other occasions, he was able to keep up with the pace and level even when he surrendered advantages he enjoyed on the hard courts of Australia.

In the big picture, Pete saw his matches with Andre as a pitcher vs. batter kind of duel. If Pete, the pitcher, didn't throw the fastball with a lot on it and brush the corner of the plate, Andre would hit it out of the park. But Pete was the pitcher—he was the one in control of how things went. Andre, in many ways, was a reactor, eager to take control—if you gave him the chance. Where Pete's natural mode was to dictate, Andre's was to take advantage. Pete won that Wimbledon final going away, and it's still one of Pete's most satisfying triumphs. His lifelong rival gave him an opportunity few others could—he allowed Pete to play, to let it rip, even though he demanded that Pete play his absolute best to win.

One of the ironies in that great rivalry was the basic feeling that Pete was dull and played a "boring" game, while Andre was the electrifying showman. The reason for that was simple: human nature. Andre got a lot of mileage out of his early career reputation as a mercurial showman. Once that image was implanted, it was there for good.

Granted, Pete was not a Big Personality, and he had a hangdog manner that fooled countless opponents into thinking he was vulnerable. But Andre was the predictable one. Near the end of his career—when he was playing incomparably better if duller tennis—all he had to do to make the crowd ooh and aah was throw in a between-the-legs shot, or show a flash of temper, and it was all good. The fans ate it up because they'd been conditioned to see Andre through a certain prism. A little of the old Andre went a long way.

Here's a final thing to think about when it comes to the Australian Open: In a very short span in recent years, Pete Sampras and Roger Federer both shattered the Grand Slam singles title mark—the old record (12 majors), held by Roy Emerson, appeared unbreakable to generations of players, including the likes of my brother John, Bjorn Borg, Jimmy Connors, and Ivan Lendl.

As I write this, Pete Sampras is retired with 14 titles, Federer is king-of-the-Grand-Slam-hill with 16, and Rafael Nadal is on track to bag a comparable number—if Rafa can remain healthy. And that's a big "If." The key to this recent flurry of excellence is the Australian Open.

It's funny, but Emerson's name comes up in many contexts; he was a pioneer of fitness, the original Iron Man of tennis. He also could play for six, seven hours a day, go out and drink beer until 3:00 a.m., and then get up in the morning and do it all over again. He was also a towering doubles player (all in, he won a record 28 major titles in singles, doubles, and mixed doubles) as well as a top Davis Cup performer who played for teams that won the Cup eight times. But his name seldom comes up, even among old-timers, when they begin talking about the Greatest of All Time.

That's because he did so much of his damage at the Australian Open, which at times was a Grand Slam in name only. And during Emmo's salad years, the best players in the world, the pros, were ineligible for Grand Slam competition. Granted, the amateur competition, particularly from homegrown rivals, was tough in that golden age of Aussie tennis. But with the top players absent, and the long trip to Australia taking a toll on visiting players' fitness, Emmo's record was sullied. He won half of his twelve majors in Australia.

Unlike Rod Laver, who was two critical years younger, Emmo didn't really make a big mark on the game in the early Open era. His achievements got an asterisk and he was somewhat forgotten. Emerson's singles title record wasn't even acknowledged, except as a stat, until Pete Sampras began to close in on it. But another reason the 12-Slam mark lasted so long was the decline of the Australian Open's prestige in the post-Emerson early Open era.

From the early 1970s until 1988, none of the top players chose to pad their résumés with titles earned at rickety old Kooyong. In my brother John's time, many top players simply ignored the event. That wasn't entirely the fault of the Australian Open, much less Emerson. The players were simply shortsighted, and the Australian Open did little to clear their vision. You have to wonder how many majors those guys of John's vintage would have bagged had the Australian Open flourished earlier.

Federer has won three Australian Open titles in ten attempts. My brother John, who finished his career with seven majors, played the Australian Open on just five occasions, but only three times in his prime. Borg (eleven majors) made the trip to Melbourne just once, and Connors (eight majors) played Australia just twice, and reached the final both times, winning once. All three of those guys were outstanding players on grass, the surface on which they would have fought for the Australian title through all or most of their careers. If Borg played as well at Kooyong as Wimbledon, he might have retired with 16 majors.

Emmo's record would have fallen more quickly, and new records would have been established on more of a steady curve, had the Australian Open evolved as a "can't miss" Grand Slam event along with the other three. The truth is that for almost two decades we were living in a world with just three majors.

Let me go back to 1991, before we leave Australia, to finish the story of my best run in singles at a major event. In the semis, I had Boris Becker by a set and I wrangled my way to a couple of break points early in the second; I could have gone up 4–2 if I converted either of them. But somewhere in there I clearly remember saying to myself, Shit, I could be in the Australian Open finals. . . .

And that's exactly when the wheels started to fall off—and Becker was too good a player not to jump in and help finish the job.

For the first time in a nearly two-week run, I got distracted. My gorgeous bubble of clarity and concentration burst as if it were made of soap. You're warned about that kind of thing, of course; all your life as a player you're cautioned about taking your eye off the ball, losing focus, and thinking ahead. Stay in the moment. . . . Forget the score. . . . Take it one point at a time. Pick your favorite cliché. But nothing really prepares you, and if you get blindsided by your own mind, things spin out of control pretty quickly. Suddenly, I had nerves again. And being a great player, Boris smelled blood. He lifted his game and turned the match around; I didn't win another set.

The big lesson I learned from my dizzying run in Oz was something I try to convey to all the kids I work with today: Be prepared for success. Work hard, expect it, and go right out to meet it. If I wasn't extra-fit, I never would have won that first round, period. If my own success hadn't come up to bite me on the butt in the semis and make me think, *Wow, I could be in the finals. . . .* Who knows?

Nearly twelve months later, the editors of now-defunct *World Tennis* magazine named my quip about the four semifinalists their Quote of the Year.

DAVIS CUP DAYS

The pleasant July 2000 weekend in the charming Spanish town of Santander should have been a high point in the tennis lives of the McEnroe brothers. John was there as the captain of the U.S.A. Davis Cup team, and I was there covering the event as a commentator for ESPN. Instead, it was an unmitigated disaster.

When it comes to pageantry, the dramatic ebb and flow of emotion and human passion, and remarkable plot twists, you just can't beat Davis Cup. To look up from the court when you're deadlocked at 4–all in the fifth set to see a sea of your nation's colors stretching to the sky in every direction, to hear the relentless pounding of drums (in Brazil), blowing of horns, ringing of cowbells (in Switzerland), or chanting, rolling down from the cheap seats—that's a rare experience, especially in a sport as basically quiet and decorous as tennis.

The atmosphere can make a humble journeyman believe he's a superhero, or make a superhero feel fear in the hollow pit of his stomach. Pete Sampras was thrown into the deep end when he first played Davis Cup, having been selected to make his debut in the final against France, in Lyon, in 1991.

Pete froze like a deer in the headlights, and got blitzed in both his matches as France's two-man team of Henri Leconte and Guy Forget won the Cup. It was enough to make Pete think twice about

Davis Cup duty for the rest of his career, even though he eventually turned in some epic performances—when he chose to play.

We McEnroes have Davis Cup in our blood; my father drilled into us at an early age that there isn't a higher honor than playing for your country. About that he was right. But that weekend in Santander was one we'd all rather forget.

For starters, John and I weren't even speaking. Some people find it hard to believe that brothers can have bouts of frosty silence, but I was accustomed to it. If I put up a win over John (it happened exclusively in doubles, but John cared about all his tennis), he would sulk and glower and ignore me. That was okay by me, even if certain people tried to interpret it as a sign of some dysfunction in our family.

Everyone is different, and John isn't all that conventional a person to begin with. He's always been very sensitive and prone to mood swings. There are things that even the blood bond of family can't—and shouldn't be expected to—overcome. John's unique personality was one of them. It would have been far worse for all of us if I (or our other brother, Mark) were insecure about our standing with John, or craved his approval. My attitude when John turned pissy was to roll my eyes, shrug, and remind myself: *He'll get over it.*

In Santander, team USA was up against a solid Spain squad led by Alex Corretja, and we had Todd Martin, and not much else. Vince Spadea and Jan-Michael Gambill, whose moment in the sun was brief and fading fast, were the singles candidates because Pete Sampras and Andre Agassi had declined to play. John thought that he could beat most of the guys on his team in singles. He was probably right.

On the job for just a few months, John was facing a legitimate crisis for which he could not have been prepared. For he loved Davis Cup with all his heart, and had long coveted the difficult and often thankless captain's job. He misjudged the extent to which other top players shared his passion, as well as the effect his captaincy would have on the motivations of his players.

Legions of people felt that John would make an ideal captain. He finally made his move when Tom Gullikson was shunted aside in 1999. The USTA, the official governing body of American tennis and thus the outfit that puts together our national Davis Cup effort, also approached me in 1999, probably looking to have a little bargaining power with John, who was hot for the job. I figured what the hell, and agreed to discuss the job. That made John hopping mad. But why not? I reasoned. I also believe in the Davis Cup mission and just having my name in the conversation was good for my future.

It didn't really seem like the right moment for me to mount a full-court press for the job. It was obvious to me that John ought to have that captaincy, and he let everyone and his brother know he really wanted it. But I also had an inkling of what would happen if John got the job, and I decided to lay low and bide my time. I withdrew my name from consideration; it just wasn't worth the grief I was getting from John. I didn't grow up with him in the next bunk without learning anything, after all.

John's record as a player for Team USA was unparalleled; he's the greatest Davis Cup player of all time, when you triangulate matches played, rate of success, and the quality of his wins. John played for more years than any other U.S. player, he took part in the most ties (that's Davis Cup lingo for the typical five-match encounter between two teams), and he posted the most wins in singles and doubles combined. Many of his matches are staples of Davis Cup lore and legend. And John *never* failed to answer the call, happily raining hell on all comers on behalf of the U.S.A.

But John is also accustomed to getting his way; he likes to be in control. He assumed that because he was a great player, his peers—the likes of Sampras, Agassi, and Jim Courier—would play for him and respond positively to his personal style. But there's a big difference between being a leader and a Davis Cup captain, because a captain calls for more in the way of management and interpersonal skills. And we all know John doesn't have the deftest touch in that department . . . but the drop volley, yes.

Davis Cup is a tough ask for the very best players. It generally entails a four-week commitment (for a team that gets to the final) on an already crowded tennis calendar. But Germany's Boris Becker liked to say that each Davis Cup tie was close to a three-week commitment, because you prepare and usually travel a few days before the Monday of tie week, and a tough tie doesn't leave you in very good shape for the following week's event, which begins the day after the decisive Sunday of a tie.

It isn't so bad during the first round of play in the elite World Group, which consists of the top sixteen nations (the first-round losers each year have to win a subsequent "relegation" match in order to retain their places at the elite level). The first Davis Cup week is in February or early March, but that's the only tie for which you know, well in advance, who you'll be playing and where.

The first tie week takes place during the relatively dead time between the end of the Australian Open and the two big, spring hardcourt events in the U.S.A. It wasn't always so well positioned. In 2004, I flew back from the Australian Open and immediately after touching down at JFK I hopped in a rental car and drove straight to the Mohegan Sun gambling resort in beautiful downtown Uncasville, Connecticut, to captain our tie against Austria. Everything at that sprawling resort is indoors; after spending two weeks in the bright Australian sunshine and warmth, I didn't see the sun for a solid week.

But by the second round, played in July shortly after Wimbledon, the players are in the heart of the tournament season and are all stressed out about the majors. Tennis players plan their schedules carefully to balance playing and rest weeks, so not knowing if you're playing Davis Cup, or where you may find yourself playing, is problematic—as is the four-round single-elimination World Group format.

In Davis Cup, nations take turns hosting ties. If you last played, say, Brazil, at home, your next tie, even if it's fifteen years later, is at their place. The greatest advantage of being host is that you also get to choose the surface (for a typical U.S.A. team, that usually means away matches on clay). Despite that, stalwart Davis Cup players put the call of the flag above all else. They make the captain's job a lot easier, especially when they're clearly the four best players available.

A Davis Cup tie, played over three days, consists of five matches: four singles and a doubles; first team to three wins advances. The singles are scripted: on Friday each nation's no. 1 plays the opponent's no. 2. Saturday is for doubles. And on Sunday you play the "reverse" singles, with the battle between the two no. 1 players always played first on that final day. In this era of computer rankings, sandbagging is impossible. The higher ranked of the singles players is automatically the no. 1 player. If your no. 2 happens to be a better player than your no. 1 on the surface being used, tough luck. The computer rules.

A talent-rich nation, like Russia or Spain, has a lot of options with a four-man team because of rules that allow for substitution. But teams have won the Davis Cup with just two men playing (the singles players are also eligible to play doubles, together or with one of the other men on the squad).

The captains name their teams on a round-by-round basis, a few weeks before each tie takes place. It's tough on morale when a top player cherry-picks the schedule and chooses to play just ties that suit his schedule or talents. That isn't likely to change until the ITF adopts a format that better suits the needs of the world's best players.

Davis Cup pays well for the typical player, although a top 10 player may earn as much in a one-night exhibition as he does for Davis Cup. Each nation has its own basic pay scale, but the ITF maintains a prize money bonus pool as well. For a Grand Slam contender, the most common reason for playing Davis Cup is pride, personal and national.

John believed that Sampras and Agassi would respond to his captaincy with enthusiasm, and be more willing to make the commitment because of his own iconic status. He was trying to make something special happen, and doing it with all his heart. He stressed that he was a player's captain, not a creature of the tennis politicians who run Davis Cup.

The first tie for a squad captained by a McEnroe was an away clash with—the backward African nation of Zimbabwe. Andre Agassi, a dedicated Davis Cup player for most of his career, stepped up. But Pete Sampras was nursing a back injury, as well as a bruised ego—he'd lost just days earlier to Agassi in the semifinals of the Australian Open. Thus, Chris "Country" Woodruff was the no. 2 singles man for the U.S.

I was in Zimbabwe as a commentator, and it was at times unnerving. The country was in the grip of economic chaos, and their "cheerleaders" were tribesmen who had the habit of jumping up on the sidelines and thrusting wooden spears at our players, although they knew exactly when to stop and dash back into their seats as play was about to resume. My dad got his wallet lifted, and we barely escaped a humiliating loss when Country atoned for his loss in the second single match with a win in the decisive fifth rubber.

The next tie, against the Czech Republic, was at home at the cavernous indoor Forum in Los Angeles. Again, the U.S. barely squeaked it out, 3–2, despite having both Sampras and Agassi playing singles. It was becoming clear that despite John's enthusiasm and imperial ambitions, the squad wasn't really jelling. How could it? You had three of the biggest egos in tennis bumping up against one another.

In John's vision, the Davis Cup team was going to be like a very tight rock and roll band. But that was unrealistic. Tennis players are often wary loners, and when they're champions and rivals, the situation can be even more edgy. In Los Angeles, the only guys who actually stayed at the team hotel, where so much of Davis Cup bonding and spirit building can take place, were doubles player Jared Palmer and a young, spunky American practice partner about whom more would soon be heard. John and Pete, who both lived in L.A., stayed at home. Andre had a place nearby, too.

Then came Santander. Sampras and Agassi were pretty much fried by the end of Wimbledon in July of 2000, and neither felt much like going to Spain to battle a tough Spanish outfit in a semifinal on their preferred red clay. That was a shock to John, who couldn't understand how they could bail on the competition in the semifinal stage. When the stars backed off, John publicly called them out. If I've learned one thing in my own nine-year tenure as captain, it's that you just don't do that kind of thing—not even if you're John McEnroe. Guys like Agassi and Sampras, they just shrug and say, "I don't need to deal with this," and walk away. Which is how it played out that year.

John bulled ahead. In Santander, he was out there on the practice court, working his tail off, as if he might even insert himself into the doubles. The players were weirded out, the tie became a nightmare, and the U.S.A. lost, 5–0.

John up and quit, ending his brief, unhappy, three-tie tenure as Davis Cup captain. And it opened the door for me.

The Davis Cup captaincy comes with its share of headaches due to the politics involved. A Davis Cup tie is a high prestige event for the ITF affiliates that run them; they're a great morale builder for outfits like the USTA. A trip to a Davis Cup tie is a great perk in an all-volunteer organization, and hobnobbing with national federation types is part of a player or captain's job. The players grin and bear it, knowing that ceremonial dinners and meet and greets come with the territory of playing for your nation.

There are ways to liven up some of those affairs. Our squad has developed a tradition whereby one of our new practice players (we take two for every tie; they're usually promising youngsters) gives a speech right after the U.S.A. captain makes his remarks to a banquet hall packed with dignitaries and tennis officials from both nations. It's the ultimate nightmare for a socially shy or awkward eighteen-year-old. To make matters worse, the veterans on the club give the kid a list of dirty words or expressions ("teabagging," "chocolate highway," "banana hammock") that the poor kid somehow must work into his speech.

Andy Roddick, for so many years our team leader and go-to guy (Bob and Mike Bryan, our ever-reliable doubles team, nicknamed him "the Closer"), loves this kind of stuff. He still enjoys telling the story of how Ryan Sweeting artfully wove the word "dingleberries" into his speech before an away tie against Russia. The butt of his story is my mom, Kay.

Dad and Mom were seated next to our team table. Andy loves to act out how, upon hearing Sweeting's speech, my mom turned to my dad, wide-eyed and baffled, and asked, "John, what's a dingleberry?"

What can I tell you? These aren't poetry professors at a conference on Shakespeare. They're young, restless, jacked up, and easily bored twenty-somethings in a pretty lonely sport, making the most of a rare chance to be part of something bigger than themselves—and they find a common denominator way of expressing their solidarity and sense of camaraderie.

That Swiss Kid Can Play . . .

After John crashed and burned as Davis Cup captain, I felt my time had come—if only the USTA wouldn't hold the disastrous experience with John against me. I've always admired great coaches and other leaders, and having played college tennis, I knew how much richer the experience of winning was if you had a team with which to share it. I was lucky that Arlen Kantarian was the CEO of Men's Professional Tennis for the USTA at the time, because I got on well with him. He asked me to write a paper detailing why I should be captain. Although Arlen supported my bid, I felt like I was back in grade school.

I wrote a six-page paper, with help from my wife, Melissa Errico.

I was up against some very accomplished candidates, including Paul Annacone and Brad Gilbert, both of whom had better pro careers than mine and extensive coaching experience with top players (Paul was Pete Sampras's coach during the latter's glory years, and Brad had resurrected Andre Agassi's once-moribund career). Plus, there was the potential anti-McEnroe backlash.

I went through five or six different interviews for the position, including one in which a former USTA president, Merv Heller, asked if I thought I was "tough" and "competitive" enough for the job. I about blew my cork; I snapped back a reply and Heller, clearly embarrassed, furiously backpedaled, claiming that he was just "testing" me with the question. He said he liked my response, although more than anything it probably made him feel like an ass.

Of course, it wasn't the first or last time I'd had to deal with that kind of question, because I was so easygoing—and that wasn't exactly considered a McEnroe family trait. My own mother was anxious about what might happen if I (a mama's boy, known to my brothers as "perfect Patrick") tried to follow in John's footsteps in tennis. She tried to dissuade me from attending Stanford and seeking a career in tennis because, she feared, I would always be compared to John, who was a genius. *What's the problem?* I wondered. I told her: "I'm always going to be compared to John, anyway, so why not just go and do what I want?"

One evening, when Melissa and I were at our rented house in Los Angeles (where she was doing some film work), the phone rang. It was Arlen. Melissa and I sat on the edge of the bed as Arlen spoke and suddenly I shouted, "I got it, I got it. I got the job!"

My first assignment as captain was to lead Team U.S.A. to Switzerland in early 2001 to meet a team featuring some promising young kid named Roger Federer.

I immediately started calling the guys, everyone from Andre Agassi to Paul Goldstein, anyone whom I thought could help. I also had my own cup experience to call on, from before I even thought I might one day be captain.

. . . .

I first got called up to play Davis Cup as a doubles player in 1993, in a tie in Charlotte, North Carolina, against the Bahamas. The Bahamas weren't exactly the Jamaican bobsled team, but it was pretty close. They fielded a three-man team that included John Farrington, a very nice guy who looked about forty-five years old.

Given the humiliation Pete Sampras had suffered just two years earlier, in France, it was a great way to debut. Our singles players against the Bahamas were Andre Agassi and Mal Washington. Although we swept the first day's singles, I had Davis Cup jitters, bad. My partner, Richey Reneberg, had already done Cup duty, so he was a little more relaxed in our match with Roger Smith and Mark Knowles (a superb doubles player).

Richey was one of my regular doubles partners over the years, a calm, nice guy who had a rebellious streak. He liked to invent nicknames for other players, and he enjoyed pranks. In Singapore one year, he and another guy got hold of one of those water balloon slingshots and started bombing the street from the hotel. Next thing, the Singapore police had shut down the entire block. Singapore is notorious for its strict—and strictly enforced—laws, including a prohibition against chewing gum. For a while, it looked like Richey might make headlines for getting one of those famous "canings." But he hid and never did get caught.

Richey also had a thing for the "Jerky Boys" comedy team (Google it to get a feel for their "sophisticated" humor), which seemed oddly out of character for such a low-key guy and born-again Christian. We were a good team, but each of us skewed more toward finesse, and we both did better with a partner who had a lot of straight-ahead power. We both had good backhands. I had quicker hands, but he had quicker feet. Neither of us had a big serve, but his was better.

Richey wasn't the most decisive guy. Receiving serve to start a match, I'd ask: "Richey, which side do you want to play, deuce or ad?"

Richey would shrug and say, "I don't care, whatever."

Or, "Richey, you want to serve first?"

To which he'd reply, "Whatever you want to do."

Well, right off, Bahamas won the first set. The second set was tight; at the changeover at 4–5, Andre suddenly got up from his seat in the stands and marched out onto the court. A buzz ran through the crowd. Andre stood in front of Richey and me, looked us in the eye, and icily said these eight words—and nothing else: "Guys. You're playing Mark Knowles and Roger Smith."

Then he marched right back to his seat and sat down. It worked; Richey and I got our act together and won.

The tie gave me my first taste of Agassi, the loose cannon. Our doubles clinched the tie, but theoretically our singles guys were supposed to play out their Sunday matches (the "dead rubbers" in Davis Cup parlance). That, incidentally, has always been an irritant, like forcing a home team in baseball to bat in the bottom of the ninth, risking injury to one of their players, when they already had an insurmountable lead of 11–1.

Anyway, Sunday morning, Andre pulled us aside and said he was pulling out and going home.

Being Perfect Patrick, I blurted, "But Andre . . . aren't you supposed to stay and play your singles?"

He laughed and replied, "No way I'm going to play, I'm fucking outta here."

But Andre promised to have a special treat for us poor peons who were going to stay. Richey was sent in to substitute for Andre in the dead rubber, playing against the older gent, Farrington—neither Smith nor Knowles was interested in playing. The proceedings were just beginning when we heard the roar of a jet, and there went Andre, just about five hundred feet above the stadium. He was doing a flyover for our benefit.

I could have sworn I saw him giving us the finger, grinning.

The Fine Art of Self-Deception

I played a couple of Davis Cup doubles matches with Richey and two with Patrick Galbraith. But despite my limited experience, I felt I was cut from the right cloth to be a Davis Cup captain. I did well in a team situation and liked it. As a kid, I found team sports like baseball and soccer more appealing than tennis. I was one of the last successful players who attended college for four years. And being the youngest of three brothers, I'd learned how to navigate relationships from a disadvantage—or how to turn my position into an asset.

I'm not just blowing smoke when I say that Davis Cup has been one of my adult, life-shaping experiences. Tennis players are, as a group, incredibly high-strung (some would say insecure) as well as stubborn. The difference between being a dominating, ruthless, take-no-prisoners stud and a guy who makes Hamlet look decisive is infinitesimal, often impossible to quantify in anything but vague psychological terms, and subject to reversal for a simple reason: in tennis, you're only as good as your last result.

As captain I would have to figure out drastically different ways of dealing with, say, James Blake, who really didn't want to hear any suggestions that went against his own philosophy, and Andy Roddick, who wasn't particularly needy or interested in intense analysis, but was always looking to improve, willing to try new things, and impatient with any real or imagined failure in others.

A tennis player is always out there, alone; he's got to believe he can get the job done because there's no fallback, no cushion like you have in team sports—even in Davis Cup, you face your greatest trials alone; there's no one to pass the ball off to when you must make a three-pointer at the buzzer. If you don't really believe in yourself in tennis, how are you going to get it done?

Okay, if I'm a player up against a weaker guy, I'll get it done. But what if the other guy has equal, or better, ability, which is almost always the case these days in tennis. The days when good players could sleepwalk through the early rounds at a tournament are long gone. Therefore, tennis players have to be good at lying to themselves; they simply have to believe they have a shot against anyone, or they end up having no shot at no one.

But that also means tennis players are going to resist change. If you follow the rule to leave the dance with the one who brought you, you're going home alone. When someone tells you that you need to do something different, or better, it suggests that what you have isn't good enough. And that can undermine your self-confidence, even if it's accurate—that's the eight-hundred-pound gorilla in the tennis room.

I knew something about all this before I became Davis Cup captain, but it wasn't nearly enough preparation—as I learned in Switzerland in my first tie as captain. My first mistake was allowing the players to bring their individual coaches. This is frequently an issue in Davis Cup, where the captain is theoretically the coach. But players, especially top players, are extremely cautious about turning themselves over to anyone but their closest and most trusted advisers. They're also reluctant to reveal their innermost insecurities and secrets. People in tennis often have multiple roles; your Davis Cup captain might end up coaching your most bitter rival.

In Switzerland, the problem was compounded and then squared: Todd Martin, a smart, low-maintenance guy with an open mind about his game, was our top singles player. My other two options, given the indifference of Sampras and Agassi that year, were Justin Gimelstob and Jan-Michael Gambill, both of whom had dominating, quasi-coach fathers who insisted on showing up at the tie. I said the problem was squared because neither the dads nor their kids got along; they had a long and bitter history as rivals, going back to the juniors. My only consolation was that the boys got along better than the dads.

One reason I'd chosen Gimelstob and Gambill was because I was desperate for a decent doubles team. I didn't want to make Todd, a fine doubles player, play three matches. In addition to the other factors, he was hampered by a bad back. But that meant I had to gamble with our doubles team. One of the great features of Davis Cup is that the doubles *really* counts; show me a great Davis Cup record and I'll show you a nation that was anchored by a great doubles team, always ready to turn a 1–1 tie after day one into a 2–1 lead.

Todd lost the opening match of the tie to Federer, but the young Swiss wasn't all that persuasive. Word about Roger had filtered around on the circuit; everyone knew he had talent. But he seemed too free spirited to become a dominant champ. In his junior career, he sometimes showed up with an absurd, hipster haircut right off the cover of some 1980s album by Flock of Seagulls. The year he won the Orange Bowl junior title in the under-18s, his hair was a blinding white, with black roots. And he always had that big, elastic smile on his face.

When Jan-Michael won the second singles, I felt we had a little breathing room. I was counting on Gimelstob and Gambill to show up big in the doubles. It didn't work out that way, mostly because Federer gave us a glimpse of what was soon coming in singles, too. His performance was mind blowing. Any time he hit a volley, or even just got his racket on a volley, the point was over.

Despite being the brother of maybe the best doubles player, ever, I'd never seen anyone put as much English on a ball at the net as Federer. When the court position called for him to cut the ball and leave it to die just across the net, he did it. When he had to drive the ball firmly, down the middle, he did that. If he had to dump it short, he would—and he'd do it in a way that left us thinking, *Holy shit, I've never seen anyone do this, put that kind of work on the ball. . . .*

It was clear that Roger had a deep artistic streak; and he would show in his later years that he could play great tennis that was also, simply, beautiful. It took him a significant period of time to learn when to use all the options in his toolbox, and when to pull the trigger on the great shot and when to resist the temptation. His record bears witness to that. While guys like Pete Sampras, Marat Safin,

Björn Borg, my brother John, and Juan Martin del Potro won majors before they turned twenty-one, Federer developed more slowly. He was almost twenty-two when he won his first major, at Wimbledon, in his seventeenth appearance in a Slam. By contrast, Pete won the eighth major he played, at age nineteen.

Federer matured as a world-class player long before he came into his own as a world-class competitor. It was easier to do well in doubles (he's an Olympic gold medalist in that discipline), where responsibilities to your partner, the guiding pressure of his expectations, and a more limited range of shot choices put a higher premium on consistency and tangible results.

We lost the doubles to the Swiss, and found ourselves—the mighty U.S.A., the most successful team in Davis Cup history—in a hole from which we didn't escape. My debut as captain was a rocky one, but relief was on the way.

Andy Roddick: Punching Bag to the Stars

Our fourth man on the team that faced Switzerland was Andy Roddick. I was pretty much set on using Todd and Jan-Michael in the singles, so I kind of took a flier by putting Roddick on the team. Earlier in the year, while I was doing my TV thing in Australia, Roddick played a Challenger event in Hawaii (Challengers are like the highest level of baseball's minor leagues). Although Andy didn't have a "can't miss" reputation, I had my eye on him as a potential player for us. During that Hawaii Challenger, I was in touch with his coach at the time, the former French tour player Tarik Benhabiles.

I told Tarik that I was thinking of picking Andy for the team that would travel to Switzerland. Andy had already been a practice partner in the U.S.A.'s tie against the Czech Republic in Los Angeles in 2000; he was the other lonely guy at the official team hotel. But this was the real deal. He would be the official fourth man on the squad, even though that didn't guarantee he would play. I didn't tell Tarik that I had very few other options, nor did I have any intention to throw Andy into the deep end of actual competition.

Tarik said, "I'm going to tell Andy you're looking at him for the team; he's going to be so excited!"

The next day in Hawaii, Andy went out and beat veteran journeyman and former Davis Cup selection Vince Spadea. Andy just crushed Vince, something like two-and-one. In fact, he was so jacked up that he won the Hawaii event, and I was thinking, *Now this is a good sign. . . .*

Come the tie against the Swiss, Andy Roddick was ready. He had flown something like eleven hours to join us in Basel, and he came straight to practice—fresh-faced, expectant, ready to go—and started bombing balls. I mean, it was like the serves were being shot out of a cannon on the battleship *Missouri.* Todd, who had stepped in to help Andy limber up, looked at me and just said, "Holy shit. . . ."

Roddick was confident, but he was also serious and respectful. When Federer beat Gambill in the fourth rubber to clinch the tie for Switzerland, I decided to put Andy in as a substitute for Todd in the final singles.

In his first Davis Cup experience, as a practice partner in Los Angeles for that tie against the Czech Republic, Andy had been the punching bag for the stars, Sampras and Agassi, who refused to practice with each other. He worked out those two icons, after which he was thrown back to the lions as a doubles partner facing the U.S.A. team of Alex O'Brien and Jared Palmer. And after that, John, the captain, wanted to get a workout in, too.

As Andy tells it, after four or five hours of regular practice, he would have to hit with John—the non-playing captain and still-fit tennis genius—for another two hours. The workload was so heavy that immediately after the tie, Andy underwent arthroscopic knee surgery.

It was a harsh welcome to Davis Cup, so I was especially pleased to give Andy an opportunity to play a match that would go into the official Davis Cup record books (that's another beef I have with those meaningless dead rubbers). Up until then, all I had heard from most quarters was that it would be a while before the U.S. has a chance to win the Davis Cup again, blah-blah-blah. . . .

Andy went out there against George Bastl, who at the time was a decent player, and just blew him away in straight sets. At one point in the match, I turned to our bench and said, "It looks like we've got ourselves a future."

THE MORE THINGS CHANGE . . .

The French expression *Plus ça change, plus c'est la même chose* (The more things change, the more they remain the same) is especially relevant to tennis. It's never more obvious than during the late winter in the U.S. While the months of gloomy winter once featured a number of significant tournaments, the big events at Indian Wells (near Palm Springs, California) and Miami now tower over a nearly empty landscape. They've held their own despite the shrinking American market because of their long history, and because they're "combined" events with full men's and women's draws.

Those events were a staple of ESPN back when I started my broadcasting career. At that point, tennis was mainly filler on ESPN, something to broadcast between those NCAA basketball tournament games and NFL draft previews. Early on, the tennis tours had to buy the time on the network (instead of the networks bidding for rights to the tournament, as networks do for major, in-demand American sports). With luck, the tours might recoup their investment in the revenues they made from commercials, and the long-term benefits of name recognition.

So ESPN would send us out to Miami, Indian Wells, Cincinnati, or Toronto for as much as eight hours a day. We'd be on from 1:00 to 5:00 p.m.; grab a bite and a break, and get back in the booth from 7:00 to 10:00 p.m. It was usually me and my compadre, Cliff

Drysdale. Once in a while, they'd throw a Mal Washington or Luke Jensen in there, but mostly it was just us. It was a grind, concentrating on tennis hour after hour through the day and evening, but I loved every moment of it. The only irritants were those bad, error-strewn matches that clearly had no bearing on anything. We had to struggle to appear interested in those.

By the time summer rolled around, tennis was higher on the public radar, and ESPN was attuned to that. I remember doing a stretch when I worked for twenty-four of twenty-seven days, going from Washington to Montreal to Cincinnati to New Haven to New York, for the US Open (when I switched to CBS). They were long days, but for ESPN it was tennis broadcasting gold—cheap, live television.

That all began to change as ESPN grew by leaps and bounds, and attracted the kind of executive talent that saw the potential tennis had as an international sport in the age of the Internet and multiple channel options. The man most responsible for the fact that ESPN now broadcasts all four Grand Slam events was Mark Shapiro, a young guy who had swiftly moved up the ESPN ranks (he's since left the network) and loved tennis.

The process started with our broadcasts of the Australian Open, which no one else wanted to touch for various reasons, starting with the time-zone issues. Australia is sixteen hours ahead of the U.S. (when it's 9:00 p.m. in the U.S., it's 1:00 p.m. Down Under), which is why the occasional night session in Australia makes such good breakfast TV in the U.S.—and why so many Americans on the eastern seaboard show up to work all bleary-eyed from watching tennis late at night.

In many ways, I still think of the Australian Open as our crown jewel. We cover it from start to finish (at the French Open, Wimbledon, and the US Open, other networks, NBC or CBS, have the rights to some key days, including the weekend of the finals). And if the odd hours restrict the size of our potential audience, we really get the tennis lovers. That's why we always plead with the programming directors to let us show great or really intriguing matches, not just top names.

But that's a battle we usually lose, because the programming directors believe that a terrible match starring Serena Williams is preferable to an epic, five-set battle between, say, Nicolas Almagro and David Ferrer. That makes some diehard tennis fans see red, but the reality is that only two players in recent years had the drawing power to trigger a spike in American viewers at ESPN: Andre Agassi and Serena Williams.

This attitude was particularly infuriating when I was working for CBS at the US Open. Granted, the business model for CBS is different from the one for ESPN, but I always felt that ESPN was invested in tennis, while CBS was just invested in the US Open, and just in American players in the tournament.

During one of my first years with CBS, during the Sampras-Agassi era, American players were struggling in the early rounds. I remember going to one of the production meetings, and the entire focus was on weekend ratings. Looking at the results, one of the program directors said, "What the hell is wrong with these (American) guys?"

I was really irritated. I wanted to say, "There are a lot of great players out there from all over the world, and they're getting better and more competitive every year. That's what's 'wrong' with them."

The programming people don't want to hear that, though. They sit there with the draw early in the tournament and pencil in the names they want to see out there for the Labor Day weekend. They tell tournament director Jim Curley and the USTA: We want Agassi twice, we want Serena Williams at night, that kind of thing. I was fresh off the tour at the time, and maybe a little too sensitive to what you might call the player point of view. These days, everyone is good; you have to be crazy to assume this or that guy is going to the fourth round, or quarters.

I ought to add that just because CBS wants something, and has plenty of leverage, many other voices—including those of the players and the holders of foreign broadcast rights—try to exert leverage on Curley as well. His job is to try to keep everyone happy, while remaining fair. Curley has to give all the players in the draw comparable conditions when it comes to rest vs. work periods, court assignments, and time of play. During the first week of the US Open, the days can be brutally hot and humid, so it's an advantage to play at night, and network types want to see certain star players on the evening card.

One of the best examples of a bad scheduling decision occurred in 1987, when that old "Super Saturday" formula (the men's semifinals were sandwiched around the women's final, which was mandated to start at 4:00 p.m. sharp) led the tournament director of the time to send Stefan Edberg and Mats Wilander out to play their semifinal at 10:00 a.m.—before a nearly empty stadium. CBS obviously wanted the other semifinal, a showdown between bitter rivals Jimmy Connors and Ivan Lendl, as its prime-time offering. Wilander and Edberg were so incensed that they called an impromptu strike, and who could blame them? You don't start at 10:00 a.m. once you get out of the juniors, never mind for a Grand Slam semi. It was a nice, polite, Swedish strike of ten minutes, after which the disgruntled pair took the court. (Wilander won, and lost to Lendl in the final.)

It was a terrible slight to those two great and popular champions, no matter how you cut it, and it underscored the deeply unfair nature of the Super Saturday concept, especially when an American player was in the semis. And it wasn't like he got a great deal, either. The Saturday semifinals meant that the guy who played the late match had to come back and play the best-of-five final less than 24 hours after winning his semi, while the man who won the early match got a good night's sleep and had many hours more to recover and get ready. I'm glad they got rid of the original Super Saturday format, but playing the men's semis on Saturday is still a problem.

The overarching question is, Should the US Open give American players all the possible breaks, short of stepping beyond the boundaries of fairness? It's a tough question, partly because that boundary isn't etched in stone. And the last I checked, Roger Federer wasn't prevented from making six of the last seven US Open finals (and winning five) by any concession made to CBS.

The reality is that every nation wants to showcase its players. Non-American fans tend to piss and moan about how much television time American players get at the US Open, which proves mostly that those fans have never been at another major, or experienced one in a foreign land. The fixation on homegrown talent is as bad—or worse. Besides, there is a huge net gain for tennis when events celebrate native players. It tends to fire up the base and advance the popularity of the game.

Anyway, Shapiro helped transform ESPN into the Grand Slam network. We made a successful, last-minute effort to get the French Open many years ago, when the USA network bailed on it. I remember, four of us jumped on a plane on the spur of the moment to cover it. I think we had someone draw up a sign (by hand) that we could hold up in front of the camera to tell viewers that it was ESPN coverage.

Securing the rights to Wimbledon put us over the top as a network vested in tennis. For one thing, it opened up the ESPN purse strings, enabling us to cover the event in an appropriate way. Wimbledon is Wimbledon; you go there and do things on the cheap and you'll look like an idiot. ESPN completed its conquest of the broadcast schedule in 2009 when it replaced the USA network as a broadcast partner to CBS and the US Open.

But there's been a downside to becoming the network of the majors; we pretty much threw every other event under the bus. In tennis, it's all about the Grand Slams. Like I said, The more things change . . .

The Women, Marching Back to Square One

Here's another way tennis has gone back to the future: When the Open era started, many tournaments were combined men's/women's events, and after a long period of segregated tours, we're back to that model.

Granted, the women originally were an afterthought—clearly the undercard at most events—and the prize money figures reflected it (at some events, the men's champion earned *seven* times more, which was ridiculous). Billie Jean King helped change all that, leading the charge to create an all-women's circuit, the Virginia Slims tour. For a long period in the 1970s and 1980s, when the women's movement, and corporate giant Philip Morris, the cigarette maker who underwrote the entire VS tour on behalf of that brand of big tobacco, were at their peak, the tour was an enormous success.

But in recent years, men's events have been far more successful and stable. Just three years ago, the WTA season-ending championships (theoretically, the next most important event after the majors) were played in a competitive market (Los Angeles) and turned out to be an unmitigated disaster. The tour finally moved the event to Doha, in the Middle East, where the sheiks are amenable to throwing petrodollars around to impress the West. Meanwhile, the men's year-end event moved from Shanghai (the men, too, are not above chasing the money) to London and the dazzling 02 Arena, a biting comment on the difference between the two tours.

As the stand-alone women's tour hit rough sledding, pioneers like former top 10 pro Butch Buchholz picked up on where sports in general was going, much to the benefit of the women. Buchholz, one of the truly great promoters who had a love of the game, was the founder of the big March event in Miami, now the Sony-Ericsson Open. Butch realized that a tennis tournament could and ought to be a "happening," a festive, laid-back, colorful mix of great tennis and fan-friendly amenities like live music on the grounds, a "fun zone" for kids, and, of course, the obligatory food court. Another feature of this new approach was having both men's and women's draws.

Buchholz knew that combined events cast a wider net for spectators, and garnered greater media attention; after all, the Grand Slams are "combined" events. And you get those benefits at a bargain price, because running one tournament, even with the additional prize money and extra days (basically, the big combined events are 10-day tournaments), was cheaper than hosting separate, equally high-quality events.

The women also found the merger increasingly attractive as they struggled in the post–Virginia Slims era, even as they won the battle of conscience raging over equal prize money. The women successfully negotiated a quota system for ensuring access to prime courts at prime times in order to guarantee maximum live audience and television exposure. That's why you'll always see one men's and one women's match at night during the US Open—even on a day when Roger Federer and Rafael Nadal might be facing tough tests, while the top two or three women, the stars whom the two-match session demands, will decimate their opponents.

Buchholz, along with the Indian Wells duo of former players Charlie Pasarell and Ray Moore, set the trend for today's back-to-the-future events. But that's also caused some discontent among the male players, who feel they give a lot (including equal prize money) and get little in return. Bring up the subject and most of the men just roll their eyes, acknowledging that this is a highly politicized issue that they can't possibly win—or look good tackling.

The depth of the typical male pro's cynicism was made clear to me when I walked into the locker room at the Australian Open in 2009, during the women's final. There was Serena Williams, opening a can of whup-ass on Dinara Safina. The room was populated with the usual assortment of doubles players, coaches, and lingerers, semiwatching a match on TV, laughing and cracking jokes about the poor quality of the blowout. Someone said, with a slight edge in his tone: "There's your argument for equal prize money."

There's no doubt that the men's game is more competitive, and I'll go into the reasons for that later. But the debate also hits close to home with me, because I have three daughters. Unlike some former players, especially some great ones, I'll do all I can to help my girls become successful players if that's what they ultimately want. (The rule of thumb seems to be that the more a given player achieved, the less he or she wants to see his own children become pros—that tells you something about the stress level at the top.) Also, I'm married to a woman who works, and in an entertainment industry where compensation can fluctuate wildly, unfairly, and irrespective of gender lines. It's driven by market forces and, like tennis, it's all about star power.

I don't put much stock in the argument that men players work harder than women, because men play best-of-five set matches (at majors and in Davis Cup) while the women are always best-of-three, with a preponderance of two-set wipeouts. Tennis is really about who is willing to pay, and how much, to watch anyone hit a ball.

Make no mistake, tennis is a woman-friendly sport. The women have always had a place at the table, even when the game went Open—and even after the women bolted to make it on their own. I guess we can thank the Grand Slams for that. I mean, just look at golf. Although that too is a skill-based game (as in tennis the men probably are better only because they're physically bigger and stronger), the lack of linkage between the genders in golf has been devastating for women; their stand-alone pro tour is in terrible economic shape, and women's golf is fast fading from the public's radar. It's not entirely fair to say that men's tennis has carried the women's game—not in the era of the Williamses, Maria Sharapova, and the Belgians, Kim Clijsters and Justine Henin—but the women are lucky the two divisions marched in lockstep, right back to where they started, but now as equal partners.

It's ironic that big tobacco took women's tennis to its peak, but Billie Jean King certainly got the job done.

Still, critics of women's tennis collected plenty of ammo recently. The day after that lopsided Williams-Safina final I mentioned above, Rafael Nadal beat Roger Federer in a five-set Australian Open final. And the round before that, Nadal and Fernando Verdasco played a five-set men's semifinal that lasted 5 hours and 14 minutes.

Look at the last three electrifying Wimbledon finals. In 2007, Roger triumphed over Rafa in a brutal five-setter. In 2008, the same men played the final (Rafa won), and that match was instantly dubbed the greatest tennis battle of all time. And in 2009, Roger was pushed to 16–14 in the fifth by Andy Roddick before he could claim his record-shattering fifteenth major title.

That Williams-Safina result in 2009 was no fluke—or the case of a "surprise finalist" being reintroduced to reality. Just weeks after the Australian Open, Safina, who dominated lesser players and showed admirable consistency, actually snatched away the top ranking from Serena. Safina was clearly the second-best player for most of the year, and that's just the problem. How can a no. 2 be so strong on paper, yet so weak on the field of play?

Venus Williams added to the body of evidence a few months later at Wimbledon, with Safina still no. 1. Venus roughed up Safina even worse than had Serena (6–1, 6–0) and in a shorter (51 minutes) match. In the interest of full disclosure, let's remember that on that same day, Serena Williams and Elena Dementieva turned in a spectacular match, the longest women's semi in Wimbledon history (Serena won it, 8–6 in the third). But players like those two (Dementieva is an Olympic Games gold medalist in singles and multiple Grand Slam event finalist) are supposed to produce those kinds of matches with some regularity; instead, they're rare occasions.

Safina remained no. 1, even after that drubbing by Venus. She earned the ranking fair and square; it certainly wasn't her fault that the Williamses declined to focus on the day-in, day-out tournaments where you earn so many ranking points. But while Safina is a big, strong girl who makes good power off both wings, she lacks that critical element of self-belief that would enable her to stand up under the mental strain of facing one of the elite champions.

If you look back on the careers of other dominant players, including Steffi Graf, Monica Seles, Martina Navratilova, and Chris Evert, you see a similar pattern. A female Grand Slam champion's path to a title is littered with lopsided 6–1, 6–2 scores. That's changed some, although the way Kim Clijsters and Justine Henin returned to tennis in 2010 after extended breaks, only to blast their way right back to the top in nothing flat, was hardly a good advertisement for the fighting qualities of the other up-and-coming WTA players.

It seems that in any generation in women's tennis, there's usually a handful of players who are fully reconciled to the demands of competition. Maybe they don't take it so personally. The model for the type was Steffi Graf, who had a strangely homemade game but the heart of a lioness and the athleticism of an Olympic track athlete (she sometimes trained with Olympic runners, as an equal).

Steffi knew what she wanted from tennis: Grand Slam titles. She was famous for appearing in the locker room five minutes before her match, and departing five minutes after it was over. She simply didn't mix or socialize with her peers. She was one of the few women who was never perceived as a diva, or accused of engaging in locker room intrigue.

For some reason, women seem to have a much harder time leaving the daily tennis battle on the court. Some top men have been aloof, guarded, and disinclined to mix much with their peers, but the guys further down the food chain happily beat the crap out of each other and end up drinking beer together. Women in a similar situation tend to stick to themselves, or immerse themselves in the cocoon provided by a support team. And the men are more interested in the game, for its own sake, and are more inclined to talk about it among themselves, or even with reporters and other peripheral types. It's amazing how few former women pros are coaches.

I believe it's unfair to judge women's tennis by the same standard as the men's game. It's an apples-and-oranges comparison, because women operate within different physical parameters. That might be more responsible than psychology or sociology for the way the talent on the WTA tour seems to drop off sharply, fairly close to the top. An athletic specimen on the order of Graf or Martina Navratilova is a rarity in the women's game, while at any given moment in time many men seem to have the makings of über-athletes.

Power is the great equalizer in men's tennis, and it's a great inhibitor on the women's tour.

The skill of the average woman pro has improved significantly in the past decade, yet the tour still hasn't become very competitive throughout the entire draw. You have to wonder, how does a player like Safina manage to lord it over all those other women, yet look almost embarrassingly undeserving of a top ranking when she plays a superb competitor?

The Serial Break-fest

The state of women's pro tennis is doubly puzzling because there's been a role reversal in tennis. It used to be the women who played a one-size-fits-all game, while the men's tour was awash in "specialists," although "experts" might be a better word. (I'd certainly say Rafael Nadal is an "expert" rather than "specialist" when it comes to his prowess on clay.)

But a combination of court speed and the advent of polyester strings (sometimes in combination with traditional gut) now allows men to take savage cuts at the ball and still have it fall in. And it has led to an absolute mastery of spin. As a result, most men play a similar style and perform equally well on all surfaces, especially now that courts at the fast end of the spectrum aren't very fast, and don't vary all that much.

The women aren't there yet, despite the trail blazed by the Williams sisters. In general, the WTA pros are locked into games that shine or look dull depending on the surface. Safina became an excellent clay-court player when she developed the fitness to go with her consistency, but Venus revealed Safina's weaknesses on grass. Maria Sharapova struggles on clay. And lately, even Venus and Serena Williams look more and more vulnerable on slower surfaces. Those four women accounted for an enormous number of titles and wins in recent years.

By contrast, the only thing that has kept Roger Federer from winning more frequently at Roland Garros has been Rafael Nadal. And without Federer, Nadal might be a three- or four-time Wimbledon champion. The only man near the top of the game who's really a slave to surface has been Andy Roddick—and he hasn't been a top-three or -four player for a few years.

Most women probably just aren't strong enough to use spin most effectively—as a tool for pushing around, punishing, and wearing down opponents. The players of today can hit big—no doubt about it. But they hit pretty flat so the margin of error is small. In tough matches, they're inclined to back away from risk, or succumb to the pressure by making more errors. And when a smart opponent takes advantage of those tendencies, the mental cookie of the typical player begins to crumble.

During the 2009 US Open, even the progressive *New York Times*, a cheerleader for women's rights, had to tackle an uncomfortable issue for the WTA, the abysmal serving statistics posted by even the top women. Poor serving is a cardinal sin in tennis, because the serve is the one shot over which you have complete control, from start to finish. It's also the easiest to work on and master, and it's such an advantage to be serving rather than receiving that the entire scoring system is based on the theory that you will hold your own serve.

For men, breaks of serve are the outstanding data points in any match; for the women, service *holds* have come to seem more critical. The conventional wisdom has been turned on its ear. You can put some of this down to the current emphasis on return of serve, and the way racket and string technologies have tilted the balance in favor of the returner. But that hasn't skewed the service efficiency statistics nearly as much for the men as the women, and they play with the same equipment. Something else is going on.

Part of it is that women just don't throw as naturally and easily as men, either by design or lack of training. And throwing is the heart of the service action. Women who have the easy, natural service that's standard issue for male players are virtually nonexistent. So serving becomes a challenge and an adventure, rather than an easy 1–2–3 process undertaken with a calm and confident mind.

To make matters worse, in this heyday of the serve return, most women just can't get enough of a wrist snap, or arm speed, to hit second (sometimes even first) serves that are both safe and capable of keeping an opponent off balance. Knowing that leads a server to fear the return, which can play havoc with a server's confidence and poise. There's no place for the doubt-ridden player to hide when she's about to serve; you do it before a hushed crowd, in an atmosphere of utter stillness and expectation. It's like shooting a critical free throw.

In a tight situation, even a journeyman male player can step up and more or less fake it—hit a serve with enough action and pace to keep his threatening rival on the defensive. The kick serve, or American Twist, is especially useful for that, because it's hit with such exaggerated spin that the ball travels high over the net and that creates a comfortable margin for error. But the kicker also dips down into the service court quickly because of the heavy rotation, and it jumps to life on impact. It's both safe and deadly.

A player's first job under duress is to avoid the silly or stupid error. His second task is to make something happen, preferably forcing an error. It's much harder for a woman to do that when she's serving, and that opens the floodgates on doubt and frustration. Also, the first thing most players do when broken is make a dramatic effort to earn back the break, which is partly why you have these serial breaks in women's tennis. It's a vicious cycle. They just take turns whacking huge returns at each other off tentative, weak serves.

Serena Williams has been the only woman to transcend this problem—she must have the best woman's serve, ever. She has the same service motion as a man, and she can hit the kicker as her second serve. Even Venus can't quite pull that off. She can hit about as hard as her kid sister, but she doesn't have the same power and control in her wrist. So her safety net isn't as deep. Venus's second serve is that "sidewinder" slice that's a little easier for an opponent to handle.

This situation is bound to change, although maybe the DNA is an inhibitor. After all, it's not like scores of women haven't been taught to serve since very early ages. But it's a process. The game will belong to the woman who figures out how to serve big—and backs it up with a combination of power and spin from the baseline. More than anything, Serena has shown us what the future might be like, while dominating the present.

The 360-Degree Game

The general decline of the late winter U.S. tournament circuit mirrors a drop in the quality of the American game. As head of the USTA's player development program, I know that better than anyone. We're hanging in there, with the two big, late-winter, hard-court events and the cluster of tournaments that make up the US Open Series. But times are definitely tough.

For an American kid, it used to be that you could take a lot of lessons and make it in tennis. But Jose Higueras, my Director of Tennis in the USTA program, has helped me realize how much more physical the game has become. We have a lot of kids in the U.S. who know how to hit a ball, but they aren't necessarily great athletes or sufficiently driven. The typical American junior isn't necessarily a rich kid, but he can go out and get lessons and court time, especially if he shows some talent. That's not enough anymore.

We used to focus on teaching kids how to hit nice, clean, efficient shots. It was a one-dimensional approach. Now, we approach a player on various fronts, and when it comes to his technique and stroke production, we act on the premise that we're looking down on a player from directly above. It's a 360-degree game, meaning that today's player needs to know how to move in every direction in response to any given shot.

That's a lot different from focusing exclusively on stepping forward and into the ball, and that's where the battle of development goes after the stroke production is ingrained. It's being fought in areas like biomechanics, fitness, and the decision-making ability under stress—all things that come into play when a player has to spend a lot of time reacting and playing good defense with an eye to making the transition to offense. The stakes have been driven sky high.

Today, God forbid you play any other sport by the time you're twelve or thirteen. Perish the thought of going to a "regular" school. It's a very different world from the one in which I grew up. Parents do—and don't—understand this. I take a lot of time trying to explain it to people like the former boxer who's trying to coach his own kid, and who almost had a fistfight with one of our USTA pros at our training facility in Carson, California.

This guy really wanted to toughen up his kid, fitnesswise. He got that part more or less right. And he believes that his twelve-year-old should *only* play against collegiate players because it will lift his game quicker. He thinks he's out there at the cutting edge.

So I was like, "Great, your kid is a monster, fitnesswise. But does he know how to play tennis? Because that still counts. Does he know how to compete? Someday, he's going to have to learn how to beat kids his own age, which is where the pressure really lies."

Your classic lone-wolf parent has enjoyed some success, especially in the women's game (think Monica Seles, Steffi Graf, or Maria Sharapova), but I can't think of a single recent case in men's tennis when a kid made it to a high level—and stayed there—with just a parent providing the training. Sergi Bruguera and Jan-Michael Gambill, who were coached by their dads, came the closest.

Most important, there's no magic bullet, and no one-size-fits-all plan for producing great players. The best young player to come along in the U.S. in recent years is work-in-progress Sam Querrey, a kid from California who never went to a tennis academy and played other sports pretty enthusiastically until he got to be seventeen or eighteen, and realized he was particularly gifted at tennis.

That kind of thing still happens, and it always will. But it's more and more the exception. And when it does happen, it takes a wise parent to know what to do next.

Take the case of Donald Young, Jr., an über-prodigy who's now twenty years old. He hit his career-high ranking (thus far) of no. 73 in the spring of 2008. Donald, a lefty, has great feel for the ball and good speed around the court, and he made the most of those virtues in a brilliant junior career. He was that familiar next great hope for American tennis.

But Donald didn't grow to be as big and strong as some of his peers, and that hurt when he began to play open pro draws, both at the top and minor-league levels. Used to ruling the roost, Donald also became prone to frustration, and didn't always compete as well as in the past.

All along, Donald's been coached by his father, also Donald, and his mother, Ilona, both teaching pros. And they don't want to let go, even though we feel pretty strongly that they're on the wrong track. As Jose Higueras said when we were discussing Young's complicated situation: "He's good, and he could make it as a pro. But he'll only make it if he does absolutely everything right."

I learned long ago that accepting the caveats of parents only leads to a terrific waste of our time, talent, and resources. When qualified players want our help, they get it—but we need to be in control because . . . this is what we do. This is our mandate: to use a formidable array of USTA human and technical resources to help kids become solid pros and, hopefully, champions. What we don't do is open a checkbook and start writing checks, although you'd be surprised to know how many people assume that's the case. The latest episode in the Donald Young saga happened at the US Open of 2009, when at a press conference Donald said that his family had gotten a letter from me saying he shouldn't be coached by his parents. Which, of course, is the one thing I knew *not* to do, even though it's the heart of the issue. And it's a tricky one, for sure. Donald is extremely dependent on his parents; maybe he wouldn't do so well traveling with a coach who isn't blood kin. That's a legitimate concern, but then I didn't feel Donald was getting what he most needed from his parents. So what do you do?

What I did write in that letter is that we—Jose, Jay Berger (the director of Men's Coaching), and I—felt that we'd given the Youngs a lot of help over the years, and believe that for him to improve he needed to leave his hometown of Atlanta. He needed to be around full-time fitness trainers and real players, not high school kids.

I guess when Donald wasn't offered a wild card into the US Open they tied it together with the letter, as if we were trying to freeze them out. But we didn't offer Donald the card for a far simpler reason: we couldn't justify it based on his results. Others simply and demonstrably were more deserving.

The Youngs are in a bind; their various endorsement deals were coming up for renewal, Donald's management picture was muddled. His parents were no longer just his coaches, they were increasingly involved in managing his career. Not long after the Open, I got a letter from father Don, claiming he wanted to put an end to the mess and move forward. I took a deep breath, invited him to call, and I spent forty-five minutes on the phone with him on a Saturday afternoon.

It was the same old routine. When I expressed my concerns with the state of Donald's development, he told me I was getting bad information from the USTA coaches whom we had sent out to travel and work with Donald. And they had all more or less reported the same thing: love the kid, the parents are a huge obstacle. The parents want to make all the decisions, and we can't count on them to take our advice. So I told the dad he wasn't going to backdoor us with that. I had good communication with, and ultimate trust in, my guys in the field.

Don Sr. changed tack: He said no one would practice with Donald at the Challengers because he's African American. It was better on the ATP tour. I was stunned by that; it strained credulity. And at the end of the day, who really knows about the truth of such charges? I certainly had heard no mention of anything like that. I assured Donald Sr. that if his son were with one of our coaches, nothing like that would ever happen. But I also was thinking, *The kid's career hangs in the balance, everyone knows what it would mean for the U.S. to produce another African-American champion, and this is what you're focusing on?*

I told Don Sr. that there were larger concerns. As well as he'd taught his son the game (and Don and Illona did a fine job with the fundamentals), Don simply hadn't developed sufficiently, strength and fitness wise. I went on to say that Donald should be putting in four hours on the court and an hour in the gym every day—like all the rest of the kids at our training facility in Boca Raton, Florida. Besides, any problem he encounters arranging practice at Challengers paled beside the fact that he was still playing, and sometimes winning, the same tournaments he won three years ago. Meanwhile, I asked, what happened to Marin Čilić, Juan Martin del Potro, and Leonardo Mayer—the guys he met along the way? Those guys are physical animals and successful pros; Donald is not.

"Is that what you really think?" Don said. "It's all about that?"

I told him, no, it wasn't all about that, just a lot about that. Sure that lefty serve of his son could get better, and so could his backhand. But those issues weren't even relevant at this point, given that Donald wasn't anywhere near where he needed to be, physically. So Don backed off a little, and asked if we had any camps coming up. I felt a little frustrated: here we go again.

Finally, I just told him, move to Florida. Pick a spot. We'll take care of you. But when Donald shows up at our site, we're in charge. If Donald wants our help, he has to accept our authority, and be willing to go out there and kill himself like these other guys do.

That's all we ask. It may seem harsh, but that's our policy. And at the end of the day, it isn't as if Donald hasn't already benefited from our program. He's probably gotten more support than any other junior (half-a-million dollars is probably a realistic number, if you want to estimate how much we've invested).

Jimmy and My Jugular

Maybe you noticed that I used the word "recent" when I wrote that no top male players were coached primarily by a parent. The big exception to that in the Open era was Jimmy Connors—and he really broke the mold.

Jimmy was an all-court player with great speed and extremely accurate ground strokes. His serve and forehand would have been vulnerable to the better guys on the tour today, but when it comes to that lust for competition, determination, and the shrewdness of the focused competitor, well, he was unmatched. And that never goes out of style. When we see signs of it in a youngster, it opens up all kinds of possibilities.

I admired Jimmy, much to my own detriment on at least one occasion. After I made the Australian Open semis in 1991, my ranking shot up to no. 50 or 60. I didn't freak out and slump, which told me I could handle my newfound prestige. At the end of 1991, I rolled into the US Open ranked in the mid-30s and pretty stoked—if a little apprehensive—about playing Jimmy Connors in my first-round match. I had a tremendous amount of respect for him; he was thirty-eight years old and still a force in the game.

Jimmy was a loner; many derided him as a punk "mama's boy." His game was created and brought to fruition by his mother, Gloria (with help from his maternal grandmother and the hands-on involvement of the cagey Ecuadorian pioneer of the pro game, Pancho Segura), and she remained the dominant presence in his life. Jimmy once admitted that he didn't feel the need for a coach, because when anything was wrong with his game, he'd just call Gloria and she'd sort it out, pronto. Via telephone, no less.

Jimmy was also suspicious of others, especially fellow players. He didn't feel he could be friends with them and still compete with his customary ruthlessness. He was convinced that it was a dog-eat-dog world; it was central to his psyche. But I admired that remarkable competitive fire, his flagrant disregard for convention and the opinions of others, and that clean, compact, almost utterly flat (spinwise) game.

For a period in the late 1980s, Jimmy had a place in Connecticut, and he would come down and practice with me in New York City.

I got to know him pretty well, and I admit I probably sucked up to him a little, because he was such an awesome player. It never occurred to me that cultivating my friendship—I could hardly be called a threat to him—was a way for Jimmy to play mind games with John, because there was little love lost between the two of them.

When we practiced, Jimmy would often bring a third guy and have us go two-on-one against him. He would go for ninety minutes, nonstop, in a full sweatsuit even if we were indoors, under the bubble at the Tennisport racket club. Connors just loved to sweat.

Jimmy and Andre Agassi (on a typical day) were the most intense practice players I've ever seen. Each one of them would hit a million balls in the shortest period of time possible. Jimmy's practice sessions rarely lasted more than a fast and furious ninety minutes. He trained himself to go, if he went at all, with maximum intensity.

By contrast, a guy like my brother John just wanted to knock the ball around to get his blood flowing and then play sets. He thought drills and hitting were a total waste of time. And Pete Sampras was the laziest of them all; he just wanted to bat the ball around for a few minutes, then play tiebreakers (instead of sets, heaven forbid drill!). And he liked to play for a couple of hundred bucks a pop, just to keep himself semi-interested. I often had to tell him, "Hey Pete, I'm not playing for five hundred. That's not real money to you, but it is to me!"

He would just break out that grin and serve them up.

At the French open in June of 1991, Jimmy, age thirty-eight, played Michael Chang, an extremely tough player who could run all day. He had something else on Connors—he'd been a champion at Roland Garros, something Jimmy never could claim. But in typical fashion, Jimmy played even with Chang and hung in there, forcing the match to a fifth set.

Connors won the first point of the fifth set and, to the shock of everyone present, strolled right up to the net, clearly waiting for Michael to join him. He extended his hand to shake and told his opponent, "That's it. I'm done." Chang, of course, looked baffled, but he shrugged and went to pack up his things.

It was a strange and sad moment—the old warrior, realizing he had nothing left in the tank, surrendered to his much younger opponent. I really admired the way Jimmy handled that, and was moved to write him a note. I wrote by hand that I thought he'd put in an unbelievable effort, that it was amazing to watch someone of his age play so hard, for so long. He was an inspiration to tennis players everywhere, I concluded. I know Jimmy got the note, although he never said a word to me about it in the ensuing months.

I knew what to expect when Jimmy and I met in that night match in the first round at Flushing Meadows in 1991. I came out firing on all cylinders, winning the first two sets and blasting out to a 0–3, 34–40 lead in the third. It was sad to see the old man going out like that. I started thinking about what had happened in Paris, with Chang. *I've got Jimmy Connors beat*, I thought. *He's done.*

You would have thought I'd learned my lesson of less than a year earlier, when I sorely wanted to believe that I had Boris Becker beaten at the Australian Open. It's hard to contain your excitement and anticipation at such moments; it's hard to do what most champions do in that situation, put the pedal to the metal. The temptation is to relax. In my shoes, a guy like my brother, or Sampras or Agassi, would have thought, *Okay, it's time to dial it up and finish off this sorry sack of shit.*

The rest, of course, is history. Connors stormed back to beat me; my only consolation, so many years later, is that I had merely been the imprudent schmo who uncorked the bottle containing the genie. After mercilessly demolishing me, Jimmy slashed and carved and savagely battled his way through a string of opponents to reach the semifinals. It was a display of courage, stamina, and heart that captured the imagination of the nation. How often does a losing Grand Slam semifinalist make the cover of *Sports Illustrated*?

I'm sure Jimmy had read that note I left at the locker room at Roland Garros, and shrewdly filed away the contents. He wasn't going to acknowledge it, either. That might make him feel a certain amount of indebtedness or thankfulness to me. And Jimmy didn't have those feelings for anyone, which helps explain his animus and his record. When we met in the US Open, he probably used that note for fuel—and insight into a soft spot in my character.

Jimmy might have sensed that in a crunch in a tough match, I would underestimate his legs, his resolve, or both; for all I know, he secretly might have been ashamed about abandoning that match with Chang. It wouldn't have been unlike him. I had seen him in a weak moment. If I were to present my neck, he'd happily sink his fangs in my jugular. And that's just what happened.

Jimmy was adept at mind games. He was so keen to keep himself distant from the pack that he would often avoid the locker room altogether, changing and killing time conspicuously apart from his peers. Top players often have what you might call a "locker room strategy," from aggressively dominating the inner sanctum of the athlete to avoiding it altogether. One of my brother John's big beefs was that tennis is the only sport where you share the locker room with not just the guy you're going to engage in intense, one-on-one combat, but also with someone to whom you might have a deep, genuine aversion. I guess golf is the same way—but then it's a stretch to call golf a sport. But don't get me started on that. . . .

John disliked Ivan Lendl, and you could feel the tension when they occupied the same locker room. Granted, John liked to strut around, scowling, his body language demanding that you give him wide berth. That could be intimidating. But he didn't engage guys in the same way as Lendl, who actually talked trash and needled people—sometimes mercilessly. When John Fitzgerald (who was actually a friend of Lendl's) came into the Australian Open locker room shortly after having his first child, a daughter, Lendl said in his mechanical, clipped Eastern European accent: "Congratulations, John. Maybe next time you vill be man enough to make a son." In conclusive proof that there is a God, Lendl ended up having five children of his own—all lovely daughters.

I watched as Brad Gilbert and Ivan Lendl almost came to blows in the locker room in Tokyo one year. Now a lot of guys found Brad's endless prattling (usually about sports) irritating. But even more glowered at the way Ivan Lendl was constantly razzing and putting others down. Somehow, the two of them got started on a game of one-upmanship. Brad suggested that he would clean Ivan's clock in a game of one-on-one basketball. Not to be outdone, Lendl said he could skate rings around Brad in a hockey rink. "Oh, yeah," Brad shot back, sticking out that Sgt. Rock jaw of his, "you want a piece of me in a batting cage?"

I could hardly believe my ears; these guys were taking it to another level, like a couple of kids in the schoolyard, until some other players intervened to talk both guys off the ledge before it came to fisticuffs. It was idiotic; clearly, it had nothing to do with either guy's skill at bowling or beer pong. They just had their backs up and neither was going to back down.

Wimbledon has two locker rooms, a spacious, well-appointed one for seeded players, and a more bare-bones one for everyone else. Yet Andy Roddick, a three-time finalist at the event, insists on hanging out in the B locker room, so he can be with buddies like Sam Querrey, the Bryan brothers, Mardy Fish, and James Blake. He just feels more comfortable in there.

Of course, you can't have individual locker rooms for all 128 players at a major. But at those events, as well as smaller ones, the locker room during the early stages of an event is like a cross between a crowded train station at rush hour and a class reunion. The camaraderie level is high. When whoever won the last tournament walks in, almost everyone slaps him on the back or drops by in front of his locker to say "Well done."

Friends who haven't seen each other in weeks say hi and catch up when they meet. At the 2009 US Open, Roger Federer watched the scoreboard as Marsel Ilhan, the first Turkish player to compete there (although he's originally from Uzbekistan), won his first-round match. Later, Federer went up to Ilhan in the locker room to congratulate the young player and introduce himself. The journeyman couldn't believe it.

Carl, the locker room attendant at the US Open, doles out the assignments at the start of the tournament. Over time, he's learned which guys like to be near each other, and he generally groups them by nations. It works out well, although the tone in the Temple of Ben-Gay changes dramatically later in the event. When it's down to the finals, the atmosphere in the locker room is almost oppressive. You've got one guy huddled with his team in one corner, his opponent and friends in the other. The tones are hushed. You can almost cut the tension with a knife. It wouldn't be such a bad idea for tournaments to give the finalists different spaces on that last critical day.

Roger Federer is probably the most relaxed guy I've ever seen in the locker room; he's nothing less than a prince—it's like he owns the place, but in a good way, like the proud proprietor of a Swiss fondue restaurant. Rafael Nadal, as nice a kid and good a sportsman as he is, gets into the mind games a bit, wittingly or not. He makes his opponents wait on him, not just between points (for which he gets criticized), but in the locker room and on the sidelines as well. When the tournament officials call Nadal's match, he goes to take another piss, making his opponent stand there, waiting. When the umpire calls them out to the center of the court for the coin toss, Rafa will often stay in his chair, fiddling with towels or his bottles while the other guy walks right out—and has to wait.

I can understand how Toni Nadal, Rafa's coach and uncle, tried to drill it into the young, impressionable eighteen-year-old of a few years ago that it was important for him to take his time, not feel rushed or obligated to do anything until he was comfortable and well-organized. But you have to grow out of that. Rafa's foot-dragging was behind that bad-blood incident at Wimbledon between Rafa and the Swedish player Robin Soderling. Ticked off by the way Rafa had the habit of making an opponent wait, Soderling did some conspicuous stalling of his own, and he even mimicked Rafa's compulsive habit of plucking at the back of his shorts. It wasn't a smart thing for Soderling to do, and it didn't make his life any easier—Rafa is genuinely liked and respected by everyone. Soderling was cast as a boorish gamesman, but many players felt that his was a point worth making, if not exactly in the way Robin chose.

When I finally left the Billie Jean King National Tennis Center that night after losing to Connors, I was in a state of shock. I was with the girl I dated all through my years at Stanford, and as we approached the house in Cove Neck, I remembered I'd forgotten my keys. It was something like 3:00 a.m., and I had to get my dad out of bed. Considering the night I'd had, seeing Dad as he opened the door, buck naked (he slept in the raw) was not a visual I cared to entertain. I told my girl, Margaret, to stand to the side until the door had been opened and Dad vanished back to his room.

After we stole inside, and just when things seemed like they couldn't get any worse, Margaret turned to me and asked, "So what do you do now with the rest of your life?"

I couldn't believe my ears, but I knew the moment marked the beginning of the end for us. Tennis was my life.

That loss to Connors trailed me around everywhere I went; it still does. In the late summer of 2009, I was at the beach with my family, playing in the water, having a great time. I could tell from their frequent glances our way that these people nearby recognized me. Finally, one of the women walked over. Just another stranger at the beach.

"Are you Patrick?" she asked, and I nodded yes.

"Oh, it's a pleasure to meet you." Then she looked a little hesitant and added, "I was there the night you played Connors at the Open in, I think, 1991. Do you remember that match?"

"Vaguely," I lied.

"I stayed for the whole thing. Right to the very end, and I was rooting for you."

Sure you were, I thought. But I just said, "That's funny, so many people tell me that, but as I remember, there weren't all that many people there by the end. And I know for sure that those who were rooting for me were few and far between. So . . . thanks."

It's always the same: I was at that match, and I was rooting for you . . . It's like Jimmy Connors had no fans in New York—and we know the truth about that.

But I suppose it could have been worse. I could have been Aaron Krickstein, who lost a similar match to Connors, but in the quarter-finals, when Connors's run was at its apex. Now Aaron has become the U.S. open rain-delay superstar because they roll tape of that Krickstein debacle during every suspension of the tournament.

Thanks, Aaron.

MY THREE SONS—THE REMAKE

My father was pretty diligent about taking me to play in junior tournaments, even though he was in way over his head when it came to technique and tactics. He always told us, "Well, I don't know anything about tennis. You guys know everything . . ."

Then, of course, he couldn't resist putting in his two cents.

At junior tournaments back in the day, there was a break between the second and third sets, which was when parents or coaches (the latter were pretty scarce—unlike today) could legitimately talk to a player. So my dad would pseudo-coach me. I rib him about it now, but the depth of his coaching knowledge was pretty much summed up in the lone piece of advice he'd give me when I was in some knock-down, drag-out with another kid: "Don't do what you did in the set you lost. Do what you did in the set you won."

I had a very good record in three-set matches as a junior; never underestimate the K.I.S.S. (Keep It Simple, Stupid) approach to tennis.

Dad didn't really live for tennis—he lived for his wife and kids. He's an up-from-the-bootstraps guy who grew up an only child on the Upper East Side of Manhattan, and he was hell-bent on having a good-sized family and making it the center of all our lives. Like any red-blooded Irishman, he liked the girls and he liked to drink, the latter with a little too much zeal at one point, but he's over that now. That's not an unfamiliar problem for the Irish.

My mom, Kay (neé Tresham), grew up in Greenport, out on the North Shore of Long Island. She had one sister who was quite a bit older, and from whom she was estranged for most of her adult life. Her sister died of alcoholism later in life, although she too produced three boys—cousins with whom I have no relationship. We just didn't figure in each other's lives.

Bill Tresham, my maternal grandfather, was conservative to the point of being backward. Mom was the top graduate and valedictorian of her high school class, but there was no discussion whatsoever of her going to college. Women didn't go to college—at least not women from the Tresham household. So Mom went to Lenox Hill School of Nursing in Manhattan. My dad was no dummy; he and some friends had scoped out the bar where the lovely nursing school students liked to unwind, and he ultimately was introduced to my mom by some student nurses he'd met there.

Dad went to Catholic University (where else, with his background?), finished in three years, and got his law degree from Fordham. The anecdote that tells you all you need to know about my mom is that when Dad finished his first year at Fordham Law he ran to her boasting about how he had finished second in his class. Mom's reaction was, "See? If you tried harder, you could have been first!"

Balloon, meet pin. . . .

By the way, Dad did exactly as Mom suggested and finished first the following year. My paternal grandfather, also John, was enchanted by Kay Tresham, my grandmother, Kathleen McEnroe, less so. Dad was a bit of a momma's boy, and Kathleen probably saw that this Kay girl was going to take her hard-working, earnest baby away. My parents worked around the problem, and when my dad went to do his Air Force duty in Weisbaden, Germany, Kay followed him, even though they weren't married. That's where Dad got the ultimatum: Either we get married or I'm out of here. It wouldn't be the first or last time Dad decided that discretion was the better part of valor, and anyway he loved my mom. Soon they were official, and John was born in Germany.

We three boys grew up in a household shaped by all those clichés about Americans in the 1950s (just think of shows like *Father Knows Best*, or, well, *My Three Sons*). The rap on American suburban life in those Eisenhower years doesn't do justice to women like my mom, who was traditional and nurturing, but also practical, tough, patient, and smart. She was the disciplinarian in the family; Dad's always been a big softie. But Mom was content to stay in the background to concentrate on building a happy, successful family.

My dad clearly loves the measure of celebrity he's earned, but Mom always dodged the press and shunned the limelight in her very proper, gracious way. She never really cared about the tennis scene, although she enjoyed our success and the way of life it brought her. She's especially proud of the fact that she's a trustee of Lenox Hill Hospital, the first graduate of the hospital's nursing school to make it to that lofty position. She loves that; when she gets her picture in the society pages of one of those glossy Manhattan magazines, like *Avenue*, it's like the most wonderful thing that ever happened in her life. But Mom's no snob. She just appreciates what she has. Down deep, I think she feels her family is the greatest thing that ever happened to her, and all the rest is gravy.

Dad was in his early thirties when he made partner at his law firm. One of the first things my parents did was go to look at houses in Douglaston, Queens. They saw one that Mom really liked, and when they went back to the car she said, "We're buying that house."

"I don't think so," Dad said. "We just can't afford that—yet."

"No. We're buying that house." And she walked right back in and told the real estate agent, "We'll take it."

Dad still complains that she didn't even try to negotiate a better price.

That's the kind of mom she is.

. . . .

When it came to tennis, Dad was very supportive from day one, and he still takes all things tennis pretty seriously. He'll call me out of the blue, all excited, and say something like, "Hey, did you see that John lost to Pat Cash in that senior event in London?" I roll my eyes and think, Are you kidding me—you called to tell me that?

Dad worked his tail off, so he wasn't around much on most weekday nights. But he took us to those junior tournaments diligently; his life at times revolved around them. My brothers used to tease me with the nickname "Perfect Pat" because I was a bit of a momma's boy myself—a Goody Two-shoes, which they found supremely annoying. I really wanted to please my mother. Maybe it was because I was the youngest of the brood; John had seven-plus years on me, and Mark was four years older.

At one point, I actually took to making my own bed. But Mom ran the house like a Swiss conductor runs a train, and I was encroaching on her territory. She would undo my handiwork and make the bed all over, the right way (her way).

Our first home in Douglaston was on the "wrong" (south) side of Northern Boulevard, but as Dad prospered we moved north to Douglaston Manor. It was a nice but by no means extravagant house; but each boy had his own bedroom. We were a pretty conventional upper middle-class family, at least until John made his unexpected leap to international fame.

I spent a lot of time bugging my brother Mark, who was closest to me in age, to go out with me to throw a baseball in the street. Mark is basically the nicest guy in the world, but I was such a noodge that he would eventually lose his temper and come close to cuffing me one. That sent me scurrying off to find John, who would come to my defense.

John would save me from Mark, so then the two of them would start going at it. My mother would go on red alert, which was my cue to run downstairs and make myself scarce. Mom would read the riot act to Mark and John, even though I had started the whole thing. That was the household dynamic. Mom was especially tough on John, probably because he was her firstborn; it had a lot to do with his eventual toughness and grit as a competitor.

The road trips to tournaments, either John's (when I was a little kid) or my own, were fun, although Dad got the shock of his life in Shreveport when he learned that the town was dry on Sundays. It was a shame; a little nip now and then improved Dad's coaching skills.

At one fourteen-and-under tournament, Ricky Peck and I were playing against two guys who would become good players, Aaron Krickstein and Robbie Weiss. Ricky and I were getting killed, because Aaron and Robbie were staying back at the baseline and lobbing us to death. We changed our own game plan, and started doing the same thing. We just stopped coming to net and camped at the baseline, throwing up lobs of our own. It all got pretty tedious, but we held our own in this juvenile war of attrition. But that made Dad see red. He let me have it during the break at the end of the second set: "That's not how you play doubles. You don't play doubles from the baseline—you go to the net!"

"But Dad," I protested, "we won the second set playing that way."

We lost that match in three sets, and sometimes when I watch doubles today I remember that episode. Especially when I see how many teams now play two-back—and win matches.

I was a little whiny, especially when I was younger. It's not uncommon among juniors. Once, I was giving a poor effort in a match. I just didn't care that much that day, and that was a rare event. But it made Dad nuts. He said: "I don't care if you win or lose, but you better try every time you go out there or you're not gonna play, period. You can quit tomorrow, I don't care. I'll love you no matter what. But if you're going to be out there, you'd better give 100 percent."

In that area, Dad did a great job. Even at his focused, most artistic peak, John was famous for the way he bitched and moaned. But one of his trademark qualities, which all the pundits took pains to note, was that for all his whining and drama, he never ceased giving his all. It was drilled into him, into all of us, to give a full effort.

The Plugger

John was an excellent student. He was just in second grade when a teacher at his parochial school, St. Anastasia's, informed my parents that John was so bright that he ought to be put into a good, competitive private school. The administration at the Buckley Country Day School was sympathetic, and allowed John to enroll, even though my father had to basically give them an IOU for the steep tuition. That began an unusual family tradition: all three of us attended the same schools (Buckley, Trinity School, Stanford University), beginning to end.

I was a good if not great student. My mom, who didn't want Mark or me to be tormented by John's superiority, always told me I wasn't a good test-taker, and it didn't take much goading to convince me of the profundity of that observation. Mom called me "the plugger" because I would just chug along. I wouldn't get to the station as fast as the other trains, but I eventually made it.

Mark was a little more of a homebody than John or I; he would often stay in to read Sherlock Holmes books while I ran around trying to keep up with John and all the other kids in our tight neighborhood. We'd play touch football, or baseball; in the winter, when the nearby pond froze, we'd lace up our skates and play hockey. All the kids in town knew one another; there was the athletic group, and then the kids who would find some bum to buy them beer, then they would go down to a wooded spot called "the field" to start a bonfire, drink, and listen to Led Zeppelin.

Mark quietly kept his distance from tennis; he just wasn't that into it, although he was good enough to make the Stanford tennis team—as a walk-on. Mark is a hefty, big-boned, 6'4", but he didn't move great, or have the burning desire to be a pro player. Still, making the tennis team at Stanford was like making the football team at Notre Dame or USC as a walk-on. It's not like anyone can go out there and do it.

Mark needed his own space, too; his older brother, the one to whom he was most easily and frequently compared, was this phenom, and I was the young plugger, trying to follow in John's outsized footsteps. Mark is a lawyer now, playing a lot more tennis than he ever did before, and helping John set up a Manhattan tennis academy. He's a real weekend warrior in all these forty-and-over events. And if you think John's got a temper—well, you don't know Mark.

One little-known fact about our tennis adventures—and Dad just loved to point this out after John got thrown out of the Australian Open in 1990—is that John wasn't the first McEnroe to be defaulted from an official match. That honor belongs to Mark, and when Dad tells casual acquaintances, their first reaction is usually, "Who the hell is Mark McEnroe?"

The incident happened when Mark was at Kent, a boarding school in Connecticut, for tenth grade. Mark hated Kent with a passion—absolutely hated it, and it was all my parents could do to keep him there on the promise he could come home and go to Trinity after that year.

Anyway, Mark played on the Kent team. He got so crazy and mad at himself in a match one time that his own coach defaulted him. Even John can't beat that.

At times during our overlapping careers, John or I would get our nose out of joint, and Mark was always the guy who listened to me rant about John or vice versa. He was smart enough not to take anyone's side; he would just be there, even-keeled, to listen.

I was still a kid, living at home, when John went out on the tour and Mark went off to Stanford. John helped my folks buy an apartment way up on Fifth Avenue, which is now worth many multiples more than what they paid. It was a lifelong dream come true for Mom, who really wanted to make that big jump from Greenport to Manhattan—and Fifth Avenue, no less! John knew that, and he helped make it happen for her.

I would come home from school or soccer practice to our Fifth Avenue pad, and I'd do my homework in my bedroom, better known as "the cell" because it was so tiny. Dad would be at work, and Mom was cooking dinner—she was always cooking. But at the same time every day, she'd poke her head in and say, "Warner's on, Pat." And I would go on to watch the sports reporter I admired, and would work with many years later on the Don Imus show, Warner Wolf.

My dad and I used to watch *The Odd Couple* and *The Honeymooners.* Those were our shows. When my brothers were around, they'd join us, too. But *The Honeymooners* was on late, around 11:00 p.m., and most nights by the time it was over Dad would be snoring away on the couch and my mom would come to wake him up and trundle him off to bed. Those are the moments that stand out in my mind when I think of our family.

All in all, we were happy. We were typical, whatever that means. And over time all of us realized, with the help of the women we married, and the work we put into having successful, satisfying relationships, that communication wasn't the high point of our home life. Maybe it's an Irish thing; you just didn't talk about anything unpleasant. On the other hand, we also didn't carry on or do things that would have demanded a much higher or more complex level of communication. We were focused, busy, and pretty adaptable to each other's needs, even if we didn't talk much about those things.

Throughout the years, Dad remained omnipresent in our tennis lives. I must have glanced up from the court or my chair at some tournament or Davis Cup city a zillion times to see my dad sitting there, absorbed. Heaven forbid he should miss a Davis Cup match! Once John exploded on the tennis scene and became an overnight sensation, it was only natural that, with his background in law, Dad would also become our manager.

. . . .

It would be easy to get the impression that we were pushed into tennis, but that just wasn't the case. Tennis was just one sport available to most of the kids of our background at that time. I got my start in tennis at the Douglaston Club, a small tennis and bath club just down the road from our house, where as a kid I would play endless imaginary matches against the backboard. It was always Rod Laver versus Ken Rosewall in the Wimbledon final. Every match went five sets. I made sure that Laver always won.

I attended good schools and played on the soccer team; tennis was strictly a weekend activity. I wasn't as good as John, even at soccer. He could have gone to any number of good, small liberal arts schools on a soccer scholarship.

I also pitched and played shortstop for our baseball team; that's my favorite sport after tennis. I had good hands for fielding and I used to hit for singles—a contact hitter. Unfortunately, when I went to Trinity, tennis and baseball were both spring sports, so I had to choose. I picked tennis mainly because Mark and John had played on the Trinity tennis team before me; I saw it as a family obligation.

Trinity had the best team in New York City, and one of the best in the state, even though it was a private school. But the competition was pretty poor for someone who took lessons and played organized junior tennis. I'd win every match easily. One time, I played a girl; she was good, too—nationally ranked in her age group. I gave her a game each set because I didn't want to beat her, 6–0, 6–0.

On Friday nights, I would go out to Glen Cove to play in this 6:00 p.m. to 8:00 p.m. youth group. I always drove home with one of the pros, who lived nearby. We usually stole some balls from the tennis club, and going home we would sometimes pelt passersby with them. Some of the other kids in the group got involved, and we graduated to water balloons. It was all pretty innocent. Mostly we had ball wars, throwing them at one another in front of one or another guy's nice house on warm summer nights. In the winter, snowball fights were the preferred form of combat.

I didn't play much with John early on—he was in a different, older age category. But I remember being fifteen, sixteen, and good enough to give him a decent hit when he was up there in the top twenty in the world. By then, John traveled in some fast company, with the late Vitas Gerulaitis and the guy with whom he amassed a great pro doubles record, Peter Fleming.

When they needed someone to feed them balls or to be the third man in two-on-one drills, it was like, "Go get Patrick." One time, Peter asked me to help him practice his overhead. I guess I was feeding the balls too short because suddenly he bellowed, "Hit them fucking deeper!"

"Yes, sir!"

It was unnerving sometimes. But it exposed me to the highest level of the game and players. But I don't remember talking much about tennis around the dinner table at home; it was just something we did for fun.

In the fourteen-and-under age division, I traveled with this kid from New Jersey, Ricky Peck. He had his own private coach, a former tour player from Texas named Rod Williams. I was with Ricky and Rod in Fort Worth, Texas, the day John lost to Borg in their first Wimbledon final—the one in 1980.

Rod started sending me letters—for twenty-five years now, he's been writing to me. He was a kid at heart, and he would do things like take a picture of Arnold Schwarzenegger's body, cut out the head, and put my face in there. He sent it along with workout instructions and schedules. Just because. When I started broadcasting, Rod wrote me letters about Roddick—what he needed to do better, or more of. And he was usually pretty accurate.

Guys like Rod have always made this game go round, and to some extent they still do. In terms of his emphasis on fitness and training, Rod was ahead of his time. But he was just another tennis nut out there, never lucky enough to hook up with a great young player who could stake him to a place at the big table. Being around a guy like that, a dedicated, in-the-trenches coach, imbued me with my basic respect for the profession.

Although I put a lot into my tennis, life was pretty normal, at least until John's Wimbledon breakout. The day after John lost to Jimmy Connors in the semis in 1977, we had five television crews running around our house, interviewing and filming like crazy. We were a little bewildered by it all because up to that point we had lived in a kind of time warp, a 1950s-style *Leave It to Beaver* world, and we weren't fixated on becoming pro athletes or celebrities. But things changed a little in 1977; the pressure ramped up.

Not long after that, when I was about fifteen, I played a junior tournament in Nashville, Tennessee. During a match, I noticed a photographer courtside. He wasn't taking any pictures—just watching—until I threw my racquet. It was the only time in the match that I did it, but that's what he'd been waiting for, and it paid off. The photo ran in the next day's paper with a headline saying, in effect, that there was another wild McEnroe brat loose in the world.

I began to see that another kind of game was being played, and it had little to do with tennis. But by then our values and priorities were well established. And one of the things our father had drilled into us was the honor and importance of playing Davis Cup. It was a nonnegotiable idea; there would be none of this cagey, *Should I or shouldn't I?* waffling about playing for the U.S. When you got the call, you answered it.

A Changing of the Guard

After my rocky debut as Davis Cup captain against Switzerland, just getting to the second round before I got fired seemed a worthy goal. We, along with the other first-round losers in World Group play, had to play a relegation match to determine if we would stay in the elite World Group.

Relegation matches (also called "playoffs") take place in September, coinciding with the WG semifinals, and determine which eight teams will make up half the World Group the following year (teams that win at least one round are automatically in the WG again the following year). You could draw a cupcake opponent in a playoff tie—a team that happened to get hot in the "zonal" minor leagues, without a singles player of top 100 caliber. On the other hand, you could draw a tough team and lose, meaning you would spend the following year battling through zonal competition just to get a shot at making it back into the World Group with a win in the next playoff round. Getting back in the WG can be a lot like that Bill Murray movie *Groundhog Day*.

We drew India in the playoffs of 2001. That nation has produced some high-quality grass-court players over the years, and a great doubles team in the 1990s, Mahesh Bhupathi and Leander Paes. Luckily, though, their fortunes in singles were at an ebb, and we got to host. We chose an indoor hard court for the tie.

The playoff week was scheduled for mid-September, but then came the 9/11 terrorist attacks, which postponed the tie for about a month, long enough for a young kid named James Blake to put up some impressive results in Asia. So I decided to put him on the team, thinking he could benefit from the seasoning.

I had a new rule for this tie: no coaches allowed. I didn't need poisonous feelings among parents (or coaches) to infect the locker room, as they had in Switzerland. Beyond that, I had to rein in my own anxiety, and a natural temptation to overmanage the tie. I was just thirty-five, and I didn't want to be insecure and display my authority just to make a statement. It was a mixed blessing that veterans like Jim Courier, Andre Agassi, Pete Sampras, and Todd Martin were fading. The USTA understood my bind, and were—to a point—open to me building a new team for the future, from the ground up.

Choosing a team isn't a particularly tricky task. Like I tell people, including players lobbying for a spot on the squad: My job is pretty easy, I'm a front runner—whoever is playing the best is in. I always wanted people to know that it wasn't about relationships and politics, especially with a changing of the guard.

Todd Martin first played for the U.S. in 1994, and he's among that elite group of players who have played 30 or more matches (his overall record is 16–14, 11–8 in singles). I was only four years older than Todd, but Todd was the backbone of the team going to North Carolina to face India. Soon after we arrived, though, it became clear that James Blake was simply playing better than Todd. I suddenly had a chance to put my money where my mouth was in terms of selection. I sucked it up and went to Todd to have the awkward conversation: I had decided to go with James for the singles.

Todd was bummed out. But being Todd, he gave it a little time to sink in, and came back to me the following morning to say, "You know, whatever you need me to do, I'll do." And he laced them up and went out to play a doubles scrimmage against our somewhat nervous team of Jared Palmer and Donald Johnson.

Palmer, incidentally, was one of the most talented doubles players I ever partnered with, and he could have had a big career in singles, too. He had the potential to be a real specimen; he stood about 6 foot 3, and had the most gorgeous one-handed backhand you could imagine, and a rifle-shot volley. He was creative, really great at improvising shots and coming up with daring angles and surprising placements. But his serve was just so-so, with lots of room for improvement.

When we were partners, I once invited Jared to come work out with me. I had a trainer who used to take me out to Central Park in New York City and bust my ass. But when Jared joined me, he quickly decided he wanted no part of it, and that was part of his problem. He was just too soft, too content to go with the flow without pushing himself. He never tried to maximize his strength, speed, and stamina.

We won the tie with India, 4–1, in the first outing for the singles duo of Roddick and Blake. The only point we lost was the doubles, in which the superior team of Bhupathi and Paes crushed Jared and Don Johnson.

In a few short months, though, I'd have to lead the team again in a first-round tie, this time against Slovakia, at home.

The Worst Fucking Idea—Ever!

The most difficult job for a captain is understanding his players and knowing what he can—or can't—say, and when he can—or can't—say it. You don't want to undermine the confidence of your guys, and you don't want to make them angry. It's surprising how easy it is to do that. Tennis pros are generally pretty high strung and stubborn, and when it comes to anyone tampering with their tennis, they can be downright bellicose.

I began to get an inkling of just *how* stubborn when we hosted Slovakia in Oklahoma City on a fast indoor court in February of 2002. We felt good, because our team consisted of Sampras, Roddick, and two excellent singles players who also played good doubles, Blake and Mardy Fish. The Slovaks had a solid squad, with up-and-coming Karol Beck and veteran Ján Krošlák playing singles. Sampras got us going in the right direction with a win over Beck.

Andy got off to a good start against Krŏslák, winning the first two sets. But as the match went on, I noticed that Krŏslák was creeping farther and farther back from the baseline to take Andy's big serve. He started getting a few balls back, and slowly worked his way into the match. He was just floating back the returns, and Andy was playing from so far behind his own baseline that he couldn't attack those weak, safe returns.

Eventually, Krošlák got a service break, which is no small thing against Andy. He's gone entire Davis Cup weeks without giving up a single break of serve—either in a match or our team practice sessions.

Up to that point, I'd bitten my tongue and said nothing to Andy, although I told the team members sitting on the bench what I thought. After Andy was broken, he came over to his chair, all pissed off. He was down a break, 1–4. I thought I saw an opportunity to teach him something. I assumed he'd win the match even if he lost the set.

I said, "Andy, you know why you lost your serve there?"

"Yeah," he snapped. "I missed that fucking forehand."

"Okay," I replied. "But it might be nice, just once in a while, to serve and volley. You know, mix it up a little. Because the guy is just playing centerfield, ten feet behind the baseline, and just floating back the returns. He's got nothing to worry about. So if you just show him a serve and volley, you'll plant that seed of doubt. It would give him something to think about."

Andy glowered at me. I'd touched a nerve.

As Andy tromped back onto the court without saying another word, I turned to the guys on the bench and said, "Yeah, I told him . . ." And they all cracked up.

Andy served the next game from the same side of the court where our chairs were (in Davis Cup, the captain sits alongside his player on the changeovers). He stepped up to the service notch. By then, I'd learned to read some of his intentions in that little ass wiggle he does before he serves and I turned to the bench. "Here it comes, guys," I said, "get ready."

I knew what he was going to do: crush a huge serve and go thundering up to the net, just to show he could do it. He uncorked this monster serve, when what he should have done was take a little off, make sure he could get nice and close to the net to exploit the element of surprise. Krošlák was playing so far back that Andy could have floated one in and crawled up to the net on his belly.

Of course, the atomic serve was a fault.

That pissed him off even more. I watched with a growing sense of horror as he lined up to hit the second serve: *Oh, no, no, no . . . he's gonna do this on a second serve!*

Andy spun in the serve and charged the net. Krošlák just blocked the ball back, at Andy's feet, and Andy hit possibly the ugliest volley of all time. He gave me a sidelong glance—he was standing just ten feet away—and yelled: "That was the worst fucking idea—ever!"

We laugh about that to this day.

The tie in Oklahoma City would be a turning point for the U.S., for after we rolled through that tie, 5–0, I felt that we were back. I knew we might not win the Cup, but with youngsters Roddick, Blake, and Mardy Fish as a nucleus, we were on our way to having a team that could pose problems for anyone.

It's a shame for Mardy that Roddick and Blake were also fast-court players, because that ensured that Mardy would get precious few opportunities to put his spectacular shotmaking and big serve to use on quick surfaces. Mardy has loads of talent; he's smooth, inventive, and there's a "bigness" to his game that puts him in the company of those who could really dominate and shut down opponents. His drawbacks were a somewhat fragile body (due partly to lack of conditioning) and an inability to keep his play level high for the extended periods it takes to build a high ranking, or win tournaments. But in Davis Cup, he could do all the damage we'd need without having to undergo a character transformation.

What I remember best about the Oklahoma tie was the way Pete Sampras—already a living legend near the end of his storied career—hung out with the younger guys on the team. He was accustomed to deluxe accommodations by then, but there's no such thing in Oklahoma City. He made cracks about it, but they were good-natured. He shared the van with the rest of the guys. As soon as they piled in, they inevitably cranked the music—usually rap.

Pete just shook his head, bewildered, and asked, "What the hell is this stuff?"

The night we clinched, we all went out to celebrate my first World Group win. Pete came along, too, along with our wives, my Melissa and his Bridgette Wilson. The girls got along well.

Melissa always liked and got along with Andy, too, and that night she danced quite a bit with him. Andy likes to dance, and he has all these hip-hop moves. He worked up quite a sweat.

I noticed throughout the evening that Pete was pretty quiet, taking it all in. He probably saw his career fading before his very eyes, for the team was changing, dramatically. He had a deep well of Davis Cup experience with comrades like Jim Courier, Andre Agassi (despite their rivalry, Pete and Andre on the same squad amounted to a definition of "elite"), Todd Martin, and even my brother John, with whom Pete won a critical doubles match in a final against Switzerland. In Oklahoma, he was both icon and odd man out. He seemed bemused by it all, took it for what it was with a faint, knowing smile on his face.

It was their day now, and it would be for quite some time.

A Davis Cup Mud Hole

James Blake, it turned out, is a sensitive guy, very self-protective and resistant to change. In 2003, we lost in the first round to Croatia, and had to play in the relegation round later in the fall. As luck would have it, we drew the Slovak Republic again, and this time they had the choice of ground. They went with an indoor clay court in Bratislava.

We would be vulnerable on clay; unlike American clubs of the not very distant past, this team was lost on dirt. Pete Sampras had almost singlehandedly won the 1995 final in Moscow on slow, indoor red clay in one of the all-time great individual Davis Cup performances (he won both his singles and joined with Todd Martin to take the doubles). Agassi and Jim Courier both won the French

Open (Courier did it twice) and felt comfortable sliding around on clay. But these new guys, they were babes in the woods.

It isn't all that easy to figure out what happened in just a few years, but this sudden aversion to clay probably had more to do with the talent and character of the players than any training or developmental factors. It isn't like Agassi, Courier, or Sampras were well trained in the art of playing on clay. Jim had plenty of clay-court experience, growing up in Florida. But his game was really developed, and at the same time and in the same way as Andre's, at a bastion of traditional, American hardcourt tennis, the Nick Bollettieri Tennis Academy. And Pete played almost exclusively on hard courts as he grew up in southern California.

The big difference between those guys and Roddick, Blake, and Fish is talent. The three young Americans all have somewhat limited games; what they do well, they often do beautifully. They just didn't have the same degree of talent as those elder statesmen. A lot of hot air gets wasted in discussing why Americans can't play on clay, but just turn it around—how many Spanish players can play on grass? Most players represent the sum of their natural talent and the prejudice in their developmental training. Great players transcend that simple formula.

Rafael Nadal ought to be lousy on grass; any pro who played anything like him in the past certainly stunk up the lawns. But Nadal is a genius—an exceptional athlete who was able to transcend his developmental history. The same goes for those older Americans who won big on clay. Great players find ways to win on all surfaces; slightly less talented guys just can't punch through the surface barrier. This is one of those debates that makes you want to go, *Duh! It's the talent!*

Andy had just shocked tennis by winning the US Open as we prepared to leave for the Slovak Republic, and he stayed in New York longer than I would have liked because he was offered the host slot on *Saturday Night Live*. I knew he might have motivation issues in Slovakia, but I still wasn't as worried about him as I was about James Blake, who was going through a rough patch. I was sufficiently concerned to invite James to New York from his home in Connecticut to practice for a few days before we left. He would hit with one of the South American pros who had tour level experience.

At the time, James was already using Luxilon polyester strings, but a lot of the guys had enjoyed improved results with half-and-half (a combination of polyester and the traditional natural gut). I suggested that James try the hybrid approach. The experiment flopped, and I thought no more of it.

James's reluctance to change things up or try something new gradually became a running joke on the team. He strung his rackets at 68 pounds of tension, no matter what. At that 2003 playoff tie, we basically played indoors, but in a damp swamp, a regular Davis Cup clay-court mud hole. In practice, James would be swinging as hard as he could and the ball would just barely plop over the net. I suggested that he drop tension to 58 pounds to get more of a trampoline effect from his strings.

He reluctantly tried it, dumped a few balls into the net, and his face clouded over. Meanwhile, the other guys—wiseasses that they are—were covertly watching, stomping their feet and calling out, "Sixty-eight, sixty-eight!"

Meanwhile, Mardy Fish was in good form so, partly out of frustration with James, I chose Mardy to join Andy as a singles player. The selection was a calculated gamble that paid off, for Mardy stepped up in that tie. Andy lost the first match to Dominik Hrbatý, so it was absolutely critical for Mardy to keep us in the hunt in the mud hole. He won his match, taking out Karol Beck. The Bryan brothers boosted our lead to 2–1 and Andy, playing more like himself, clinched the tie with a win over Beck.

Weeks later, I found out from James's coach, Brian Barker, that James had been so discombobulated by my suggestion that he use Luxilon combined with gut that it only exacerbated his tailspin, and contributed to the funk that led him to lose his place on the team to Mardy. I learned quickly that James needed to be handled with kid gloves, and tried to remember it in every subsequent tie.

Some time later, we finally got James to drop down to a compromise 64 pounds of string tension.

We almost threw a party to celebrate.

THE FRENCH OPEN: WILD CARD McENROE

In late April, the tennis action shifts to Europe and a demanding clay-court circuit that culminates in Paris, at the French Open, aka Roland Garros, the scene of one of my most humbling moments.

It happened in 1991, at the time when my quest to become a good singles player finally started to pay off. It was a long time coming, too, because it turned out that I had a lot to learn.

After my doubles successes in 1989 (in addition to the French Open, Jim Grabb and I won the title at the tour's year-end playoffs, to which only the top eight doubles teams of the year were invited), I was ranked around no. 400 in singles. I fully expected to make it in singles, and I was lulled into a false sense of security by a perk that came with my last name: virtually unlimited wild cards.

Being John McEnroe's brother greased the tournament skids for me. Tournament promoters, especially at smaller events, liked that I had a recognizable name, and I was always a good story, creating media exposure for the event. Also, every tournament promoter was interested in building some kind of relationship with a star as big as John, and giving his kid brother a free pass into the main draw could be a benefit somewhere down the road. At one point, between October of 1988 and November of the following year, I was a wild-card entrant—and first-round loser—in seven straight tournaments. It pains me to admit this, but I believe I hold the ATP record for having been awarded the greatest number of wild cards in one year—forgive me if I don't really want to research the issue.

But after a year and a half of spinning my wheels, I found myself thinking, *You know, you're not gonna make it. Unless you get into super incredible shape, you're not gonna make it as a singles player at all.* That realization hurt my pride and it made me anxious about my future. Should I focus on being a "doubles specialist," which could yield a nice, easy living? The funny thing was, at tournaments where I was a direct acceptance based on ranking (or merit), I did better. Granted, it's not hard to improve on an 0–7 record, but it was something to think about.

I came to realize that wild cards were a form of poison. I felt guilty taking them, because down deep I knew I was only given them because of John's achievements. Sure I was good in doubles, but did that entitle me to a free pass in singles? Being showered with wild cards blunted the urgency I felt to make it, and it subtly undermined my confidence.

In the off-season of 1989, I realized that I wouldn't be satisfied as a "doubles specialist"—and that I didn't want those tempting wild cards. I thought: *You know what? You need to work hard and play tennis hard. You need to earn your way.*

And that's when things started to fall into place. In the winter of 1989, I stayed out at our family home in Cove Neck, and got into the fitness routine. I felt good enough about myself to accept wild cards into the Hong Kong and Singapore events in the spring of 1990. I reversed my decision for two reasons: I knew how hard I'd worked, and I'd won enough matches to have a shot at making the singles cutoff for the French Open—especially if I had a little help. I made the quarters in Hong Kong, but I lost to my former Stanford teammate Dan Goldie in the quarters of Singapore, narrowly missing the cutoff for direct acceptance into Roland Garros and Wimbledon. I was bummed out, but I kept slogging away.

This process of breaking in, which all but the best players have to go through, is tough; I still believe that the toughest match to win in all of tennis is the last round of qualifying for a Grand Slam event. I try to communicate that to all those talented young kids I come across in the USTA development program.

I tell them, don't be tempted by the easy way, even if it does present itself. If you win a couple of matches and know in your heart that you earned those wins, you feel different about yourself. Capitalize on that feeling. And for gosh sakes, lay your foundation, fitness and trainingwise, so that when an opportunity does come your way—as it did for me, finally, at that 1991 Australian Open—you can make the most of it.

Yeah, This Kid Is For Real

You can't say the words "Roland Garros" in this decade without thinking: *Rafael Nadal.* Nadal won 31 consecutive matches on the red dirt of the Philippe Chartrier Court (aka Court Centrale) before he lost one: That's four titles, plus. . . . No one, not even Björn Borg, can match that 31-win run.

I first got a glimmer of what Nadal would become before he even played at Roland Garros (an injury kept him out in the first year he was a direct acceptance), in the Davis Cup final of 2004, in Seville, Spain. We all knew of him by then; although he was ranked in the 50s, word was out that he was a comer.

We weren't expecting Nadal to play—not on a squad that featured two former world no. 1 singles players, Juan Carlos Ferrero and Carlos Moya. But the Spanish threw us—and Ferrero—a huge curveball by nominating Nadal to play singles behind Moya. Nadal had just turned eighteen a few months earlier, and here he was, in a Davis Cup final, about to lock horns with our top singles performer and the US Open champ of the previous year.

By the time we stepped out on the floor of the Estadio Olimpico de Sevilla, the Davis Cup one-day attendance record, established at White City, the Sydney, Australia, shrine of Davis Cup, had been shattered. Over 27,000 Spanish fans had assembled in stands specially reconfigured to accommodate tennis. When I looked up from the floor of the enormous soccer stadium, the sight of all those red and yellow Spanish flags, rippling and stretching as far as the eye could see, was overwhelming.

Moya roughed up Mardy Fish in the opening match pitting the Spanish no. 1 player against our no. 2. And while that took a little pressure off Nadal, I thought Andy Roddick was in with a decent shot. As we walked out into that sea of spectators awash in red and yellow, Andy said, "Look around. Does it ever get any better than this?" Whatever else lay in store, I knew Andy wasn't intimidated. His competitive instincts flourish under duress.

Nadal was green but the expectations of the home crowd were obvious. Andy and I knew that, and were hoping that Nadal would feel the pressure. By the time the match began, it was pretty late in the chilly day, and the court was playing heavier because of the moisture in the air. That might be good for Andy. The ball would travel more slowly, making Andy's serve less effective, but it would stay relatively low on the bounce. That would keep Nadal's big, viciously bouncing topspin shots down closer to Andy's wheelhouse.

For players who aren't trained on clay, dealing with those high-bouncing topspins and clay-court kick serves is daunting. Having to hit the ball from shoulder height is awkward, and it puts terrific stress on muscles unaccustomed to such a specific challenge, so it's also exhausting.

Andy won the first set, in a tiebreaker, but Nadal took the second relatively easily as his booming ground strokes began to find their mark. At one point, Andy hit a nasty ad-court kick serve that pushed Nadal ten feet behind the baseline and pulled him eight feet wide of the sideline. Whereupon the lefty Nadal smoked a return that didn't even cross the net—it came in at a severe angle outside the net post, and got just enough of the line in that near-side corner to skid away, a clean winner.

Andy and I reacted automatically, making eye contact. *Yeah, this kid is for real. . . .*

I had a flash memory of Roger Federer, hitting all those razor-cut volleys against our doubles team in my debut as Davis Cup captain. This was a similar epiphany. This guy is something special, something different. We could see, up to that point, that Nadal had the attitude—that signature mix of boyish exuberance and competitive steel. Now we knew that he had the game, too.

As the third set spooled out toward the tiebreaker, I sensed the match slipping away. Nadal was finding that clay-court groove. But if Andy could just hang in there and serve his way through the tiebreaker, it might discourage the kid just long enough for Andy to put the hammer down and snatch the win.

Andy saved two set points late in the third and got to the tiebreaker. He blasted and clawed his way to 5–4. As he prepared to serve, he shot me a look, a question in his eyes: *This is getting desperate, but I've got a shot. . . . Where do I serve this one?*

As a captain on foreign turf, before a frenzied crowd, the last thing you want to show is insecurity or confusion. I'd been thinking, *5-4 in the breaker, he has to go with his biggest gun, he's got to go right down the middle—just hit the crap out of it, right down the "T". . . .* So I leaned slightly forward, raised my hand to shield my mouth, and hissed, "Middle."

Andy hit a huge first serve that missed by a hair; a serve that would have brought him to set point.

Then, he hit another fault. 5–5.

It was over. We'd missed our chance. Nadal won the set, and although he suffered bouts of cramps in the fourth set, he broke

Andy twice early on and won it handily. Six months later, Nadal would bag his first French Open title and begin his remarkable 31-match streak.

The French, Being the French

Until the explosion of Open tennis, the European clay-court circuit was like a summer party on the Riviera, a chance for the classic "tennis bum" to soak up the sun, steal kisses from the odd heiress, and hit some balls on the exotic, slow surface that dominated in Italy, France, and Spain. Roland Garros is the only Grand Slam event on clay—the other three were played on grass for most of tennis history. The Anglo communities were apt to pass it off as the French being . . . the French.

But in this case, we're not talking about being different for its own sake. Clay has unique aesthetic and game-influencing properties. It calls for a different skill set than grass or hard courts, yet it's not so different that the demand is unreasonable. We're lucky the French didn't try to emulate the British, because the game is much richer for having a thriving clay-court tradition, despite the headaches it causes for American players.

The difference between clay-court and hardcourt tennis also has interesting cultural overtones. Europeans like to slow down and enjoy life more than Americans, and clay isn't just the slowest commonly used surface, it's the one that calls for the most deliberation and strategic thinking. Until the recent, dramatic slowing of most U.S. hard courts, the American game was based on power and efficiency—unloading a bomb of a serve, and then ending the point before it could even be said to begin, with a follow-up volley.

The French phrase for clay courts is *terre battue* (literally, "broken earth"). You may have noticed that my broadcast colleague, Dick Enberg, *never* misses an opportunity to say those two words. The surface is made from an underlayer of firm clay, covered with a top dressing of crushed red brick. A clay court is organic; it reacts to changes in weather, and its playing properties are influenced by the amount of top dressing you apply. Because a clay court is absorbent, it takes a real rain shower to halt play, and the courts dry fast. You can resume the battle quickly, even after a thunderstorm.

By contrast, American hard courts are synthetic, with a cement base. In keeping with our national obsession with standardization, the original cement courts that were the basis for the American style of play were virtually identical from coast to coast. Their playing properties were unaffected by humidity or temperature, although a light drizzle rendered them unplayable. These days, though, the application of a rubberlike top coating allows you to at least fine-tune a cement court for speed.

We value the practical and inexpensive in the U.S., and hard courts require no maintenance. Clay courts need a fair amount of TLC; most European tennis clubs employ attendants who sweep and water the courts, paint or apply tape lines on it, smooth divots, and make sure the courts have just the right amount of top dressing, even on windy days that blow the stuff around like desert sand.

The aesthetics of clay-court tennis can't be beat, but even in Europe that's a losing battle—more and more of the new courts they build are hard courts. But clay is the best surface for developing consistency, a strategic understanding of the game, and those big, troublesome, topspin shots. For a long time, that was enough to get a player a high degree of success. But at the elite level, players now need to add aggression and a willingness to end points to the consistency bred on clay. That's where hard courts come into play. The recent surge of top-class Spanish players weren't trained exclusively on clay; they attended hardcourt finishing school, where they built on the foundation of mobility, stamina, and strategic savvy that they developed early on clay.

Monte Carlo, the Italian Open, Madrid, and the French Open are the highlights of the loaded spring clay circuit. That's one major and three mandatory Masters Series events that offer the highest number of ranking points, and commensurate prize money. It's only fitting that Rolex, the high-end watchmaker, is the title sponsor in Monte Carlo, because you could call it the James Bond tournament.

The site, the Monte Carlo Country Club, is an enclave of the rich, royal, and powerful. Patrons and club members regularly have lunch on the terrace while watching the players—or is it well-paid peons?—grunting and sweating on the main stadium court. From the stands, you can look out, beyond the sculpted gardens and attractive, maroon earth tones of the courts, at the blue Mediterranean, where dazzling white yachts sit moored until their passengers decide to visit the fabled Monte Carlo casino, or maybe the tennis.

You can see how traveling around the Riviera and the Mediterranean nations all spring and early summer can appeal to young, footloose guys. I was one of them, even though I was pretty well traveled by the time I earned my degree in political science in three and a half years at Stanford. I'd played national and international-level junior events, and before college graduation I'd already won a main-tour doubles title at San Jose (with Jim Grabb). It was no cheap win, either—in the first round, we beat one of the great American doubles teams of the Open era, Ken Flach and Robert Seguso.

I played singles at the French Open for the first time in 1991, a direct entry thanks to my successful Australian Open. I won two matches—this was huge for me, given the surface—and had Andre Agassi to face in the third round. I was playing well. I'd won my first-round match in four hours, and my next one took almost that long. But despite the long matches, I felt great. I was confident, fit, and strong.

We played on the Court Centrale, or stadium court (it's now named for the great French tennis administrator Philippe Chartrier). I hit a pretty flat, clean ball, which Andre always liked because it enabled him to get grooved and maximize his accuracy and consistency. Despite my confidence, it quickly became apparent that I was in trouble.

Playing Andre that day was like walking into a buzz saw; everything I tried, he had an answer. I quickly devolved from opponent into his personal yo-yo. I didn't miss too many balls, which only prolonged the agony as, time and again, Andre set me up and then finished me off with a well-placed shot.

A few of my buddies from my Stanford days were in the stands. I remember looking up at them when I was behind 2–6, 2–6, 0–4, just two games from losing, and instead of hiding their faces and Stanford caps, they were yelling and screaming, "Come on, Mac! Come on!"

I felt bad for them, and bad for me. I walked over toward them and muttered, "Man, I'm just a human punching bag out here."

Soon it was over, in a mercifully short hour and forty-two minutes. I won all of four games. My balloon was pretty much deflated; I thought I had this clay-court thing somewhat figured out, but this set back my thinking. Andre unwittingly gave me a preview of how the game would come to look a decade later, when guys like me could no longer count on winning their fair share of matches just by hitting a clean, pretty, flat ball, and keeping the error count down.

When we shook hands, Andre said, "Hey, tough luck. That's about as well as I can play."

Incidentally, Andre wasn't always so gracious in victory. In another match, on hard courts at the Canadian Open in the summer of 1993, Andre was in a showboating mode. He toyed with me. One time, he pulled me in with a drop shot, drove me back, and then hit another dropper. He was running me ragged, and I'd had about all I was going to take. I looked at him and yelled across the net: "Andre, that was bullshit. Do me a favor—just play. Beat the shit out of me, that's fine. I can take it. But don't pull this shit."

After that match, which Andre won 6–1, 6–4, he sought me out to apologize. That was the young Andre, the arrogant Andre, the one who once was so far ahead in a Davis Cup match in Argentina that he cavalierly hand-caught serves by an inferior opponent, just to get on with things and close the poor guy out. All that changed, over time. We became friends, and Andre gradually emerged as a great ambassador for the game.

But I think about that blowout in Paris every spring, because it foreshadowed the way the game would become a spectacular, if carefully calibrated, shoot-out, featuring players who took huge cuts, used plenty of spin, and had loads of stamina. One valuable lesson I learned that day was that the length of match is hardly all that matters, because I was more tired after Andre whupped me in under two hours than I'd been after enduring two matches nearly twice as time consuming. The intensity of each point against Andre just wore me down.

Swinging From the Heels

Andre lost the final in Paris that same year to Jim Courier, his stable mate at the Nick Bollettieri Tennis Academy in Bradenton, Florida (Jim successfully defended the title in 1992). Both men were part of a new breed—guys who liked to step into the court and dictate, using the big forehand. Jim was a pioneer of the "inside out" forehand, the shot you hit crosscourt, from anywhere near the center of the court to well over on the backhand side—to a fellow righthander's backhand.

Up until that point, you could get away with being a really good tennis player, if not a great athlete. You could hit through guys with steady, deep strokes, and more or less take turns playing offense and defense. But getting good began to be less about stroking technique and the classic setup-and-hit sensibility than about how well you hit on the run, how fit you are, how well you can play defense, or transition to—or from—offense. If you want to get in the game, you'd better be ready to rip the ball, open up the court, and seize your chances. And do all of that on the fly.

There's no guarantee that if I came up today, I could figure out a way to match my career-high singles ranking of 28. But racket speed (how quickly you accelerate through your stroke) wasn't a big issue twenty years ago—today, it's the grail.

I was taught by the same shy, soft-spoken Mexican-born pro as my brothers, Tony Palafox. He encouraged us to actually arrest the racket on impact—actually slow the stroke—to keep the ball on the strings that extra split second. You could see that in a lot of John's strokes, because his timing was exceptional. That approach also was conducive to hitting a slightly heavier ball, with just a smidgen more control.

But then along came young, high-flying Jimmy Arias, one of the first great players produced by the Bollettieri academy. Jimmy, who got as high as no. 5 in the world in 1984, was the first guy to actually lash out at the ball, accelerating with increasing violence, right through the follow-through. He would swing so hard that the momentum would lift him off the ground. But at the same moment in history, engineers unveiled the "oversize" rackets (the aluminum Prince Pro was the first of that line), which made it much easier for others to follow Arias's lead—even if they didn't have Jimmy's gift of timing. To this day, Jimmy says that's the main reason he couldn't hold his high ranking. He lost his edge.

There's truth in that. Diminishing the role of timing has been a leveler of the playing field, although the advantages provided by better equipment are by no means obvious to the naked eye. Robert Lansdorp, the coach who helped develop Tracy Austin, Pete Sampras, Lindsay Davenport, Eliot Teltscher, Maria Sharapova, and many other fine pros, likes to say that the one shared attribute of all great players is exceptional timing. In fact, when he evaluates a potential protégé, it's the very first thing he looks for. I think he's dead right about that.

The search for increased racket-head speed has led many pros to play with ever-lighter frames. The advent of polyester strings also had a huge impact in recent years. The old truism dictating that the harder you swing, the less control you have, has been turned upside down. With the new, less elastic strings, swinging from the heels gives you *more* control.

Top players today are almost immune to the second-oldest fear in the book, hitting the ball out (the oldest fear is feebly driving it into the net). And kids today are taught to get in position—quick—and whale on the ball. It's all about positioning and racket speed.

Slice, or underspin, keeps the ball low after the bounce. In the past, it was useful as a setup tool, or an attacking shot behind which you would charge the net. Now its main purpose is to keep the other guy from attacking, because if you leave anything hanging in that strike zone between the waist and shoulders, it's good-night Irene. And the game is tougher, physically, point-in, point-out. You need to get used to that at a young age and be ready to withstand the punishment.

It's surprising that despite these constantly escalating demands, there's been no dramatic rise in injury or burnout. The players who burned out at a relatively young age (Pat Rafter and Lleyton Hewitt, who kept playing in spite of it) or were forced into premature retirement by injury (Marcelo Rios and Miloslav Mečíř, both former Grand Slam finalists) aren't at all typical of the aggressive, power baseliners. In fact, Rios (a former no. 1, despite never having won a major) and Mečíř, both of whom suffered crippling back injuries, also had strikingly smooth, efficient, seemingly stress-free games.

The human body is an amazing machine.

Prawn Tennis

After I was eliminated from the French Open in 1994, I went straight to England to prepare for Wimbledon. I was working out with Richey Reneberg at Queens Club, site of the major Wimbledon tune-up tournament, on the day of the Roland Garros final. After practice, we sat around the lounge with some of the club members and watched the final, in which upstart Alberto Berasategui faced off with his Spanish countryman—and the defending champion—Sergi Bruguera.

Berasategui hit his forehand with such an extreme western grip that he made contact with the back, rather than front, face of the strings. It was hard to find the guy's backhand, he overplayed so far to that side. And when you did get to it, the shot was less than menacing; it was a crazy, two-fisted flick, but so well protected by his court positioning that the stroke was irrelevant.

Berasategui walloped one forehand after another with sizzling pace and loads of topspin. But Bruguera played impregnable defense, appeared tireless, ran like a deer—and hit with so much topspin that Berasategui often had to leave his feet just to reach the ball with his subsequent swing.

While we were watching, one of the elderly club members suddenly rose to his feet and roared, "Lawn tennis? That isn't lawn tennis. It's prawn tennis!"

Richey and I looked at each other, snickering. It seemed a nonsensical statement, made by an old-school fuddy-duddy who was still enamored of the stylized, serve-and-volley pas de deux that once characterized tennis on grass. But then, the prawn, or shrimp, swims backward (tail first), and these two guys were certainly taking turns pushing each other way *back*—way back and off the court. The geezer had hit upon a description that can only be called inspired.

For weeks on end, Richey couldn't get over that comment. He'd walk around and suddenly adopt this heavy British accent and thunder: "That isn't lawn tennis, by Jove—it's prawn tennis!"

The game was changing, no doubt about it; the "prawns" were emerging as the kingmakers—if not always the kings—of clay. Soon there were simply too many powerful, consistent, athletic grinders out there—guys like Albert Costa, Thomas Muster, Juan Carlos Ferrero, Alex Corretja—for the more artistic, versatile, attacking players to handle, round-by-round. You might get by one or two of them, but another always seemed to lie in wait.

My brother John struck one of the last great blows for the attacking game back in 1984, when—against the odds, even then—he reached the Roland Garros final and met the pioneer of fitness in tennis, powerful, punishing Ivan Lendl. I saw much of that match because on the same day my partner Luke Jensen and I were penciled in to play the Boys' Doubles Final (under eighteen). Our opponents were Eric Winogradsky and this lumbering fifteen-year-old who was already saddled with a colorful nickname: Boris "Boom Boom" Becker.

The four of us sat in the locker room, as astonished as anyone to see John take a two-sets-to-none lead over Ivan Lendl. Our boy's match was scheduled for Court no. 1, at the time the second largest of the show courts. But an official came to the locker room early in the third set to tell us that the final was going so fast that they were probably going to hold us up and put us on the Court Centrale.

Holy shit, I thought. My brother's going to win the French and I'm going to play right after him, on one of the great center courts of the world!

On top of that, my parents had made a last-minute trip to Paris to see the final (John's, not mine, in case you were wondering). This promised to be some day. Diehard tennis fans still remember what happened next. At 1–1 in the third set, noise escaping from the headset of a courtside cameraman got to John, and he had one of his trademark fits. As often as John rallied from a meltdown to play with newfound focus and energy, this time it was different. Although he continued to play at an extremely high level, it was almost as if a spell had been broken.

The outburst pulled John out of that serene state players call "the zone." Suddenly he appeared to realize that he was facing one of the most ruthless and brutally powerful baseliners in the history of tennis, on a slow red clay court where a serve-and-volley player like John could run, but not hide. His game declined just enough to provide hope for Lendl. They seesawed back and forth, but Lendl won the third set.

Early in the fourth, the tournament official came and told us to take it easy; if John won in four, they would still put us on the Court Centrale. The decision enabled me to keep watching, and when John went up, 4–2—two games from the title—it looked like my folks could just rest easy in their center-court seats on a great day for the McEnroes.

But Lendl battled back to take set four, and the official told us, "Sorry, boys, but I've got to put you on Court One, now."

So out we went. During our warm-up and most of the first set, I was distracted; I spoke enough French to follow the score in the stadium. I could hear it called after every point. The fifth set was tight, and I feared that it wouldn't end well for John—nor for me, for that matter, because Luke and I lost the first set of our final.

It was soon over in the stadium; Lendl came back to win, 7–5 in the fifth. The only good thing was that I could forget about John's fate and concentrate on my own. When I looked up to see my parents walking down the cement aisle to the player guest box at my court, they looked like they'd just seen a ghost.

It was funny, in a sick kind of way—my folks had to pretend that they really cared what happened in my match after watching their other son lose in an epic final. They'd have to clap and cheer and try to show some enthusiasm when I knew my doubles final had to be the last thing on their minds. I have to hand it to them, they made a good effort. Thankfully, I didn't have to fish them out of the Seine that night; Luke and I battled back to win our doubles, even if it wasn't the win the McEnroes were looking for on that Paris afternoon.

That night, I had dinner with my folks back in town. When I spoke to John later, he ruefully said, "You know, that was my chance. That was my chance to win the French."

Being seventeen and trying extra hard to be Mr. Positive after seeing my brother absorb such a heavy blow, I said, "Oh, no. Don't worry, you'll have another chance."

John just looked at me like I was nuts. Without smiling, he repeated what he'd said: ". . . that was my chance."

John would go on to dominate the tour that year, putting together an 82–3 singles record that remains the best-ever single-year winning percentage (96%) in the Open era. It's a record unlikely to be broken, even though Roger Federer came within a hair in 2005 (with 95% on 81–4). But in his heart, John knew that his chance in Paris had come and gone.

Everything had come together to create the best possible opportunity for John that year, and he failed to capitalize on it. Expecting that to happen again was like expecting lightning to strike again in the same place as before. The very fact that he'd squandered such a golden opportunity was enough to make him feel jinxed, no matter how many more times he would play. Down deep, he knew he'd blown it—for good.

John understood something I didn't know at the time. When greatness calls, you'd better be ready to answer and do everything in your power to seize the moment. If you don't you may never get another chance. That's how champions think, and it helps explain why they're so relentless, why their reaction when they get a nose out in front is to hit the gas, not coast, or nudge the brakes.

In my world, there's always another chance. John also must have thought that I was underestimating the basic degree of difficulty he faced in his quest for greatness. It irritated him that I would even suggest that if he plugged away, he'd get another chance. He was saying: "This isn't going to happen again. Stop living in this world where it's very easy to be great. Because it's not."

Europe on Five Sets a Day

No matter where you're from, traveling abroad is a rite of passage; I enjoyed it and made the most of it once I became a full-time player. I sometimes rented a car and drove from event to event in Europe; a road trip was a great escape from the day-to-day anxieties of playing, and it kept me from getting too lost in the tournament fun house with its courtesy cars, caterers, locker room attendants, and such—all amenities that create a firewall between players and what you might call the "real" world—you know, where you may have to read a map, ask a question in a foreign tongue, find a restaurant and read the menu posted in the window to make sure you're not about to walk into a joint that serves only exotic reptile meat.

I always felt comfortable in Europe; for a period, I was coached by an Austrian, Gunther Bresnick, and dating a pro from Vienna, Petra Ritter. I spent a fair amount of time driving to and from Austria from various points where I played in Europe.

Sometime around 1993, I was invited to the wedding of my former Stanford teammate Jeff Tarango. I was pretty tight for a while with Jeff, even though he had a reputation as a contentious, difficult guy. He had a unique talent for pissing off people in the locker room.

Tennis has produced its share of . . . characters . . . and Jeff was an outstanding example. In his autobiography, *Open*, Andre Agassi tells the story of a bitterly fought, incredibly close junior match with Jeff—one that ended, Agassi insists, with Jeff making such a conspicuously bad call in his own favor to win the match that the only reaction Andre could muster was utter disbelief.

When we were on the tour, I sometimes trained with Jeff in Los Angeles. We would take our rackets to the beach and play "beach tennis"—volley drills in the deep sand. Those were killers, because we could keep the ball going in the air at close quarters for a long time. But all that lunging and pushing off in the sand was great for your quads and calves.

I didn't see that match between Andre and Jeff, so I have no opinion on that call. I do know that Jeff was a junior with an astonishing, rare gift. He was one of the few players who could, conceivably, have played Andre close enough to get in a position to win a match. In juniors, Jeff was 13–0 against Pete Sampras, and 9–0 against Michael Chang, the two best players of his time in southern California. Unlike those two, Jeff decided to attend college.

At Stanford, Jeff blossomed into a collegiate star. He played no. 1 singles and doubles, and led us to the NCAA title in 1989. Jeff's production dropped off when he turned pro; his highest ranking was no. 42. But I wouldn't blame Jeff's decline on lingering too long in college.

He was one of those prodigies whose game and competitive skills matured early. It's not an unusual story: Al Parker, Tommy Ho, and Scott Davis were just a few of the more spectacularly successful juniors who were unable to surpass their junior achievements. Donald Young seems headed down that same road as I write this.

When Jeff left college, he met Sampras again for the first time as a pro in 1990 (the year Pete burst on the scene and won the US Open). Jeff expected to pick up where he'd left off, even though Pete had already risen to no. 7 in the world. Jeff lost 7–6, 7–6 (both tiebreakers went to 7–5, you couldn't ask for a closer match), nothing to be ashamed of, against the hottest young player on the planet, and a guy destined to shatter the Grand Slam singles title record. But Jeff took it pretty badly. He later said, "It kind of burst the bubble I had, thinking I'd always be better than those guys."

Anyway, Jeff was a pro when he fell in love with a French girl, Benedicte, and they planned their wedding in the south of France for the final weekend of Wimbledon (I guess Jeff figured his presence in London would not be required). So I decided to be a loyal buddy and go, along with a few of our old Stanford teammates, even though I was entered in the tournament in the pretty Alpine Swiss town of Gstaad.

Gstaad began the day after the wedding, so I requested a Tuesday start (it's a common appeal made by anyone who's got a reasonable excuse). The tournament turned me down; it looked like I'd either have to blow off the wedding or try to find a way to get to Gstaad late Sunday or very early Monday. As it turned out, there was no viable way to do that by air. I said to hell with it; I'm going to the wedding, and the reception, and then I'm driving to Switzerland. So, after the ceremony and the big party, I got in the car—this tiny Peugeot that would do maybe 110 kilometers per hour if you kept it floored—at around ten at night. I had the company of our Stanford buddy Barry Richards. But I didn't trust Barry to stay awake, so I took the wheel, drove all night, and pulled into Gstaad in broad daylight.

I rushed to the hotel and slept for two hours before my first-rounder with a good Italian clay-court player, Renzo Furlan. Sometimes, when you don't expect anything, good things happen. I won the first set and pushed the second one to a tiebreaker. But when I lost that, the fatigue hit me and I had nothing left in the tank. Renzo crushed me in the third.

I vowed never to play Gstaad again, because I saw no reason why the tournament couldn't cut me the same break other players routinely got. That's a common story. Players are accustomed to having their path cleared of stones, and gravitate almost superstitiously to a place where they've had good experiences (mainly, winning) and avoid places where they've struggled, or felt they got stiffed somehow by the organization. The Hungarian player Balázs Taróczy, who played in John's era and rose as high as no. 13, won 13 singles titles in his career, almost *half* of them (six) at the de facto Netherlands Open, aka Hilversum. The guy kept going back to Holland because he had good experiences there and they treated him well.

Tournament directors live in fear of offending players, especially the stars. Any bad experience—food poisoning, a missed airport pickup, even a few horrendous line calls that cost someone a match—can alienate a player for good. It doesn't matter who screwed up, or whether the tournament had anything to do with it.

Jeff Tarango was difficult, but it took a little help from Benedicte to make him the poster child for nut-job tennis players worldwide. The incident took place at Wimbledon in 1995, during Jeff's third-round match with the German Alexander Mronz (an old boyfriend of Steffi Graf). The crowd got on Tarango, who was easily cast as the ugly American because of his aggressive, confrontational manner. As usual, Jeff pushed back, telling the crowd to "shut up."

Bruno Rebeuh, a professional chair umpire, immediately hit him with a code violation for "audible obscenity."

Jeff went ballistic, arguing that "shut up" isn't an obscenity. He demanded to see the tournament referee, who was unsympathetic and ordered Jeff to continue playing. Whereupon Jeff called Rebeuh "one of the most corrupt officials in the game," incurring an additional violation, for unsportsmanlike conduct.

That did it for Jeff; he walked to his chair, packed up, and left the court. Benedicte left the stands, but instead of following Jeff to the locker room, she went up to Rebeuh and slapped him—twice—across the face. In a sick sort of way, it was a wonderfully "French" thing to do, and a lot of people found it more amusing than mortifying.

The tabloids went nuts. The broadcast media from around the world went nuts. Jeff continued to go nuts. In his subsequent press conference, Tarango stuck to his guns and ended up incurring $63,000 worth of fines (no one was crazy enough to try fining the slaphappy, hot-blooded French beauty Benedicte). And for months afterward, Jeff stood by his contention that Rebeuh was corrupt, an official who enjoyed his semicelebrity too much, loved to mingle with the stars, and played personal favorites.

I never had any reason to doubt Rebeuh's integrity, but anyone who's played the tournament game at least understands Tarango's suspicions. In tennis, you're at the utter mercy of the umpire; it probably doesn't help that the guy sits in a chair, high above you. All of us have lost matches because of horrendous calls, and many of us have strong feelings about the competence or evenhandedness of certain officials. You're out there alone on the court, and you know the old saying; even paranoids have real enemies. You may even remember my brother John's famous remark, directed at the predecessor to the Hawk-Eye electronic line-calling system, the machine called Cyclops. The device was of limited use, because all it determined was whether or not a serve was long. After Cyclops beeped to judge one of John's serves, he complained audibly to the chair umpire: *Maybe I'm paranoid, but that machine knows who I am. . . .*

Hawk-Eye, the digital ball-tracking system that covers every line on the court, has been a great addition to the game, even if Roger Federer has an ongoing feud with it. Roger actually looks offended when he challenges a call and Hawk-Eye fails to uphold his challenge. It's actually pretty funny to see Roger glower or make a gesture of frustration when he's rebuffed.

The big fear when visionaries called for adopting some form of electronic line calling was that it would eliminate human interest along with the prejudice that sometimes made it easier for a lineperson to miss a call—consciously or not. A simple Cyclops-like system that would emit a signal or light a bulb when a ball was out, with no linesmen on the court, certainly would have seemed soulless. But Hawk-Eye is basically a backup, like a court of appeals. The eagle-eyed as well as myopic linespeople are still with us, but now a player is allowed three incorrect challenges per set, and an additional one in the event of a tiebreaker.

Using the challenges wisely adds an additional element of strategy to the game, and it's an intriguing spectacle to see a stadium full of people, along with the two players, raptly watching the replay screen where Hawk-Eye re-creates the path of a ball in question.

Someday, of course, we'll have a disaster. A player will have exhausted his three or four challenges, and become the victim of a call that instant replay conclusively proves wrong—and the umpire will be powerless to do anything about. For that reason, maybe the powers that be ought to consider a system whereby the chair umpire has the discretion to consult Hawk-Eye if it looks like a player who's exhausted his challenges was robbed. But after almost five years of Hawk-Eye line calling, that disaster scenario has never occurred. The Lords of Tennis really got this one right.

It's also a pity that Hawk-Eye is presently too costly a system to use on all but show courts. Players sent out to play on field courts have no challenge system to fall back on in the event of linesperson incompetence.

John had an attitude-shaping experience in 1976 that highlights the degree to which a player is at the mercy of the umpire—or in that case, of the tournament referee, who's the overlord and ultimate authority at every event. Nothing in my experience rivals what he suffered when he was just seventeen, and playing the US Open qualifying tournament. He was already on the verge of busting out that year, and went into the tournament just days after winning an official ATP match at South Orange against tough New Zealand veteran Onny Parun.

John made it to the last round of qualifying for the Open, and found himself facing a solid player, a twenty-seven-year-old whose top career ranking was no. 105, Zan Guerry. It was a close match, but John appeared to win it after three hard-fought sets. When the umpire called "Game, Set, and Match, Mr. McEnroe," it looked like John had his first ticket into the main singles draw of the US Open.

But Guerry challenged the call on match-point, and the umpire went to check the mark (this was during that three-year period when the US Open was played on green Har-Tru clay, which is faster than red clay but slower than cement). Again, he called, "Game, Set, Match, Mr. McEnroe."

However, Anita Shukow, the referee for the qualifying event (whose job includes settling any disputes involving the on-court umpires), had been sitting nearby. She rose and went out on the court, found a mark, and proclaimed, "If that's the mark, the ball was in." She ordered the point replayed.

John was stupefied: *If* that's the mark???????

Of course, John was so discombobulated that he ended up losing the match. It wasn't nearly as critical or historic as that loss to Ivan Lendl, but John was no less devastated, and he'd never forget it. He soon made his breakthrough, and he let it be known wherever he played that he did not want Shukow anywhere near any of his matches. Of course, he had no authority to make such a demand, but most tournament directors knew he was deadly serious, and none wanted to risk his wrath. They kept her away from him.

Like I said before, tournament officials live in fear of offending top players because they are so dependent on them for their jobs.

. . . .

Jeff Tarango and I found ourselves on opposite sides of the net in a doubles match in the first round at the 1997 US Open at a time when both our careers were on the wane. I was still recovering from a botched operation on my shoulder and I didn't want to drag down one of my regular doubles partners. I chose to play with an obscure fellow American, Bill Behrens.

By then, the television folks had sized me up as a potential television commentator, and I moonlighted in the booth between attempts to play. At that very tournament I was working as a studio analyst for CBS. So during this tight match, Jeff started giving me shit—saying stupid stuff like, "Go back to the commentary booth, you don't belong out here."

I could hardly believe my ears. He knew I was coming back from surgery. This was, theoretically, my friend. I'd trained with him and attended his wedding. And to top it off, I'd played him six times and owned him, 5–1, 2–0 at majors. You'd think he'd have a little respect, or at least sympathy.

That kind of thing happens pretty often in the heat of competition; players trash talk each other, and it's almost always taken as a heat of the moment thing, and forgiven. The aggression has to find an outlet, and some guys are more prone to losing it, emotionally, than others. I don't usually hold grudges, but this incident with Tarango was a tough one to get over. It was a few years before I would even acknowledge Jeff when our paths crossed, but eventually we mended fences.

The Kings of Paris

If the French Open was the site of one of my most painful losses, it was also the place where, very early in my career, I became a Grand Slam champ. Jim Grabb and I won the doubles in 1989, the same year Michael Chang became the youngest singles champion in French Open history while tanks rumbled through Beijing's Tiananmen Square in Michael's ancestral home, China.

In the quarterfinals at that tournament, Jim and I played Tomas Carbonell and Carlos Costa, who's now Rafael Nadal's manager. They served for the match at 6–4, 5–4, but we managed to break, then went to win the tiebreaker. On the changeover at a set apiece, Jim breathed a huge sigh of relief and said, "Well, we've got a little breathing room now, even if it goes five sets."

I looked at him, unsure if he was pulling my leg. For in 1989, the best-of-five format was used only in the final two rounds of the doubles. I said, "Grabber—it's a best-of-three match. They served for the whole thing four games ago."

"Really?" Jim's jaw dropped and he was lost in thought for a moment. "Wow, lucky we won that game, huh?"

Actually, it was probably better that Jim didn't know at the time that they were serving for the match. He'd played well when we were at the brink, and maybe the extra pressure would have inhibited him. That's what it was like playing with Jim—he was kind of a space cadet, but also a terrific, old-school type doubles player (he won two majors, finished no. 1 for the year in doubles on two occasions, and won a remarkable 23 out of the 26 doubles finals he played).

Jim was six-four and powerful, with a big serve and excellent range. He had an excellent "big-man volley," meaning he could really stretch and still get plenty of stick on the ball. So if I got my return down low, he'd be ready to swoop across to intercept the next shot and end the point. Given that my serve was okay at best, it really helped me to have a big, active net person. (I had good results with another big man, Jonathan Stark, for the same reason.) Jim also was a streaky returner; when he was feeling it, we were a tough team.

Jim, who's from Tucson, Arizona, has a real calm demeanor and an intensely analytical mind. He reminded me of the brilliant basketball coach Phil Jackson, because he was into all that Zen stuff, and enjoyed talking about out-there things, like the meaning of life.

Heaven forbid tennis pros think about such things! Richey Reneberg gave Grabber a nickname that stuck, "The Thinker." Richey would always be making jokes and The Thinker would just roll his eyes—he was pondering loftier things. What did he care about Richey's infatuation with the Jerky Boys?

Communication and getting along is a huge part of success in doubles, and that helps explain why doubles is usually dominated by a fairly small pool of players who often change partners. Relationships go stale, people get on each other's nerves, especially when they're really dedicated and have ambitions. Just developing a knack for managing the doubles relationship becomes a distinct asset at that highest echelon of the game.

Jim and I never got to that level despite our promising start, because both of us also wanted to have good singles careers (we had a similar degree of success at that; he topped out at no. 24, four places above me). Jim was a very positive guy to play alongside, even if he tended to retreat into himself a bit when he was struggling with his game. But that's a lot better than taking your frustrations out on your partner.

Our biggest win in Paris that year was in the semis, over Andres Jarryd and John Fitzgerald, a really solid, veteran team, before a good crowd on the Court Centrale. The final was a different story. The men's doubles is always played on Saturday, after the women's singles final, and that year Aranxta Sánchez-Vicario beat Steffi Graf, 7–5 in the third, in one of the all-time great singles finals. By the time the trophies were presented and they got the court ready for the doubles, it was after 6:00 p.m. It was also cold and damp. Scores of fans, having seen a great women's match, had all gone home to warm up.

In the final, we played Eric Winogradsky (who now coaches the talented Jo-Wilfried Tsonga) and Mansour Bahrami, a self-made doubles specialist from Iran. Bahrami had fled Iran, and he spent time sleeping on park benches in Paris as he worked to realize his goal of becoming a pro tennis player. Mansour had remarkable touch and ball-handling skills, but he was older, and never rose higher than no. 192 in singles. His payoff came in the mid-1990s, when he carved out a niche for himself at veterans' events and exhibitions as a kind of Harlem Globetrotter of tennis. He was a very entertaining, charismatic guy.

It was a pity that the atmosphere for our big moment was basically depressing, but what did Jim and I care? We were a couple of young studs, fresh out of college, eager to make a mark and on the verge of winning a Grand Slam title. We won the final in four sets, barely squeaking out the last set in tiebreaker before just a handful of fans, as dusk descended over Paris.

I opened up my wallet that night, taking my dad and mom out to dinner at a well-known Parisian bistro, Brasserie Lippe. Then Jim and I went off to do what most young guys do—chase women at nightclubs. What I remember most from that night is walking around for what seemed like hours, in the predawn, trying to find a taxi that would take the world's newest Grand Slam champions back to their hotel.

As a coach I'm more in the "stoic" or low-key school. But this photo was taken during our finest moment, the 2007 final, in which we won the championship over Russia. Even I couldn't contain myself.

By Fred and Susan Mullane (Camerawork USA, Inc.)

My courtside seat as Davis Cup captain is right in front of the U.S. bench, behind which is the section usually reserved for USTA honchos and dignitaries. That's why I'm not the only one in this picture reacting jubilantly to an Andy Roddick win during his match against Dmitry Tursunov of Russia.

By Fred and Susan Mullane (Camerawork USA, Inc.)

When my infant daughter, Victoria, was brought on the court after we clinched the 2007 Davis Cup championship, she was so mesmerized by the glittery confetti that had fallen into the Davis Cup itself that my wife, Melissa (in white cap), and I just put her into the Cup itself.

Can you tell the boys and I are happy after clinching the Davis Cup in 2007? That's James peeking out from behind Andy Roddick's right shoulder.

Port Washington TA Enrolls Pupils in USLTA

Several youngsters at Port Washington TA with their new USLTA membership cards presented to them by Lucy (Mrs. Harry) Hopman. Young chap at left is Pat McEnroe, 5, youngest player at PWTA and brother of John McEnroe, nationally ranked No. 7 in Boys 12.

HY ZAUSNER, head of the Port Washington Tennis Academy, Port Washington, N.Y., has launched a new plan which is unique in concept and scope. In order to assure that all the students in his program, run under the supervision of Harry Hopman, would be eligible to play in USLTA-sanctioned tournaments, he had each participant take out a membership in USLTA. As a result, over 500 names were added to the USLTA membership rolls.

MAY, 1972

That's me at the far left, right in front of Lucy Hopman, whose husband, Harry—the great Australian Davis Cup captain—ran the highly productive Port Washington (NY) Tennis Academy. At five, I was the youngest player in the group.

Here I am (on the far left) at the Yale Bowl for a football game with my childhood pal Mike Errico and his sister, Melissa. If I knew at the time that I would eventually marry her I would have at least asked her to stand in the middle for the photo.

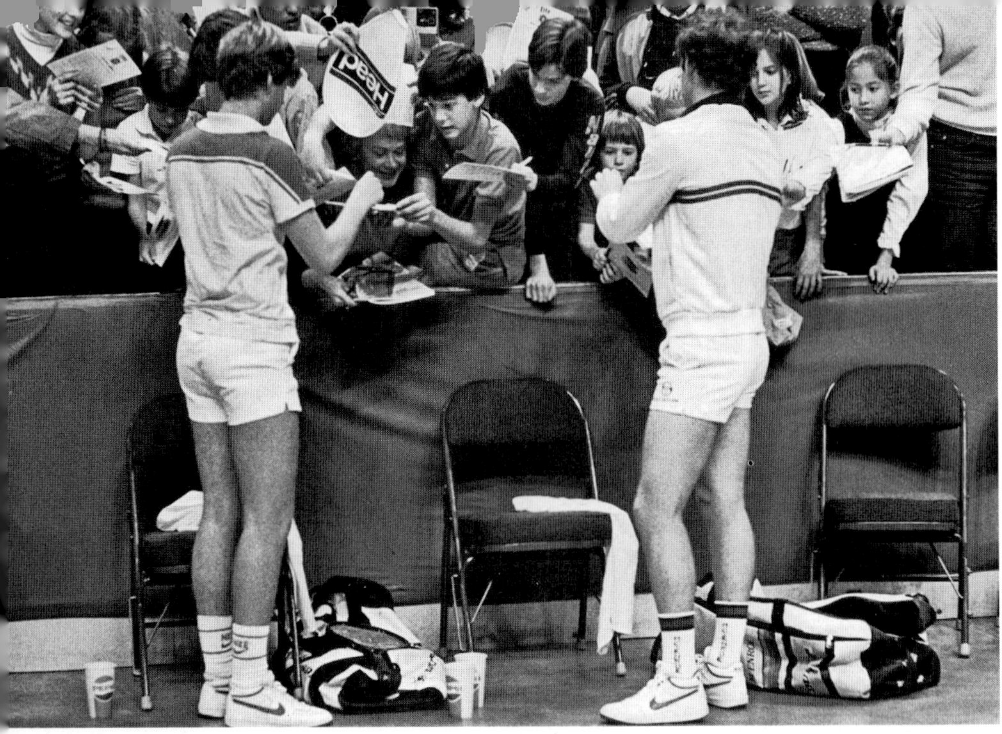

Playing doubles with my brother John was always a rock star moment because of his fame and popularity. Here we're signing autographs after a match. John and I played doubles a fair amount very early in my career, but less and less as the years rolled on. We posted our best win in 1992, at the prestigious Paris Indoors Masters Series event.

My brother John may have had a better serve, but I clearly had better hair. This photo was taken in Montreal, in 1987. If you look closely at the cooler on the right you may recognize the WCT (World Championship Tennis) logo. WCT was the early Open-era pro tour formed by that seminal figure in American sports, Lamar Hunt.

That's my dad, John, old-fashioned Aussie-style bucket tennis hat managing to stay seated on his head as he leaps to his feet to applaud a shot by his first-born, John McEnroe, at Wimbledon, circa 1981.

One pretty big, pretty happy family. That's my dad, John, on the far left, with me, John, my mom, Kay, and Mark. Dad lived for such family moments, as his beaming face suggests.

That's me with my father, John, a real Davis Cup road warrior. This tie took place in 2007 in the Czech Republic city of Ostrava, on indoor clay. We won it, 4-1.

Rafael Nadal has caused us plenty of problems in Davis Cup action, but not at this tie, which took place in Winston-Salem, North Carolina. We won, 4-1, through no fault of Nadal's. Injury prevented him from playing that tie.

My brother John and I worked a few matches together at the 2009 US Open. One of the reasons I felt we made a good pairing was because we have such different temperaments. Courtesy of ESPN

Cliff Drysdale and I have had a lot of interesting and popular boothmates over the years, but when it comes to making tennis fans sit up on the couch while they're channel-surfing, you just can't beat Andre Agassi. I practiced with Andre as a player, battled him on the court, coached him in Davis Cup, and called matches with him. He was equally adept in all those roles. Courtesy of ESPN

There was a time in tennis when everyone and his brother was a little bit Bjorn Borg, a little bit Guillermo Vilas. You can see in this image that as an impressionable kid playing in one of my first few tour events, I managed to be a little bit of both. The two-handed backhand has always been my best shot; later in my career, I worked on specific strategies intended to set me up to end points with the stroke.

I'd love to report that they put me on the cover of *Tennis Week*, which has since gone belly up (regrettably), because of some singular on-court achievement, but I suspect that, the picture having been taken in the 1980s, it was more about the magazine trying to be with-it at the height of the New Wave era in music.

WIMBLEDON: A WEEK TOO FAR

Grand Slam events are two-act plays, the first seven days, and the second week. For most top 50 players, success at a major is defined as getting to that all-important second week, when the draw is pared down to the last 16. That's when the men are separated from the boys, even though most of the men end up thrown to the big dogs. It doesn't matter; you make the second week at a major, and you're entitled to throw your weight around in the locker room.

The first week at a major is chaotic. Matches are unspooling all over the place; every time you turn around, there's an upset, a bitter and glorious five-set epic, a bizarre controversy like that incident that got Jeff Tarango suspended from the tour and turned his wife, Benedicte, into a regular Joan of Arc for umpire-hating players and fans everywhere. It's all part of the Grand Slam scene, a riveting weeding-out process that sets the stage for the *real* tournament, which takes place during the second week.

I had a legitimate shot at making the second week at Wimbledon as a singles player just once in my playing career, in 1991. In all honesty, as much as I loved Wimbledon, I never assigned the tournament a high priority. The slick grass, which produced so many bad bounces, didn't suit my game. My most glaring weakness, a shitty second serve, was a huge liability. And I wasn't athletic enough to compensate for those shortcomings. Even my doubles game suffered at Wimbledon; I never got a whiff of a Wimbledon doubles final. I played singles at Wimbledon just five times, partly because of late-career injury problems.

In 1991, in the first round of my very first Wimbledon, I straight-setted Emilio Sanchez, a very good clay and hardcourt player with whom I had one thing in common: Each of us was overshadowed by a sibling; in his case it was a sister, Aranxta Sánchez-Vicario, a multiple Grand Slam title winner. I'd won a few matches in the warm-up events, and I was feeling pretty good about my game. My next opponent was a crafty Dutchman Jacco Eltingh, whom I'd never played before. I found myself thinking, *Hey, maybe this isn't such a bad tournament for my game after all. . . .*

Jacco probably was a better player than me on grass—he had a bigger serve and he was more athletic. But it wasn't a mismatch and I liked my chances as we went out to play on one of the field courts behind the old Court No. 2 and 3 grandstand. The match quickly became a full-blown war. We battled it out through five tough sets, until we reached 5–6 in the fifth, with Jacco serving—at deuce. I was two points from making the third round in my first Wimbledon. In the back of my mind, I also was aware that our side of the draw had a few holes in it. Whoever won the match would have pretty good chances to make it into the second week.

Wimbledon has always relied on a characteristically British method of dealing with rain showers, something Rube Goldberg might have dreamed up. Rain is the bane of Wimbledon, because the grass becomes slippery as ice in even a light drizzle. So the courts have to be covered by tarps as soon as the first drops begin to fall. Once grass gets wet, it can take a long time to become playable again, especially during the typically damp British summer.

Originally, officials posted a semaphore-like message using painted white dots on the scoreboard to advise grounds staff about the imminence of rain. The crew watched the scoreboard; the number of dots posted indicated the likelihood of rain, putting the grounds crew on varying degrees of alert. It was one step up from smoke signals, and by the time I played at Wimbledon the system had given way to the use of a tiny electric light. When it was on, rain was coming. Once you knew about this esoteric feature at Wimbledon, you could watch the scoreboard along with the grounds crew for a rain alert. It wasn't the only quaint feature at the world's most famous tournament. Before the main scoreboard went electronic (and that wasn't so long ago), they actually had a person running around like a mouse on a narrow passageway inside the scoreboard itself, manually (and frantically, over the first few days) flipping wooden numbers to update the scores for the spectators looking up from the walkway below.

Anyway, at 5–6 in my match with Jacco, the light was on.

I went into my receiving crouch as Jacco bounced the ball, preparing to serve the critical deuce point. I was ready to pounce and pull the trigger on a big return that would earn a match point. Suddenly, the grounds crew, which consists of about a dozen men, came dashing onto the court. Jacco and I both started, looked at each other, shrugged, and laughed. Then we bolted to pick up the bags lying beside our chairs on either side of the umpire, because the grounds crew doesn't care what or even who is in the way—they want to tarp that court as quickly as possible, and if you're not careful your bag gets covered by the tarp and so maybe do you.

After a few hours' delay, Jacco and I returned to the court. I won the first point, and found myself one swing away from the win. But I lost the next point; we were back at deuce. I battled back, and had a few more match points. But I couldn't convert any of them. I wound up losing, 12–10 in the fifth.

It was a bitter pill to swallow, especially when Jacco wound up in the quarterfinals thanks to the soft draw. It could have been me. One of the toughest situations in tennis is playing a guy you have a decent chance of beating, knowing that the winner has an excellent chance to win a few more matches before he faces the reality of a Borg, Sampras, or Federer.

Although I avenged that loss to Jacco with a straight sets win on hard courts a couple of years later, he ended up 2–1 against me by virtue of another win that he snatched right out of my hands. That one played out in Australia in 1995. I had Jacco down 15–40 on his serve at 3–all in the fifth set, but he slipped the noose and won it, 6–4 in the fifth.

You get guys like that in a career, someone that seems beatable but proves maddeningly elusive, like a magician. Once he wins a close one, he can take up residence in your head, and if you're not careful, he signs a long-term lease and lives there, an annoying source of anxiety and torment. No matter how well you're playing, you see the guy's name opposite yours in the draw and your confidence begins to leak away.

Most everyone, even Roger Federer, is tormented by someone. That's why it was often said that once Rafael Nadal matured as a Grand Slam champion, "He was in Federer's head."

Glacial Gunfighters

On the first day of Wimbledon, I always make it a point to get out hours ahead of our broadcast time, just to stroll around, breathe in the atmosphere, and check the lay of the land before the gates even open to the public.

I get there before the nets are up. No matter how often I've done it, I always feel a little bit like I did on my first trip to Yankee Stadium—and never more so than when I walk through that dark little tunnel leading out to Centre Court, toward that gorgeous turf, tennis's most significant quarter acre.

Those first mornings I go up to the roof of the broadcast center where I do a lot of my work. The BC is a huge brick building on the perimeter of the club, overlooking Court 18 and other field courts stretching away toward the No. 1 Court stadium. I watch the grounds crew as they tweak the wooden netposts, check the lay of the chalk lines, or make last-minute adjustments to the umpire's chair, or fiddle with the knee-high fences that stand between the players and public on many of those courts.

But mainly, I'm waiting for the guys with the big stick. The one I call the Wimbledon pole.

When they arrive, the men set up the eight- or ten-foot-tall pole with a tennis ball balanced on top. One of them operates a little triggering mechanism, and the ball drops to the turf. Then they measure the height of the bounce. It's pretty comical.

During my playing career, I had a little ritual; I liked to bounce the ball three times before my first serve, and two times before my second. At Wimbledon, I wouldn't bounce it as much as throw it at the ground, just to make it rebound high enough off the spongy surface to reach my hand. In fact, on at least one occasion I decided not to bounce the ball anymore at all. It was a frustrating waste of energy.

These days, though, when the bounce testers drop the ball off the big stick, it bounces about waist high, even with no force behind it. This change may have saved Wimbledon, which just about fifteen years ago stood in danger of becoming an anachronism, an arcane tennis ritual having no real relation to the contemporary game. Advances in racket technology and a generation of gifted, hard-serving attacking players led by Pete Sampras threatened to turn grass-court tennis into something like farce—a serving contest, with rallies as rare as blue skies over London.

Who can forget matches like the Wimbledon semifinal Stefan Edberg lost to Michael Stich in 1991? There was only one break of serve in the entire match, and it was Stich who was broken; yet he went on to win the match, 4–6, 7–6, 7–6, 7–6.

By the middle of the 1990s, the media, pundits, fans, and even some officials and players were arguing that Wimbledon was, of all things, killing tennis—grass-court matches had degenerated into ghastly rock fights between remarkably fit, powerful giants who served thunderbolts. British tabloids ran contemptuous headlines; after yet another routine win by Sampras, the headline in one of the tabs was a simple: *Sampraszzzzzz!*

Granted, there was a frosty kind of majesty to some of the Sampras vs. Goran Ivanisevic, or Boris Becker vs. Stefan Edberg or Richard Krajicek matches. It took the nerve of a gunfighter to wait, point after point, game after game, sometimes set after set, for that lone, oh-so-crucial moment to strike.

At times, a player gambled an entire match on a single swing of the racket on a service return or passing shot. And the opportunity may have presented itself in a way that could only be called random—a double fault at 15–all, and then a lucky let-cord return winner of a good serve, and suddenly the guy who hadn't been broken in two sets, and won one tiebreaker and lost the other, is down 15–40, double break point, in the crucial third set. And he did very little wrong or different to put himself into so deep a hole.

The curious combination of tedium and tension was sometimes excruciating. Entire matches were determined by the outcome of six or seven critical points. Little, run-of-the-mill mistakes that meant nothing on clay or hard courts could be pivotal. Those things happened because on grass you could just take 80, 90 percent of the points and throw them out—they were filler, more or less, a pile of aces, volleys, or overheads that the receiver never got near. They weren't fought over, they produced no message indicating where a match was going. They were time markers, along the way to the few, critically important points.

If you were a coach or particularly vested fan, you just brought along a roll of Tums and watched the parade of winners and unreturnables and hoped that when the stars aligned and created opportunities, your guy would have the poise and nerve to take advantage of them. A lot of what happened didn't really have much to do with how either guy was hitting his forehand or backhand that day.

Still—the idea that Wimbledon was just a serving contest at any time in its history is patently absurd. Even at the peak of the "grass is boring" era, only the very best players won the tournament. An ace-blasting journeyman could score a huge upset here and there in the draw, but that happens everywhere. There isn't a more distinguished roll of champions than Wimbledon's. The debate was less about the credibility of the results than the entertainment value (or lack thereof) of grass-court tennis.

The glacial gunfights and the protests they engendered suggested that the officials at All England Club had fallen asleep at the switch; the game had passed them by. Serves them right, some thought, because the AEC was just a stuffy, prestigious private tennis club that had morphed into a national institution. The pro game should be run by real pros, right?

Some thought that the game on grass was passé, but apparently all those guys in the green and purple AEC ties never got the memo. Two of the other four majors (the Australian and US Opens) had moved to new venues in response to the increased demand for relevance (as well as seats) in the Open era. Significantly, both had abandoned the private club, and turned away from grass in favor of slower, more common, and versatile hard courts. The British wouldn't dream of leaving Wimbledon, the AEC wouldn't think of abandoning grass, and on top of all that the players were still obliged to wear predominantly white. Serves them right.

But the one word you'd never, ever associate with the Lords of Wimbledon is "panic." So, just as the "grass is dead" movement reached a fevered pitch, the tournament was already considering—and making—the changes that would radically transform Wimbledon's lawns, and the way tennis is played on them. The club is pretty coy about this, having admitted publicly only to ripping out the mixed strains of grass in favor of 100 percent perennial rye grass (a hardier, more durable grass), starting in 2001. But Wimbledon veterans, including most players, think the balls are slower as well. And many say that the courts are firmer and harder than ever before.

Hence, the waist-high bounce off the Wimbledon pole.

Those subtle, basically invisible changes, combined with the evolution of the world game, were to have a huge impact. These days, a typical Wimbledon match is nothing like the matches played by nearly everyone up through the era of Pete Sampras. Now it's chockablock with exciting, dramatically supercharged rallies, and in the last three years we've seen Wimbledon men's finals move the needle off the charts on the drama meter.

Not long ago, players who preferred clay, including many Spanish and South American stars, frequently left Wimbledon entirely off their schedules despite the tournament's status, and the prize money and rankings points on offer. They felt it was pointless to challenge all those hard-charging serve-and-volley players who ran amok on the lawns. Some formidable clay-court experts were miserable competitors at Wimbledon. French Open winners Thomas Muster and Gustavo Kuertin (who won at Roland Garros three times) were particularly awful on grass; after experiencing great frustration as youngsters on grass, they threw in the towel and just went through the motions—when they even bothered to play.

One year, a group of mostly Spanish players, led by former French Open finalist Àlex Corretja (a popular guy known for his outstanding sportsmanship), threatened to boycott the tournament because certain of their number had been demoted in the seedings—bumped down the list while other, lower-ranked players who happened to be good on grass were moved up.

That was an interesting issue. The AEC always reserved the right to come up with its own seedings. They reasoned that seedings based on rankings, without taking surface proficiency into account, were potential tournament killers. For one thing, the only tournaments on grass were Wimbledon, two or three warm-up events right before it, and a minor tournament played in Newport, Rhode Island, after Wimbledon ended. There's very little reliable data for handicapping on grass.

For Wimbledon, losing a number 4 seed who had little chance of surviving two rounds on grass could wreak havoc, putting a semifinal berth up for grabs among players who had no real shot at winning—and were likely to be rubbed out mercilessly by the first good grass-court player they encountered. When that happened, everyone lost—the tournament, the fans, the international tennis audience.

This became a serious institutional and political problem when most of the other majors agreed to seed strictly on the basis of the ATP rankings, which don't take surface proficiency into account. Wimbledon wouldn't yield on this point; they retained the right to seed as they saw fit, coming up with their own grass-specific seedings, in which a player's record at Wimbledon and history on grass were a significant factor.

Although Wimbledon's position was well thought out, and produced a more realistic seeding than a blind computer ever could, Corretja and his cohorts held fast. Seedings, they insisted, are rewards earned under all kinds of conditions over a twelve-month period. The whole idea of the rankings was to create a simple, objectively based performance index, and it was grossly unfair to deny a player a seeding he had earned with his all-around performance over twelve months. Plus, denying a clay courter an appropriately high seeding made the grass-court challenge even tougher, because it set him up to meet a tougher rival earlier in the tournament.

Was Wimbledon played for an elite little band of guys who happened to be good on grass, or was it part of a larger, integrated community of players governed by a set of transparent, results-based rules?

The aggrieved Spanish players also sensed undercurrents of anti-Spanish sentiment in the course taken by the WASPs who run Wimbledon, a feeling that was encouraged by the opaque way the seeding committee at Wimbledon did its work. Nobody really knew the committee's criteria, or how it arrived at a decision—even if it was hard to challenge the grass-court seeding order the committee eventually produced. Wimbledon took note of the discontent, and it helped that the game was changing in a way that would close the gap between best grass and clay players. The AEC eventually articulated a firm set of standards for seeding, and the disagreement melted away, even though Wimbledon still hasn't adopted the color-by-numbers approach. It still reserves the right to ignore the official ATP rankings when it seeds the tournament.

Wimbledon wants to make it look like nothing has changed, not since the days of King Arthur, while they work furiously—and with notable success—to not just keep up to date, but one step ahead of the game, without compromising the event's cachet.

The Oh-So-Not-So British

Court 18, which sits right next to our broadcast center, isn't one of the prime "show courts" on which the club likes to put the top players. It's scooped out of the side of the hill, so the stands built into the slope at the north baseline are very steep. But if you stake out a spot in the temporary bleachers on the west sideline, you'll be sitting six or seven feet away from the player at that end of the court. You can hear every muttered aside—or desperate F-bomb—he or she drops.

An hour before play starts on the outside courts at midday, the fans are already lined up to get seats at Court 18; it doesn't even matter who's first up. It could be a men's doubles, or even a mixed doubles. In New York, the equivalent of Court 18 would attract only the coach and blood relations of the players battling it out.

The Wimbledon grounds-pass holders sit on the grassy, terraced knoll now known to everyone as (Tim) Henman Hill in tribute to the best British player of the Open era, and a perennial Wimbledon contender in the 1990s. Countless Brits, the bulk of them young, have had their hearts broken as they sat on that hill and watched in horror and despair as Henman, their great hope, lost yet another quarterfinal or semi to a Becker, Sampras, or Ivanisevic.

Henman was an excellent top 10 player, one of the last survivors of the era in which the serve-and-volley player went extinct. He was sneeringly (or lovingly) referred to by some of his countrymen as "a perfectly nice English middle-class boy," and some punk reporter once sniffed, "He's the human equivalent of beige." But I'll tell you what—he had a solid serve, an excellent volley, and he moved really well. His record at Wimbledon demolishes the notion that he was some kind of Casper Milquetoast. Henman would have become a national hero if he was the first British male to win Wimbledon since Fred Perry in the 1930s, and he came awfully close. But he lacked just that extra smidgen of power that might have gotten him over that historic hump.

Henman was overshadowed by his pal and frequent golfing partner Pete Sampras. He had one great chance, in 2001, the year Sampras was upset at Wimbledon by a relatively unknown Swiss, Roger Federer. In the semifinals that year, Henman was up two sets to one on Goran Ivanisevic when the match was halted by rain. He lost his momentum while the rain pattered down, and Ivanisevic—a wild-card entry—beat him. But let's remember that despite carrying the burden of the entire United Kingdom's hopes and expectations on his shoulders, Henman consistently punched above his weight. He made four quarterfinals and four semis, which is a pretty remarkable record of consistency in a major for a guy who had to work hard to keep a place in the top ten.

British fans are among the most knowledgeable in the world; they're fair-minded, and as much as they hunger for a national tennis hero, they always show their appreciation for high-quality tennis. That they recognize it at all puts them a few steps ahead of fans in some nations. The British know how to have a good time, too. Who else would consider it "fun" to camp out overnight on the sidewalk along the club's wall in hopes of scoring a ticket? Henman Hill is a world within the world of Wimbledon. The fans who cover the knoll daily—and sometimes they're thick as ants on a heap—have a commanding view of much of the grounds, but the only place they can watch tennis being played is on the enormous Jumbotron attached to the side of the nearby Court no. 1 stadium. The spectators might as well be in Trafalgar Square, but in England, a trip to Wimbledon is a ritual.

Ball Crushers and Shotmakers

As my broadcasting colleague Mary Carillo likes to say, "Jocks win Wimbledon." That was especially easy to forget during the "grass is boring" era. It often appeared that the players, their shirts unstained by perspiration, stood around and waved at balls flying by, rarely making contact, rarely having to do a lot of running even when they did. But that was deceptive. On lightning-fast grass, the sheer pace of what play there was, the low bounces and the bad bounces, all were part of a grass-court equation ensuring that only great athletes won the event. They just weren't able to do it with their consistency or shotmaking skills on full display.

Back then, you had to be ready to stretch and bend and spear and make last-moment adjustments. The last man standing at Wimbledon almost always had that little extra in the way of mobility, which is style neutral. Players as different as my acrobatic, artistic brother John and the resolute, understated baseliner Björn Borg both were great athletes. They always seemed to find a way to get or keep the ball in play. Give the other guy a chance to screw it up, is one of the most valuable of tennis maxims.

I controlled things better on hard courts than on grass. I was able to do more with my weak second serve on hard; I could hit a better kicker (because of the height of the bounce), and move it around more effectively. I had a good service return, especially when I got a good look at a ball. But big servers on grass often don't give you that look. I did beat Becker in an exhibition on grass once, probably because it was inferior grass. That helped me because I was able to get enough returns back, while the bad bounces made my serve better. At Wimbledon, the grass was too . . . good. I'm sure I would have done better if Wimbledon had gone to slower, higher-bouncing grass in my playing days.

I'd compare the surface at Wimbledon today to that of a medium-to-fast hard court, with one caveat—natural turf accentuates spin better than a typical cement court, if not as well as a clay court. Back in the day, any old slice serve or approach shot would slip away from the receiver like a watermelon seed squeezed between your fingers. It used to be that a typical player's topspin shot would hit the spongy turf, slow down, and sit up just high enough for the returner to wallop it. Now, topspin is a viable option on the harder turf.

But you have to be vigilant today, because you can't get away with as much. Leave a ball hanging—hit a little fluffball, or fail to make clean contact—and the court will punish you.

Serving, the ball still skids on grass if you really crush it, but to really get the effect of slice you have to hit the ball very well. Play a good, crisp, clean shot and you can force the action—create what Andre Agassi always liked to call "progress." When I practiced with Andre, or watched him in Davis Cup practice, he would always talk about getting "progress," a nice way to describe the art of having a good shot reap a reasonable reward in the form of pushing your opponent back, and into a more defensive position, or just out of position.

On a very slow court, the hard, flat shot doesn't give you much progress; you have to put a lot of topspin on the ball to make it jump at the guy, achieving that desired end of pushing him back, while also forcing him to hit the ball at an uncomfortably high point. The courts at Wimbledon now allow you to do that, as Nadal, who hits with vicious topspin, demonstrated. It's a significant component in his success.

One hallmark of the Wimbledon champ that remains the same in this new era is second-serve proficiency. Wimbledon winners tend to be guys with great second serves. Nadal may not have great pace on his serve, but it has plenty of action, and his placement is very precise. That makes it hard to attack, and the most reliable way to get a player on his back foot is by attacking his second serve.

Years ago, you could put your kick serve in the closet, right next to your topspin forehand, when it came to Wimbledon. Flat or slice serves (to exploit the slipperiness of grass) were the way to go. These days, the kicker is effective because of the higher bounce. Wimbledon used to belong to the ball crushers; now it belongs to the shotmakers.

Nadal: Pitch Perfect in a Wimbledon Opera

I watched Nadal, and his entourage suffering in the player's guest box, intently as the young Spaniard flopped into his chair on the changeover at the end of the fourth set of the Wimbledon final of 2008.

Toni Nadal, Rafa's coach and uncle, dropped his head to the railing in the player guest box. Rafa's father, Sebastian, stood up and he must have told Toni not to do that, because in a moment his brother was bolt upright again. It was a momentary lapse, a show of despair from a straightforward, even-tempered guy who's anything but obsessed with winning and losing. What he's obsessed with—and it shows in his nephew's conduct and words—is character.

Toni Nadal used to make Rafa play with poor quality equipment, just to show him that he had to buck up and play with the tools at his disposal. He forbade Rafa jamming his feet into his shoes without untying the laces: "Just because you get them for free doesn't mean you can ruin them; many people work very hard just to be able to afford the shoes you get for free." He made Rafa sweep the court before and after practice session, even after the boy had become a Grand Slam champion. And he made Rafa carry his own bags. In 2005, Rafa scored one of the first big titles on hard courts, winning the big Masters 1000 event in Montreal over Andre Agassi. My ESPN booth-mate, Cliff Drysdale, and I worked that match, and were faced with having to call our first match in Cincinnati fewer than twenty-four hours later. We groused and complained about having to be at the airport to catch a flight on a small commuter airline at six in the morning after the Montreal final, and when we got to the airport we were surprised to see we weren't the first of the tennis people to arrive.

Toni Nadal and Rafa were already standing in line, patiently waiting to check their bags. "Well," I said to Cliff, "if Rafa can do it, I guess we can, too." By then, Rafa's great rival, Roger Federer, was traveling exclusively by private jet; in fact, after Novak Djokovic beat Rafa and Roger in back-to-back matches at the same Montreal event in 2007, Roger decided to spare Rafa the indignities of the Com-Air check-in line and gave him a lift to the next event in his private jet.

I imagine Toni appreciated the gesture, too. He's salt of the earth, a man of good intentions and conscience who always seemed interested in turning his nephew into a good man, not merely a great tennis player.

He was working with good clay.

If Toni had surrendered to despair at the end of that fourth set of that epic 2008 Wimbledon final, I could only imagine what Rafa himself felt. But it was impossible to tell. Beads of perspiration dripped from his damp, dark hair as he sat. He looked curiously at peace with himself, not by any means resigned. He held his chin high and gazed off into the distance, as if he were watching some strange object crawling across the horizon. He was devoid of visible emotion, although he had plenty of reason to be captive to feelings, most of them bad. Nadal had won the first two sets by identical 6–4 scores, setting the stage for the one thing no one had expected: a blowout. A comprehensive beat down of the man who, many had already decided, was the greatest player ever to swing a racket.

A year earlier, Rafa had lost his second consecutive, heartbreaking five-set final to Federer on Centre Court at Wimbledon. Alone in the shower, he cried. Yet there he was, granted a tennis player's most profound wish—a chance to play the same guy under nearly identical conditions, for almost exactly the same stakes, one more time. A third time, no less. Third-time lucky, or three strikes and you're out, it was going to be one or the other. And as Nadal sat on that changeover, who could imagine it would be the former?

He'd been a hair's breadth from winning this match in straight sets, 6–4, 6–4, 6–4. But he faltered, ever so slightly, and lost his momentum. With the help of rain delays, Federer had found a way back into the hunt. He chipped away at Nadal's huge lead, and won that third set. And not long after that he had stared down one match point and faced another in the tiebreaker.

All day, Nadal had been scoring big with his topspin forehand to Federer's backhand, and he went to the well once again on that second match point. As the ball left Nadal's racket, I thought: *This is over. Federer hasn't made a backhand down the line all day.*

Anticipating Nadal's shot, Federer ran toward his backhand corner, loaded up, and hit down-the-line for a clean, sizzling winner. I'll always remember that stroke as the single greatest shot of that Wimbledon fortnight, and the perfect symbol of Federer's genius. It was a gorgeous swing and a perfect placement, and it was the most difficult of shots, made under the most intense pressure a man can face on a tennis court.

I turned to Dick Enberg, my colleague in the ESPN broadcast booth, and just asked: "How does this happen? How does he make that shot?"

Dick, I think, was speechless.

After Federer hit that frozen rope down the line to wipe away the second Nadal match point, he went on to win the tiebreaker and level the match at two all. Nadal was powerless to do anything but slump into his chair to await the start of the fifth and final set.

This was the match, and the tournament, that Nadal most powerfully burned to win. It was on a pale green field of battle, where, for years, no one had really expected him to do well, much less emerge as the champion. Legions of Nadal's gifted, Open-era countrymen, all of them proficient and deadly on slower clay surfaces, were routinely shot to pieces by efficient, aggressive, attacking players employing the shorter backswings, penetrating serves, chip returns, and flatter shots that can pay big dividends on surfaces faster than clay.

Yet there he was. More than once during the match, he'd taken a covert glance at the Royal Box, where his eyes must have picked out Prince Juan Carlos of Spain, seated in one of those dark green wicker chairs with the green and white stripes. Nadal had been introduced to him, and sheepishly admitted that they were something like buddies. One of the main reasons Rafa wanted to win Wimbledon was to bring honor to Spain, to show that a Spanish player could win at Wimbledon, even though none had managed it since Manuel Santana in 1966, in an era that might have been three hundred years ago.

And there he sat. He was, at least, taking that third strike like a man, with stoic equilibrium.

Throughout that final, the new-era grass at Wimbledon had enabled Rafa to use his best weapon against Roger with deadly efficiency. Rafa lashed that high-bouncing, topspin forehand to Federer's backhand side, both on the serve and in their baseline battles, and he scored with it, thanks to the altered playing properties of the grass.

That shot was Rafa's magic bullet on slow clay, where it was even more lethal, as demonstrated by his domination of Roger in four consecutive French Opens starting in 2005 (one semi and three finals, in that order). The only thing more surprising than Nadal's proficiency with that shot has been Federer's seeming refusal to do anything that might counteract it.

Most great champions have a broad and deep stubborn streak, and all of them want to win on their own terms, as if adjusting or adapting to an opponent is somehow a confession of weakness. The last thing a champion wants to do is let an opponent—especially a rival—feel that he's forcing you to get out of your comfort zone and making you try things you wouldn't ordinarily do. Great players just don't like to capitulate to a rival's terms, but they will sometimes accept the challenge, just to show they can still win.

For an all-out attacking player like my brother John, that was out of the question and in many ways it made his life easier. He was coming right at you with the serve and aggressive net game. If you could pass him more often than he could destroy your defenses with his volley and overhead, you had him. More than likely, he would take away your game and shut you down. Great talents who lean more to the all-court or baseline game, like Federer and Pete Sampras, are less aggressive and thus more inclined to let you choose your weapons and take it from there.

Pete Sampras used to do that, sometimes to the dismay of his coach, Paul Annacone. Pete occasionally decided that he was going to beat an opponent at the guy's own game, instead of making his own life easier by taking the guy out of his comfort zone. You may remember that now legendary U.S. Open quarterfinal match between Pete and Àlex Corretja—the one that cemented Pete's reputation as a warrior of unparalleled grit. It was a brutal five-setter that Pete won despite growing woozy and vomiting in the early stages of the fifth set tiebreaker. He would close out the match with a combination of an ace and a double fault by Corretja to end the tiebreaker 9–7.

Annacone had encouraged Pete to attack Corretja, and take away the set play off which Corretja lived. He liked to get a good kick on his serve to the backhand, which gave him enough time to run around all but the most aggressive return and dictate with his forehand. Paul had all kinds of ideas about how to neutralize that strategy, but Pete decided not to follow any of them. He wanted to beat Corretja at his own game, and he finally did—but we all saw what it cost him. Roger took much the same attitude into his matches with Rafa on clay. It got to the point where many pundits suggested that Roger was simply living in a state of denial, unwilling to admit that there was no way he could play on Nadal's terms and still win.

I understand the mind-set, and I'm always reluctant to advise a player to try to outfox an opponent. Trust your game—it's an important lesson to learn. Have faith in your best shots and do your best to create situations where you can hit them, but be open to making adjustments if you need a Plan B to fall back on. That Nadal topspin forehand to the Federer one-handed backhand, high, was a gift that just kept giving, and the cornerstone of Nadal's successful game plan against Roger. There comes a point where even a talent like Roger has to recognize reality and formulate a counter-strategy, even if it's as simple as adjusting your receiving position to make it easier to step around the kicker to the backhand and hit a forehand return.

On those few occasions when Roger did surprise Rafa by stepping around the backhand, he won the point. Early in the Australian Open final of 2009, Federer stepped around a high-bouncing serve to his backhand and just powdered the ball. I thought, *Okay, here we go. Roger has seen the light.* But he didn't follow up with more of the same. He immediately fell back into the old, familiar pattern of sticking to a game plan that worked against everyone else on the planet. And he lost the match.

The weird thing is that Roger is a pretty mellow, rational guy. He never acts like he's got anything to prove, and seems to enjoy winning in a surgical, clean way. He's the one guy who, despite or because of his sheer brilliance, you expect to make adjustments that demonstrate his mastery of strategy and tactics.

But it isn't like Federer didn't benefit from the properties of grass, 2.0, either. One of his most effective shots is the short, crosscourt slice, and he hits an amazing forehand; because of his racket head speed, he gets a lot of spin—action—on the ball but it still travels with a pretty low trajectory, unlike typical topspin shots. The grass rewards those shots. The 2008 Wimbledon final was a fine example of the way a court with great playing properties gives with one hand, and takes away with the other, even when the players have dramatically different styles. And it doesn't get much different than Federer vs. Nadal.

. . . .

Everyone knows how that 2008 final turned out: Nadal finally won it, 9–7 in the fifth, under light conditions so poor that had it not developed into the greatest tennis match of our time, it might have been called because of darkness before the last ball was hit.

I was really curious to find out what Nadal had been thinking on that changeover at the start of the fifth set, and I learned soon enough. He told us in response to the very first question asked at the official post-match press conference. Did you think you'd blown it after failing to convert those two fourth-set match points?

These were his exact words: "I just reminded myself that I am still here. The match is not over, we are at two sets all. When I lost the fourth set I was sitting down, and just say [to myself], 'Well, I am playing well, I am doing well, I am with very good positive attitude, so gonna continue like this and wait, wait what's happening. I feeled confident with myself, so for that reason I was confident on the match. . . ."

And that, right there, is one of the keys to Nadal's success and a pretty good explanation of how the guy was able to complete what started out as an impossible mission—to catch and eventually eclipse Federer (albeit briefly), and to bring him down on his own turf.

Every player in a tough match, even at a small club tournament, tells himself: *Hey, it's about now. Forget what happened two moments ago, or back in the first set. Stay in the now. Love the game, indulge your passion for it.* Players strive mightily to think that way, and it's a message I'm always trying to drill into my kids. But it may be the hardest of all things to do in this game. And Nadal had the poise, mental discipline, and the deep confidence to not only think but live that mandate in what had to be the darkest hour of his career.

In the aftermath, people inevitably compared the match with its predecessor, "the greatest Wimbledon battle of the Open era," John's clash with Björn Borg in 1980—the five-set war that featured what is now known simply as The Tiebreaker. John won that fourth-set tiebreaker, 18–16, saving a handful of match points along the way. Like everyone else, John expected that his performance in that tiebreaker might break Borg's steely spirit, but the Swede overcame the devastating effect of that lost breaker to take the match, 8–6 in the fifth.

The comparison is specious, and if anything it's unfair to Nadal. In 1980, Borg was already a Wimbledon champion; he was gunning for an outrageous fifth consecutive Wimbledon title, while John had just one major title, earned at the previous year's US Open. Borg, like Federer (who already had five Wimbledon trophies in 2008), was the more accomplished, experienced favorite.

Sure, you can appreciate the pressure Björn felt as John, an explosive upstart, set about hunting him down. Roger probably experienced the same apprehensions. But could anyone have more confidence to draw on, more reason to believe that he could, and would, win than Borg—or Federer?

John, also the hunter, did not win his ultimate Wimbledon showdown. Rafael Nadal did. And it was all the more astonishing because there's a real chance that Nadal might never play another Wimbledon final. He certainly escaped some treacherous times on his way to that title, and as much as the grass playing field has been leveled, I wouldn't call his style ideal for grass. The injuries that would prevent Nadal from defending his Wimbledon title and enabled Federer to re-claim his no. 1 ranking in 2009 also must be taken into account.

Rafa knew how rare an opportunity he faced, and you can bet it was going through his head as he watched the chalk dust fly after a Federer ace, or another of those wicked, penetrating, forehand winners. Sitting on that changeover after set four, Nadal had every reason to channel my brother at that French Open of 1989, and think: *This was my shot. This was my window of opportunity.*

Nadal believed in himself to an extraordinary degree at Wimbledon in 2008. But even that deep feeling of confidence isn't enough to get the job done, because in tennis you're always a victim of changing circumstances. You face unpredictable developments (like squandering match points) that can make you do crazy things—panic and overreact to a lost opportunity, retreat into a shell of false bravado, play passive tennis because you think you can always come back to win, or just because you're, well, scared stiff. You can undermine yourself in a dozen insidious ways, especially if you act for the sake of acting.

It's much tougher to say, as Nadal did, *just wait . . . be patient . . . see how things work out and focus on the immediate task at hand.*

It's funny, but there's nothing earth shattering or especially insightful in Nadal's explanation of what he was thinking. If you're unfamiliar with tennis, you might even shrug and say it amounted to a string of typical jock clichés.

Some players say something like that, and you think, *The guy is full of shit. He's just talking.* But when Nadal says such obvious, simple things, you really believe him. When he says he feels content even though he lost in the semifinals of the US Open because "being one of the last four is good, no?," you believe him because—because you just know it's coming from his heart, and because he's right. He makes his point in a way both innocent and preemptive, like a wise child pointing out the obvious to a confused and overly analytical adult.

Nadal told himself, during that fourth-set changeover, you're playing great tennis, just keep going. Any other tennis player on the planet would have been more likely to think: *Holy shit! I just fucked that up. I blew my chance to become a Wimbledon champion. . . . How do I get out of this without losing too much face?*

If I had to choose a match to serve as the template for greatness, Nadal's performance in the 2008 Wimbledon final would be at the top of the list.

VILLAGE OF THE DAMNED LUCKY

I was going to collect my laundry in Wimbledon Village during the Wimbledon women's final a few years ago. Walking down the High Street on that quiet Saturday afternoon I went by Starbucks and glanced inside. The place was nearly deserted; clearly, everyone was glued to the TV at home. There sat the Federers, Roger and Mirka.

I stopped and went inside. They looked like any typical well-to-do couple, out for coffee on a quiet afternoon. Roger was dressed in a nice sweater, slacks, and expensive dress shoes, nothing flashy.

"Hey Patrick," Roger said. "What's happening in the women's final?"

"It was pretty close when I left. What are you doing?"

"Just relaxing," said the guy who, in fewer than twenty-four hours, would attempt to win yet another Wimbledon title. "Nice afternoon, isn't it?"

We chitchatted for a few minutes, saying nothing about the upcoming final. Far be it from me to spoil a day off for one of the hardest-working and most successful of pro athletes.

I had to smile as I left the place. Roger and Mirka are so damned . . . normal. They know how to enjoy the simple pleasures, and have figured out something a lot of other people in Roger's position haven't:

That if you feel normal, act normal, and enjoy being normal, you can avoid a lot of the drama that often swirls around stars and celebrities. But let's not go overboard. Roger certainly likes his five-star hotels, fine dining, and his private jet.

Early in his career, Roger liked to use the expression: It's nice to be important, but it's important to be nice. Okay, so it's a little goofy. But Roger was always cheerful and sincere, the antithesis of those champions who were, or wanted to present themselves as, rebels or hard cases. Only later in his career did Roger adopt that ever so slight, but well-earned swagger he sometimes displays. The guy has lived the saccharine cliché he used to quote; it's ridiculous how unaffected he is.

To some extent, that was also the kind of encounter that could only have taken place in Wimbledon Village. If the world body of tennis has a heart, this little hilltop enclave is it.

All four majors are played on the outskirts of international capitals—Melbourne, Paris, London, and New York. The Australian Open site, Melbourne Park, is situated just a short walk from downtown. Flanked by the Yarra river on one side and a massive commuter train rail yard on the other, it's basically built between two major travel arteries leading to the center of the nearby city.

In Paris, the Stade Roland Garros is at the edge of the upscale suburban neighborhood of Boulogne, alongside a park of the same name and a major Parisian commuter freeway, the Peripherique. The tournament's well-heeled neighbors seem locked in a perpetual war against Roland Garros's plans for growth. The USTA Billie Jean King National Tennis Center is sandwiched between a rail yard and a vast metropolitan public park created partly from the remains of the epochal New York World's Fair of 1964. The park is usually filled with people far more interested in soccer and pickup baseball and basketball games than tennis, despite the hordes of tennis fans who descend on the US Open.

Wimbledon is, yet again, a little different. The tournament evolved in unique symbiosis with the community surrounding the All-England Club; it's no mere accident that the tournament adopted the name of the town, instead of becoming the British Open (for that's really what it is). Wimbledon is a London suburb, but you don't get nearly the same sense as you do in Paris of the metropolis nearby.

Wimbledon has three parts: a town at the foot of a big hill, complete with department stores, restaurants, supermarkets, pubs, and big rail and bus stations. Then there's Wimbledon Village, a ten-minute walk up a fairly steep hill and, finally, the All England Club, about the same distance down the far side of the hill from Wimbledon village as is Wimbledon town.

You can almost see the All-England Club from the main drag in the village, the High Street. Since the tournament takes place during summer holiday time, enormous numbers of people choose to rent out their homes and apartments to players and other tournament goers, many to escape the inconveniences created by the tournament. Some of the palatial homes, the kinds of places a top player might rent, go for twenty, thirty thousand dollars for the three or four weeks during which a player uses them.

Believe it or not, Pete Sampras used to rent a home on a street called Borg Road (it was named that long before the Swedish star appeared on the scene). When he moved, the next player to take the place was a Swiss kid named Federer. I suggest that if you have a kid who plays tennis and is lucky enough to play Wimbledon, that's the house you want to rent. Take a loan, if you must. Unlike most British homes, it even has air-conditioning—Sampras had to buy one while he was a tenant there, and I'm pretty sure he never lugged it back to Los Angeles when he quit the house.

Lesser players as well as officials, tournament staff, and the media, generally pay about two hundred dollars a night and up for good rental accommodations, often sharing a town house or large apartment with friends.

Top players often bring their families and support team, including a chef. Rafael Nadal was an exception to that. In 2008, he stayed with his uncle Toni and one or two others in a relatively modern, small, attached town house, just a short walk uphill from the club. Rafa slept in a small room usually occupied by an adolescent boy and furnished in what you might call Contemporary Ikea: the walls were still decorated with posters and handmade cards the kid got for a recent birthday.

The choicest rental homes are the ones closest to the AEC. But the action, such as it is, takes place on top of the hill, on the High Street. If you want to see how Andy Roddick's model wife, Brooklyn Decker, looks without makeup, or hope to bump into a Billie Jean King, Pat Rafter, or Stefan Edberg, you're better off skipping the crowded entrances to Wimbledon and hanging out at the Starbucks, or one of the numerous other boutique coffee joints in the village.

Wimbledon is the closest thing tennis has to an annual convention. Everyone who's ever made a mark in tennis seems to attend, long after his or her playing days are over. You may bump into Martina Navratilova at the door of the Indian restaurant. Stop at the brick-oven pizza place or go shopping at the Tesco mini-supermarket and you're likely to end up waiting in line behind a Pat Cash or Ilie Nastase.

After his matches, Andy Roddick will often call up San Lorenzo, the Italian restaurant (in the town), and order his dinner. His trainer Doug Spreen or wife Brooklyn will swing by there to pick it up while Andy does his post-match routines. Last year, I was eating dinner with friends at one of the Village's Indian restaurants when Sara Foster, the actress girlfriend of Tommy Haas, came in to pick up a takeaway order. Tommy was in the semifinals at Wimbledon for the first time in his career, after upending Novak Djokovic. I made some passing remark about Indian maybe not being the best choice for his pre-semi supper, but Sara laughed and said that Tommy had been eating Indian every night of the tournament.

Surprisingly, players don't really get hassled much by autograph hunters or aggressive fans. It's like the village is a celebrity DMZ, with an uneasy truce between locals, visiting fans, and players.

Although the village can be crowded at night, you get the feeling that all the gritty and grimy elements of life get washed down into the hollow of Wimbledon town. The only real exception is the handful of major pubs that become swamped as young, dehydrated fans make their way up to the village from Henman Hill. The police put up temporary fences to keep the kids from spilling out into the road, but that makes it hard to wade through the crowd if you happen to be walking by. Most everyone clutches a pint of beer in one hand and a cigarette in the other. And lest you get the wrong idea, you don't really see a James Blake, Juan Martin del Potro, or Maria Sharapova running around, semi-wasted on warm beer.

The top players may go out for dinner; some of the younger ones may even go to the one private nightclub that has a door policy (unless they have to play the following day). But the stars mostly remain holed up in their lovely English rental homes after nightfall, and leave chasing girls or general carousing to the qualifiers, journeymen, and doubles-only players.

Everyone in the village seems to eat, sleep, drink, talk, breathe, and even play tennis during Wimbledon. It's like a giant oxygen tent for tennis nuts.

Federer: No Safe Place to Hide

Cliff Drysdale is my longtime comrade in arms on ESPN broadcasts. A South African, Cliff was a contemporary of Rod Laver, and one of the pioneering pros known as the Handsome Eight. The group included the Aussie icons Laver, Ken Rosewall, and John Newcombe; they signed to play on what would be the very first pro tour of the Open era, World Championship Tennis. Cliff went on, among other things, to become the first president of the Association of Tennis Professionals, now the ATP Tour.

A suave, sophisticated guy, Cliff also became a little salty as he got older—the kind of guy of whom people would say, "He's seen it all." His wit is acerbic, and he cultivates a gruff manner, saving his best and most biting barbs for those he knows best. His off-air personality contrasts sharply with his smooth public persona. Cliff's been toughened up by life, but he hides it well. He was married early in his life to the former Jean Forbes, a vivacious, talented fellow player who died at a young age (the sister of author Gordon Forbes, Jean haunts the pages of that legendary tennis memoir, *A Handful of Summers*). Cliff's daughter, Kirsten, developed a rare spinal disease that left her wheelchair-bound.

I'd known Cliff for a long time, and I'd never seen him cry—not until that July day in 2003 when Roger Federer won his first Grand Slam title at Wimbledon. As soon as the last ball was hit, Cliff welled up and soon tears rolled down his cheeks; he made me think of a proud papa watching his son triumph.

Federer has always had that effect on a certain kind of tennis fan—the one who cares just as much about *how* a pro plays and conducts himself as how well he or she does. Tennis is a game steeped in aesthetics and etiquette. Nothing, including frantic attempts to expand the basic audience or the sometimes shocking behavior of the players, has done a lot to change that.

Sure, clothing companies pushed the envelope once tennis abandoned the "predominantly white" clothing rule. And promoters at many events, including the U.S. and Australian Opens, have added all kinds of bells and whistles, like Jumbotrons, kiss cams, and loud rock music during changeovers. But gorgeous tennis, sportsmanship, and personal appeal have never gone out of style. And Roger Federer is about all three, and most of all about beautiful—but absolutely deadly—tennis.

Federer fans are a borderline cult; you can imagine hordes of them lighting votive candles before Nike posters of "full-flight" Federer, as their hero is caught and frozen in midair, ripping off a signature, smoking-hot forehand winner. Tennis is very popular with women, who make up an enormous part of Federer's (and tennis's) fan base. One reason tennis attracts so many female fans is because you can watch the game and focus on the individual performance, rather than the combat or score. Tennis can be balletic or bullish, and it hits some of its greatest heights when it pits those two qualities against each other, as it does in the historic battle between Federer and Nadal.

If you had to choose a player from any era to represent what tennis has always been about, you'd be hard pressed to make a better choice than Federer. Tennis has largely been a middle-class, aspirational sport—the inroads it has made in "diversity" are partly due to the fact that there are simply more hungry players out there now. Promoters try to play up the mano-a-mano combat in tennis, but the game is full of niceties that no one really wants to give up—raising your hand in apology when you inadvertently hit a let-cord winner, offering to give up a point, or play one over, if you feel you got the benefit of a bad call or some extraneous distraction that threw off your opponent.

It's also a habit of players to hold up new balls to show an opponent when they're about to serve with them (new balls are put into play after the first seven games, then every nine games thereafter). I always liked that, and it ticked me off, more than it should have, when guys ignored that basic courtesy.

Tennis strives to be a popular sport while retaining many elements that make it elitist in the same way that the Marine Corps, or a good school that clings to a strict disciplinary or even dress code, is elitist. The game is focused on being inclusive, but it's exclusive in that it asks you to embrace tennis traditions. It doesn't matter that many players who have no use for the conventions of tennis succeed, and often at a really high level. That's part of the cost of doing business in a fully professional, performance-driven era. The game just absorbs individualists and geniuses like my brother John and Agassi; they become curiosities who help dispel the notion that tennis is a white-bread game, and they get tennis a lot of attention because of their flair. There always should be room for them.

Federer, though, is the ultimate mainstream tennis guy. He's even-tempered, rational, good-natured, and prudent, just what you might expect from a typical Swiss. And this much is for sure: No one with a game as pretty has ever enjoyed anything like the success of Federer, who's pretty much become the consensus GOAT (Greatest of All Time). If the guy were less successful, he'd be one of those players who is taken for granted and never gets his props because he's so . . . regular.

It's hard to say anything original about Federer's game anymore. His toolbox is bottomless, his athletic gifts are superb, and it's easy to underestimate his grit because he has a habit of making the most difficult shots and matches look easy. That match-point backhand winner he hit down the line in the 2008 final against Nadal is a great example of his ability to make the impossible look routine.

But Nadal's ability to find and exploit that backhand is responsible for the oxymoronic reality that Swedish champion Mats Wilander summed up in the neat phrase: "It's weird that the guy (Federer) may be the best player of all time, but there's one guy in his own generation he can't beat."

At the end of 2009 the head-to-head advantage for Nadal was 13–7; that's significant when you compare it to some other rivalries. Sampras pretty much owned Andre Agassi at every major but the Australian Open, but the final H2H was close: 20–14 for Pete. My brother John went 7–7 with Björn Borg, and 20–14 with Jimmy Connors; but he trailed Ivan Lendl, 21–15. So 13–7 is a pretty significant lead.

But H2H stats can be deceptive. For one thing, even great players had nemeses: Pete Sampras went 4–5 against the lean and powerful German Michael Stich. Even more critically, Roger gets unduly punished for losing to Rafa on the Spanish player's best surface, clay. Roger was good enough to beat everyone else on clay and every other surface, but you can't say that for Nadal. He often lost while Federer waited for him in a final on a surface better suited to Roger's game. Nine of Nadal's wins over Federer were on clay. All but one were in finals. Rafa beat Roger in just two hardcourt finals, and one on grass.

It's bad luck for Roger that Rafa is a mold-breaking rarity. Few players ever played even remotely like him. He's a natural right-hander, but he became a lefty as if the tennis gods had ordained it, just to prove that Federer is indeed human. Nadal's powerful forehand naturally goes to Federer's backhand (a ball hit squarely always wants to go crosscourt), and having a lefty serve is a decided advantage, too. The southpaw serves wide in the ad-court are especially effective against the right-hander's backhand. And since most players are right-handed, playing a lefty demands a big mental readjustment.

Given all that, Roger has handled Rafa pretty darned well on all but clay courts. Andre Agassi probably described Roger's talent best in the locker room after he was roughed up by Federer in the US Open final of 2005. "I felt like I had nowhere to go," Andre said, after losing in four sets. "Nowhere to go against the guy where I felt safe, where I could buy time. Even with Pete (Sampras, Andre's career rival), I felt I could go to his backhand and I wouldn't be in danger. It's not like that with Roger."

That's one of the big keys to Roger's success. He's so dangerous that his opponents are under constant pressure, while his remarkable ability to transition from great defense to lethal offense ensures that if there's a weakness in your game, he'll eventually find and exploit it. Roger can always turn the tables with one swing of the racket. Rafa is the only guy who's been able to handcuff him, at least on clay. A number of players out there can hit with enough topspin to trouble Roger, especially on the backhand side. But they aren't as quick or strong as Rafa, so Roger can often take away that play and keep them at bay. He can't do that with Rafa. Generally, guys who can trouble Federer have one thing in common: They're very strong on the "left" (backhand for a right-handed player) side.

However, Juan Martin del Potro's upset of Federer in the 2009 US Open final also suggested for the first time that if your game is big enough—and if Roger agrees to play it on the terms you choose—it's possible to overwhelm him. The question is, will del Potro, or anyone else, be able to do it on a consistent basis?

The same day that Federer's first major win made Cliff cry, I went over to the player area, a grassy, open space filled with picnic tables built right on the roof of the media center. Alan Mills, the legendary Wimbledon tournament referee (he's since retired), liked to go out there to smoke a cigarette whenever he got a chance. I approached him and said of Federer, "Geez, Alan, this guy's pretty good. How many of these Wimbledons do you think he'll win?"

Alan looked at me, took a drag, and, after thinking a moment, said: "As many as he wants."

Then he stubbed out his smoke and returned to his office.

Sampras Ice and Roger Grass

Pete Sampras came along at one of those moments in history when a variety of forces converge to create exceptional opportunity. Pete was the final, evolutionary product of the old game—the game that would be shunted aside as the Open era unfolded in the new century and a new style better suited to slower surfaces became standard. Pete was just a few years this side of that great divide, and it made his job a little easier.

Power has always been the holy grail in tennis, and maybe it always will be, even though power alone no longer suffices to get the work of greatness done. Pete was like a Pancho Gonzalez, or a Lew Hoad. He was a great athlete, both rangy (6–1, 170 pounds) and explosive. His game was extremely clean; even if it lacked the dazzling variety you see in Federer, it was lethally efficient. If you wanted to come up with the Platonic ideal for a tennis player, you'd pick Roger or Pete, depending on whether you have a weak spot for a beautiful, versatile game, or a streamlined, power-based one.

Pete won the Wimbledon title seven times—two more than his take at the US Open (his perfect 7–0 record in Wimbledon finals is a record; no man has ever so dominated a major). That record may hold up for a long time, as will two other Sampras marks: Pete finished no. 1 in the world for six consecutive years; Nadal prevented Federer from accomplishing that in 2008, and for obvious reasons it's a record any player will have just one chance to equal or surpass. Sampras spent 286 weeks at the no. 1 spot in the rankings, but Federer has that record in his sights as I write this.

Talk about Sampras for any length of time and inevitably the question pops up: How would he have fared against Federer, when each man was at the peak of his game? They met just once in a high-stakes match, at Wimbledon in 2001, where Federer won a tense, five-set struggle that ended Pete's 31-match win streak at the event. Roger was just coming into his own, but Pete was in eclipse by then, in the midst of a two-year dry spell that only ended when he unexpectedly won his farewell slam in 2002.

One of the great things about Pete was his straightforward, no-frills approach to the game on most surfaces. He was coming right at you, stop him if you can, although his pride and sheer love of the game sometimes led him to take his foot off the gas and try to beat an opponent at his own game. Tim Gullikson shepherded Pete to his first Wimbledon title and the doorway to greatness, but Pete's coach and close friend succumbed to brain cancer before he could finish his work. Paul Annacone took over the job and the results speak for themselves.

Tim and his twin, Tom, were from Wisconsin. They fought their way onto the pro tour from a lowly start as teaching pros at a tennis club in Ohio. Tim had a no-nonsense, practical view of life. A big fan of the NFL's Green Bay Packers, Tim often told Pete: "You're like the tennis version of the Packers' famous Power Sweep play. Everyone knows it's coming, but no one can do anything to stop it. That's just how you have to play tennis."

You could call the attitude arrogant, but Tim's assessment was accurate. So this question of Federer vs. Sampras is a tricky one, partly because no one Federer has played, with the exception of del

Potro, can bring the heat the way Sampras could. Rafa can impose himself on Roger, push him around a bit. No one ever pushed Pete around; he stood his ground and forced the issue, win or lose.

Roger is quick, crafty, athletic, and he has great nerves, but he doesn't really smother people the way Sampras did. Sampras has said that he would have taken the game right to Federer, come what may. Both guys have a knack for winning easy; Roger is so poised and smooth that he hardly appears to make an effort. And Pete—well, you can beat some guys 6–2, 6–3, and come off the court exhausted. But you could lose to Pete 7–6, 6–4, and never break a sweat. He'd just cruise along, holding easily, content to wait patiently for his moment to strike. And he made the most of his opportunities. He left you feeling like you were never in it, even though the scorecard suggested it was a pretty close match.

Still, I'd give Federer the edge, hands down, on any surface but grass—if both men had their A games. But back in Pete's heyday, I'd give Pete the definite edge at Wimbledon. It was almost impossible to break Pete down on grass, because in every one of his service games he'd hit a couple of unreturnables (it's pretty hard to hurt a guy when you can't get your racket on the ball). And knowing that Pete would be knifing to the net behind these monster serves always put that much more pressure on the receiver. All Pete ever had to do on grass was get hot in one return game in any given set, and make two shots to go with an error or two by his opponent—and that was that. He would have overwhelmed Roger with power and attacking tennis, in a way that no player in this era of baseline tennis even attempts.

However, if they played on the "Roger grass" of today, rather than the "Sampras ice" of yore, and with today's slower balls, it might be a different story. Under present conditions, Roger would get more looks, he'd get more balls back in play. And once the ball is in play few players have come out on top of Federer on a regular basis.

The 20-year-old newcomer, del Potro, managed to overpower Federer in the 2009 US Open final. But Federer was still basking in the afterglow of an amazing summer, in which he completed his career Grand Slam in Paris and topped Sampras's all-time singles title mark with his fifteenth major at Wimbledon.

I'd hardly call that win conclusive.

Dead Man Serving

I always got a kick out of Pete, he was a different breed of cat—come to think of it, he was a lot like a big cat, the way he made so much power in such a leisurely manner, the way he was almost lazy but supremely confident in his own power, and his ability to call upon whatever reserves he needed to tide him through a crisis.

I think of Pete as a Sandy Koufax or Joe DiMaggio-type guy—aloof, reclusive, a little different—and indifferent to what anyone else might think or say about him. He was a real gentleman on the court; he always played by the rules, but unlike some guys he never traded on his character. He never hammed it up or used it to work a crowd. Pete was all business; he did things fairly and squarely, he kept things simple and clean.

It's funny, Pete can be a prick. I don't mind saying it because I think he knows it. In fact, I think he enjoys it. Pete has never had a problem saying no to people, and often with that sly smile on his lips. That smile, though, was a defense mechanism. It's hard, and it takes a certain kind of courage, to look someone in the eye and tell him "no." A smile helps defuse the situation.

You couldn't expect Pete to cut you a break, as I learned to my financial detriment at the lucrative (now defunct) tournament, the Grand Slam Cup. That was a year-end event that lasted through most of the 1990s. It brought together the best performers in the majors of any given year in Munich, Germany.

The prize money was nothing short of insane; the winner could walk away with as much as $2.5 million if he also happened to win a Grand Slam event that same year. My brother John called the payout "obscene" and refused to play the event. I confess that I didn't have such highfalutin moral qualms; my palms just broke out in a sweat when I saw the prize money breakdown in 1995. You got a hundred grand for just showing up, and something like a quarter-million dollars for actually winning a match.

I drew Sampras as my first-round opponent. Ordinarily that was like a death sentence, but Pete was coming straight from the Davis Cup final in Moscow, where he'd just completed what might be the greatest single achievement of his career. He'd played two singles and doubles against a strong Russian squad on very slow red clay. He swept all three matches, coming as close as humanly possible to single-handedly winning the Cup.

The day after the U.S.—or Pete—won the Cup, he showed up in Munich. I'd watched the Davis Cup final, riveted to the television. Pete was so tired at the end of his first singles match that he cramped, and had to be carried off the court by his teammates. I admit my reaction upon seeing that wasn't exactly noble. *Holy shit*, I thought, *maybe he'll pull out of the Grand Slam Cup. I could make 250 grand if I just beat the alternate!*

What I didn't take into consideration was that players who entered the event automatically got a $250,000 bonus for each major title they'd earned that year. So Pete, who won two Grand Slams that year, was guaranteed half a million dollars just for showing up to play a match.

Things went from rosy to bad to worse for me when the tournament, reluctant to lose as big a drawing card as Pete, scheduled our first-round encounter for the latest possible slot, on Wednesday. That gave Pete a couple of days to rest.

The indoor courts in Munich were lightning-fast, and I quickly lost the first set, 6–1. But I started playing better in the second set, and I was hoping Pete's legs would go dead. When we got to the second-set tiebreaker, I felt that if I could just find a way to pull it out, I was in there with a shot. I hung in there until the tiebreaker. By then, Pete was completely out of it—a dead man serving.

But Pete dug deep, yet again. He won the tiebreaker, 7–1. I still had a big paycheck to balm my wound, but what really got me was that Pete pulled out before he played his next match. He picked up his $750,000 and said, "Fuck it, I'm outta here."

Sometimes when I see him, I still say, "That has to be the easiest seven-fifty K you ever made. Couldn't you at least give me a break and pull out *before* we played?"

Of course he couldn't. Nobody else would have, either—and that's as it should be.

Pete took pride in the fact that there was no bullshit or anything two-faced about him. The one character that made a lasting impression on him, he said, was Holden Caulfield, the prematurely cynical, alienated young hero of the J. D. Salinger novel, *The Catcher in the Rye*. We all know Caulfield's deal, right—he hated "phonys." Pete appeared to care about three things: his results, his money, and his family. He was no fame whore, and he sometimes got irritated by the way Andre Agassi traded so effectively—and profitably—on his more flamboyant, iconoclastic personality.

Pete liked to gamble, and he didn't much like to practice. We hit a few times in Australia, and after a desultory warm-up, he would suggest that we play tiebreakers, for a couple of hundred bucks a pop. It was his way of keeping up his interest level. I was no fool; I couldn't afford to drop five hundred bucks or a grand on a practice set, especially not against Pete Sampras. So I always made him give me odds. One time, I hit a lucky streak and won a fair amount of money, which pissed off Pete. When we quit, he looked disgusted. He just threw the money on my racket bag and stalked off. I didn't take it personally. Pete was, well, Pete.

As much as he was willing to gamble, Pete was also cheap—very cheap. Andre Agassi has told the story about how, after the two men had gone out to a fancy restaurant for dinner, Pete tipped the valet a buck—and specified that he give it to the kid who actually brought his car around. When the valet looked at him, stunned, Pete broke out that fuck-you smile, hopped in his car, and drove off. (Pete, when asked about the incident, shrugged and said he was very young at the time.)

But Pete kept close track of his money, as I learned at an off-the-radar event, the World Team Cup. The team tournament is held every year in Düsseldorf, Germany, as a warm-up for the French Open. It offers players a chance to get some matches on clay and to make some decent money as they prepare for the French Open. But a lot of the top players skip the event, and while it can be an interesting and meaningful competition, the results can hardly be called significant. Still, winning is always better than losing, and in 1993 I was part of the winning U.S.A. team, along with Pete, Michael Chang, and my doubles partner, Richey Reneberg.

Everything clicked and we ripped through the field; Richey and I didn't lose a match, and our squad shut out Germany in the final, 3–0. The rules of the competition were a little strange; the top player on the team decided who got to play, and the prize money was distributed through some complicated formula. All I knew is that when Richey and I eagerly tabulated the numbers, we stood to make over a hundred grand each; for us, that was a huge windfall. Monopoly money.

Somehow, Pete eventually got wind of how well we'd done, and he got pissed. He called me weeks later and said, "Hey, you guys made too much money."

"What?" I wasn't sure I understood. "What do you mean?"

In what became a pretty weird conversation, Pete suggested that Richey and I got too big a chunk of the pot. As he was nominally the team captain, I wasn't sure what that meant—all I knew was that I wasn't the one who created the distribution formula. Ultimately, Richey and I did get the sum we'd calculated, but the controversy left a sour taste in my mouth.

Pete likes to play cards, too. Down Under, he enjoyed going to the Crown casino, which was part of the enormous hotel complex where many of the players stayed at a reduced tournament rate. Pete would always try to get some guys to go to the casino with him.

They got all excited, because they'd be going out with the great Pete Sampras. Heads would turn. Gorgeous women would try to get their attention. They would sit down at a table reserved for the high rollers in the Mahogany Room.

Poor guys. Their puffed-out chests collapsed when they sat down at that table and saw Pete plunk down a couple of grand. Their eyes became wide pools as they thought of their expenses and rankings, the wives and girlfriends waiting back home. They'd think, *Holy shit! I can't do this. . . .*

It got to the point that the guys would duck Pete when he was looking for company; they didn't want to seem like deadbeats, but the game was just too rich for their blood. You know what they say about running with the big dogs; it was as true in the casino as it was on the court when Pete Sampras was around.

The Channel Slammer

Pete Sampras and Roger Federer have dominated the GOAT debate, both at Wimbledon and in terms of their overall careers. The other names that come up often are those of Rod Laver (with his two Grand Slams and eleven majors), Ivan Lendl, and Björn Borg. The most intriguing record undoubtedly belongs to Borg. He won the same number of majors as Laver, but they were all earned at Roland Garros or Wimbledon. Borg won 41 percent of the Grand Slam tournaments he entered (he was 11 of 27) and his 89.8 winning percentage in Grand Slam events is also an Open-era record.

Borg's six French Open titles remain a record, although it's presently threatened by Rafael Nadal. Borg missed Roland Garros a few times while he was still at the peak of his powers, because he chose to play in the highly remunerative but utterly meaningless World Team Tennis league in the U.S. during the tournament, a decision that looks absurd in hindsight. As it is, the guy lost just two matches at the French Open, both to the same man—the flashy Italian serve-and-volley player Adriano Panatta.

And consider this: Björn is still the only Open-era player to win the French Open and Wimbledon in the same year more than once. He did it three times. In a row. That "Channel Slam" is one of the rarest accomplishments in tennis. In the Open era, only Laver, Borg, Nadal, and Federer have pulled it off. It may be the ultimate definition of all-around stamina, determination, and superiority, because the tournaments are on vastly different surfaces but are played a scant few weeks apart.

Björn won the last of his eleven singles titles on the day after his twenty-fifth birthday; a year later, he shocked the tennis world—and no one more deeply than his rival, my brother John—by announcing that he was done. John had visions of his rivalry with Borg lasting for years; as it was, it ran its course in just under three years.

Björn struggled a bit after he retired. Cutting loose from the discipline and sense of simple purpose that helped keep him moored, he went a little wild on the party front, and he also made some poor business decisions. Who could blame him, given that all he'd done up to that point in his life was play tennis? Those difficulties, combined with a few ill-fated comeback attempts, tarnished his image. But he's reinvented himself in recent years, emerging as the figurehead of a successful line of men's underwear. The many women he dallied with would probably nod approvingly. Björn still looks rock solid and indestructible at age 50.

John has always had enormous respect for Björn, and he almost always behaved like a gentleman when he played Borg. On one occasion early in their rivalry, John started to freak out during one of their matches. Björn stopped playing, called John to the net, and in an almost paternal tone tried to calm him down. Borg never meant anyone harm and he always behaved like a combination of gentleman and stoic. Federer, that other classy sportsman, is more thoughtful and sophisticated; Borg was spartan, and emotionally restrained. He was all about action and physical superiority.

What I love about him now, though, is that he doesn't really care when he goes out there to play an exhibition or a senior tour event. John and Jimmy Connors both still act like any match they play is a Wimbledon final. Björn plays it for laughs; he has no big, hungry ego to feed and maybe he never really did. Maybe that's why he just up and quit at age twenty-five, after he lost the 1987 US Open final to my brother. He probably decided, "Who needs this crap?," which is very different from what many people suspected. They suggested that he limped away with a shattered ego because he feared that John had his number.

When you look at the records Borg amassed, and how often he skipped the Australian Open and some of those French Opens, you have to wonder how many majors he would have ended up with if he came along a little later and played until a reasonable thirty years of age. Sixteen? Eighteen? Twenty? And while he wasn't nearly as well rounded a player as Federer, he was the equal of anyone, including Roger, as an athlete.

Put some modern equipment into Björn's hands and I'd say all bets are off. He had a big serve, and he was hitting that buggy-whip forehand that Nadal likes—the one where the follow-through ends up over the same shoulder as the racket arm, instead of the opposite one. Björn was a model of consistency from the baseline; his defense was impregnable. His two-fisted backhand had sting and his topspin forehand was as accurate as it was consistent.

Björn wasn't just extremely fast, but tireless. If anyone could go toe-to-toe with Nadal on slow clay for five hours it would have been Björn. And how great might he have been if the courts were slower back then, playing right into his strengths? When you look at Borg's record closely, you can't help but come away thinking, *How soon they forget*. . . .

A Miracle on People's Monday

Wimbledon has been cruel to a number of outstanding players who, but for a stroke here or there, could have won—maybe should have won, given their career history, the nature of their games, or both. Ken Rosewall never won Wimbledon; neither did Ivan Lendl, who went as far as skipping the French Open, where he was usually a favorite to win, in order to improve his chances to win a major on grass. Ivan never quite got his nose over the finish line, losing in five semifinals and two championship matches at Wimbledon.

Or take the bouncing Aussie serve and volley stylist, Pat Rafter. His game was well suited to the grass courts of the late 1990s, although his trademark kick serve didn't work as well on spongy grass as on hard courts (he won the US Open twice). Rafter played back-to-back Wimbledon finals in 2000 and 2001, losing both—the first to Sampras, the second to a guy with a hard-luck story much like Rafter's own, Goran Ivanisevic.

A 6–4 beanpole, Goran was long, lean, and flexible. His left-handed power, especially serving, blinded people to his athleticism. Those qualities might have been enough to earn him a Wimbledon title had he played in any era but the one dominated by Pete Sampras. Goran's oft-declared life ambition was to win Wimbledon; he ate, drank, slept, and dreamed Wimbledon. And Lord knows he tried and came close. Goran was a semifinalist twice, and he played four finals—losing three before he finally and magically bagged the trophy. He did it when almost all hope was gone, as a desperate, twenty-nine-year-old wild card entry playing the final days of his career. He's still the only wild card to win a major. The record may last forever.

Goran was a great example of a guy who, for most of his career, lacked some subtle but essential qualities of a Grand Slam champion. It's hard to succeed at the highest level without a reasonable amount of variety, and that was a problem for Goran. He basically teed off in a pretty predictable way on any ball that came his way, despite having developed his game on clay. He didn't know how to change things up, employ different strategies against different players, or stick the ball to the same place time and again, patiently waiting for an error or an opening. Despite all that, his big lefty serve and athleticism got him as high as no. 2 in the world.

The one thing you absolutely could not afford to do in those glacial gunfights of the Sampras era was relax, take your eye off the ball, and play a couple of loose or sloppy points. Against good grass players, opportunities to break were few and far between, and being broken spelled disaster, mentally as well as on the scoreboard. That was especially true for a guy like Goran; breaking his serve ought to have been like drawing a winning lottery ticket. Instead, the very top players could usually bank on Goran giving them an opening now and then with a mental lapse.

Goran tended to get a little sloppy, maybe a little tight, at the most critical of times. He blinked exactly when he should have been squinting. It was partly because he never did develop a really good volley game, even though he had the tools. His volley let him down on some very big moments at Wimbledon, which was a mental discipline issue because his technique and athleticism were solid.

Still, Goran's triumph in 2001 remains one of the ultimate feel-good stories in tennis, partly because it happened on "People's Monday." Rain had forced Wimbledon to reschedule the men's final from Sunday to Monday, and Wimbledon's policy during unforeseen extra days is to let people in for free, on a first-come, first-served basis. All you have to do is go stand in line, or "queue," as the Brits say. Some years, the backlog created by rain also forces club officials to mandate play on the middle Sunday of the two-week tournament, which is usually an off day for everyone. The same policy applies.

The atmosphere on People's Monday in 2001 made even the most jaded or snooty of tennis fans grin from ear to ear. Hordes of young Aussies and Croatians queued for over twenty-four hours to get in, and they turned the staid Centre Court into a tennis version of Woodstock. They sang, chanted, and horsed around. When Jack Nicholson walked in and took his seat in the fancy reserved section, he got a standing ovation. To top it off, Ivanisevic and Rafter produced a terrific match that found Goran ahead, 8–7, and serving for the match in the fifth set. 40–30—match point.

Goran hit a double fault; the crowd gasped, collectively.

At deuce, Goran hit another double fault. Throughout all of Croatia, and much of London, there was weeping and gnashing of teeth, for Goran was an icon at home and one of the most beloved figures at Wimbledon. But this time, Goran called on reserves many people didn't think he had. He could barely breathe for nerves, but he worked out of his jam—only to see Rafter loft a beauty of a lob to dispel Goran's second match point.

Somehow, Goran got to advantage again, for another match point. And this time, after missing his first serve, Goran hit an unreturnable second to earn the prize he'd chased for his entire career. Even Sampras, Goran's nemesis and not exactly a paragon of sympathy, admitted that he was thrilled to see Ivanisevic finally win it. He could afford to be charitable, for the win didn't come at his expense; it was earned partly through the tears of agony Sampras had so often forced Goran to shed.

Goran was the quintessential fun guy in tennis. You always knew when he was giving a press conference, because in the locker room all the guys would crowd around the TV monitor to listen. You just never knew what this loose cannon and mortifyingly unpolitically correct Croatian would say. At the height of the tensions in the Balkans, Goran volunteered that he wished his racket were a machine gun, so he could line a bunch of Serbs up against some wall and mow them down.

In another of those press sessions—they were always a cross between therapy, a roast, and a confession—he admitted to being "two Gorans," and re-created an entire dialogue between his two selves: one the familiar knuckleheaded, self-destructive, temperamental wild man, the other a calm, wise, veteran pro who knew exactly what he ought to do, and why. My wife, who knows a thing or two about theatrical personalities, adored Goran.

I liked playing against Goran in doubles; it was a blast. He clearly didn't care if he won or lost, he just liked being out there, screwing around, playing to the crowd. He was there to have a good time with his partner and two opponents whom he treated more like fraternity brothers than enemies—despite the fact that his game was huge and his serve a combination of bludgeon and rapier.

Goran's ball had amazing action; that big lefty slice was like a David Beckham free kick, curving like a banana as it burned toward you at warp speed. Once in Milan I played Goran indoors, on the kind of fast carpet that made his serve even more difficult to handle. He quickly went up a set and a break, and by then it was pretty clear that he was going to win. One game, he hit three aces in a row. I'd had it. I walked back behind my baseline and stepped over the low wall separating the court from the spectators. They watched, shocked, as I walked up a few rows and into an aisle until I was roughly in line with the net post. Then I got into my receiver's crouch.

Never one to miss a chance to goof around, Goran merely tapped his next serve into the box. It was the only six-mile-per-hour ace he ever hit. If I were him, I'd claim that as a record for slowest ace ever hit. I doubt anyone would ever challenge it. So that's *two* unusual records for Goran; he was that kind of guy.

Goran had his last hurrah against one of my Davis Cup teams. We played Croatia, at their place, in a first-round match in 2003. Andy Roddick missed the tie with a wrist injury, and Goran was coming off what would be a career-ending shoulder surgery. He was also closing quickly on his thirty-second birthday, but determined on a swan song. The Croatian tennis officials, who already had a pair of top-flight singles players in Ivan Ljubičić and Mario Ančić, understood Goran's inspirational value. So they put Goran on the team, thinking he might be useful in doubles.

Mardy Fish lost the first rubber in straight sets on the ultra-fast indoor carpet, but James Blake—a good indoors player—stepped up and played one of his finest Davis Cup matches, taking out Ancic. I saw a chance to snatch a surprise win and rolled the die. I elected to play Blake and Fish (ignoring Robby Ginepri and Taylor Dent), figuring that if we took the doubles the pressure might get to Croatia and we could slip out of Zagreb with a win.

It was clear from the start of the doubles that Goran was in bad shape. He was barely serving at 100 miles per hour. But this was Goran. Even in that diminished state, his slider, placed in the corner, was hard to handle. At the start, Goran was hitting double faults left and right, and we won the first two sets with relative ease. If we could get Fish and Blake off the court quickly, they would be fresh for the reverse singles, and we'd need just one win to clinch.

But Goran dug deep; he was clearly prepared to leave it all—including his shoulder—out on the court that day. The Croatians eked out a third-set tiebreaker and went on to take the last two sets. The next day, Ljubičić upended Blake to clinch the tie.

It was Goran's last Davis Cup match, and he went out in a blaze of glory—as befitting a true Davis Cup warrior. Goran compiled a 48–15 (28–9 in singles) record playing for Croatia, but he never did play on a team that won it all. But that was all right—he'd gotten his Wimbledon, so it was all good.

Throwing the Sink, and the Kitchen

I hate to write about Andy Roddick as a hard luck story; he's been in the mix at or near the top for his entire career, he's won a major (his beloved US Open), and he led the U.S. to a Davis Cup final win. Plus he's wildly popular and makes a ton of money. I just hope that sometime in the next few years, Andy gets to pull a Goran at Wimbledon. He's still got time, if not a great deal of it. He's still got the game. And the way he's ticked the final hurdle to lose the race to Roger Federer three times in the Wimbledon final really makes me wonder if fate isn't working up something special for Andy.

Roger's game matured at almost the same moment as Andy's. The first time they met at Wimbledon, in 2003, Roger tagged him in three sets in the semifinals, and went on to win his first major (Andy won his own Slam just three months later). Since then, Andy has struggled to solve Roger's game. His head-to-head with Federer at the end of 2009 was a painful 2–19. But none of his three losses to Roger in Wimbledon finals stung as badly as the most recent, in 2009. In one of the all-time great finals, Andy lost in five, stretching Federer to 16–14 in the fifth. It was Roger's record-setting fifteenth major.

Andy's problem has always been that Roger simply has a little too much game for him. As Andy himself has said, Roger probably is not just the greatest player to heft a racket, he's probably the most complete. And that spells trouble for a meat-and-potatoes player like Andy, because Roger has a solution for everything Andy throws at him, and Andy has thrown the kitchen sink. Then the kitchen.

To his credit, Andy has tried some stuff that isn't really in his comfort zone, just to avoid losing in a predictable way. At the Australian Open in 2007, during a period of resurgence, Andy tried to get very aggressive, looking to come in to the net at every opportunity. But Roger is a great defender, and Andy's attacking game—unlike that of a Pete Sampras—just isn't good enough. Long story short: Andy got shot to rag dolls, losing 6–4, 6–0, 6–2.

At times, Roddick has tried to play Federer from the baseline, looking for a chance to hit his big forehand. But Federer knows how to stay away from that forehand and outmaneuver Roddick. Andy's backhand hasn't ever been a weapon, and a player as skilled as Roger knows how to punish Andy for that. But Wimbledon still rewards the very best servers, so Andy always has a chance on grass—against anyone.

Andy came close to denying Roger that fifteenth major last July. That was astonishing. For Andy is no longer a top three player. What he is, though, is a consistent, seasoned, tough, hardworking competitor who'll take anything you give him, and a guy who has the sand to make a big statement. And at Wimbledon, he was within a lucky net cord or errant Federer service return from winning the title. It would have been a moment comparable to Goran Ivanisevic's 2001 win on the same court, for Andy too is much loved for his devotion to the challenge, and his consistent excellence—and frustration—at Wimbledon.

I thought that for the most part, Andy outplayed Roger in that 2009 final—to whatever degree that's possible. Roger was the one more often playing from back on his heels, but the match was thus a testament to Federer's defensive skills.

Nothing has ever come easily to Andy, except for that gigantic serve. The last Wimbledon loss to Roger was devastating, but fading out now would go against everything Andy's been about. He's slipped and reinvented himself at least two times, once under the guidance of Jimmy Connors and more recently under Larry Stefanki. Andy's still got holes in his game, and that won't change. But this is a guy who dropped fifteen pounds early in 2009 as part of a general makeover (it helps explain his outstanding performance at Wimbledon), and one who's managed to make the year-ending ATP World Tour Finals eight years in a row.

For a guy who gets a lot of crap for failing to win more than one major, that's pretty damned consistent. Whether he can stay in the hunt remains to be seen; a heartbreaking loss can have a strange, delayed effect on a player. No one knows that better than Andre Agassi. When Agassi lost that US Open final to Sampras in 1995, after a brilliant summer during which he amassed his career best 26-match winning streak, he was so devastated that his game went off a cliff, not to return until 1998.

Andy doesn't have that kind of time to work with, or the game that would stand the strain of so big a swoon. Then again, he doesn't have a spirit that can be broken so easily, either.

I worked hard during the 2009 Wimbledon, and I pretty much stayed away from the players and the locker room. In addition to the usual stress, I was worried about our upcoming, tough Davis Cup tie against a nation that loves to play us, Croatia. The tie was going to happen the weekend after Wimbledon ended, on Croatian turf.

The USTA had chartered a private jet to whisk us all off to Croatia the morning after the Wimbledon final. As Andy got further and further into the tournament, I got progressively more and more concerned. *This is great*, I thought, *but I wonder if Andy is in?*

On the day before the final, I bumped into Ken Myerson, Andy's agent, and the woman who arranges Andy's travel, in Wimbledon Village. They both told me Andy was on the flight, he'd be ready to go. I told them that whatever happened in the final, Andy could take a few days off and join us in Croatia on Wednesday; maybe he'd appreciate a little time to unwind and recover from the final.

But as the final between Andy and Roger evolved into an epic, I became pessimistic. (I was calling the match with Dick Enberg for ESPN, in case they wanted to re-broadcast it after NBC's exclusive "Live" rights expired.) What if Andy lost, 6–4 in the fifth? I knew that he'd be crushed, and the closer he came to winning, the more the blow would hurt. As the match went on, it became clear that any chance that Andy might play against Croatia was fading.

When the match was over—Roddick won more games (39) than anyone ever had at Wimbledon, even though he lost the match—I had to scramble to do the ESPN SportsCenter show, live. Before I went on the air, I had a text from Andy: *We need to talk.* I immediately thought, *This is not going to be good.*

Doug Spreen, our official Davis Cup trainer and Andy's personal trainer, found me at the broadcast center and said that Andy was devastated. Doug didn't know what was going to happen. I suggested that Andy not worry about it until he did his cool-down, his press, and the host of little chores that await a Wimbledon finalist. Then we'd talk.

Bobby Feller, our ESPN producer and a good buddy of mine, knew what was going on. Halfway through the ESPN show, he could also see that my mind was racing, a million miles away from the business at hand. He gently suggested that I go; Chris Fowler and my other colleagues would handle the rest of the postmortems.

As it turned out, Andy's house in the village was very close to the place I rented. I texted Andy that I was heading to his place as I started walking up the hill from the club.

When I arrived, Doug Spreen, Ken Myerson, and Larry Stefanki were sitting around on the ground floor of Andy's multistoried house. Andy and Brooklyn were upstairs. The atmosphere was funereal; there was no point saying stuff that would try to cheer up anyone, so we more or less sat there in silence, drinking beer. Soon, Andy and Brooklyn came downstairs.

The words didn't come easily, but I felt I had to say almost exactly what I'd said on the air right after the match. "I know you're gutted, but that match was like my brother's final with Borg in 1980. You played your ass off, you played great. It just didn't work out. But you made more fans with this loss than with any win you ever had. I know that's not going to make you feel better, but it's a fact and all you can do is . . . go on."

We talked a little. Even then, Andy knew that despite losing, he had a lot to be proud about. Among other things, he knew he was now as much a part of Wimbledon lore and legend as anyone—more a part of it than some guys who have actually won the tournament. It was cold comfort, of course, but that's better than no comfort.

Eventually, we got around to talking about Davis Cup. Andy hemmed and hawed a bit; he told me that he never in his life had gone into a Davis Cup tie not feeling 100 percent there, 100 percent committed to winning. But he found it hard at that moment to imagine that he could get himself into that frame of mind overnight. I wanted to say, "Well, take maybe twenty-four hours to think about it before you make up your mind." But my heart wasn't in it. I could tell he'd pretty much made up his mind.

So I gave him an out, saying, "You know it really looked like you tweaked your hip there in that fourth set. . . ."

Myerson immediately looked at me and silently mouthed the words: *Thank you.*

Given all Andy has done for Davis Cup, it was the least I could do.

RED, WHITE, AND STOKED

Davis Cup has a problem. Two of its four weeks are scheduled right after Grand Slam events, Wimbledon and the US Open. If your top players are contenders at those events, it's tough to ask them to bounce back as Davis Cup heroes. In 2009 I saw our chance to advance to the semifinals with a win over Croatia dissolve before my very eyes; Andy Roddick had done too well at Wimbledon, but not well enough to surf into Croatia on a wave of euphoria. Asking him to rebound, in his depleted physical and mental condition, to play an away tie on a surface he dislikes, was more than I wanted to put him through.

It can be frustrating, knowing that the unwieldy Davis Cup format is too demanding on the players the competition needs most, the top stars. Rafael Nadal has been in a pretty fortunate position; he can pass on a fair number of ties because the Spanish team has good depth. As a result, Spain joined the select group of nations that have created Davis Cup dynasties. Rafa didn't even play the tie that put them over the top, the huge upset over host Argentina in the championship round of 2008.

Roger Federer is so focused on winning Grand Slams that he doesn't even pencil Davis Cup weeks into his schedule, although he'll often play a relegation-round match just to keep the Swiss in the World Group. Andy Roddick has always stepped up, but with his chances to win another major fading, he may decide to focus exclusively on tournament play. Can't say I blame him.

Davis Cup is a terrific competition, and elements like the choice of ground ensure that every team gets fully tested—and that most nations get the honor of hosting a Davis Cup tie. It can mean a lot for a nation like, say, Israel or Chile, to have Nadal and his crew come to their place. The format also accounts for a lot of the color that's associated with the event, and it invites heroics. Early in 2009, thirty-two-year-old Nicolas Lapentti of Ecuador led his team into a tough tie against South American rival Brazil. Playing all three possible matches, Lapentti spearheaded a surprising upset, clinching the tie on his aging legs with an 8–6 in the fifth win over Marcos Daniel. Lapentti returned home exhausted, but a national hero. It was one of the all-time great performances by a player over thirty years of age in the Open era.

Unfortunately, some of the best elements of World Group play (including single elimination and the choice-of-ground system) are also the Davis Cup's worst enemy. The format makes it hard for a top pro to plan his schedule and Davis Cup ties are difficult to promote properly in prosperous, sports-rich nations, where they face the most competition from other activities. Big arenas are often booked solid before you can lock them down. The promotional lead time isn't all that long, although that's gradually improved.

For most nations, the system works fine, but a few tweaks could make it better at an acceptable cost. The irony is that in spite of almost universal participation, the nature of the Davis Cup format dooms it to a kind of perpetual regionalism. One of the most glaring obstacles is created by the overarching importance of television. Your nation may be playing a critical tie in a time zone that makes it impossible for you to watch, live—or for a network to have much interest in carrying it. There are ways Davis Cup can be made to seem like a bigger deal, like World Cup soccer or the Winter Olympics.

A lot of people have put forth ideas about that, but my choice would be to play the first two rounds as we do now, with the choice-of-ground rule, because that's good for smaller nations. But then bring the four finalists to one location for a ten-day semi and final. The ITF might even consider going to best-of-three set matches, although I know that's heresy.

Davis Cup is famous for those best-of-five epics, like the one my brother played in St. Louis with Mats Wilander of Sweden in 1982. John won that, 8–6, in the fifth. At six hours and thirty-two minutes, it was the longest continuous men's pro tennis match on record until Frenchmen Fabrice Santoro and Arnaud Clément surpassed it by eleven minutes at the French Open in 2004. Best-of-five with no final-set tiebreaker—a feature of both Davis Cup and the French Open—certainly enhances the stud factor for those lucky enough to prevail in those matches.

But imagine Federer and Nadal deadlocked after two hours and twenty minutes at a set and four games apiece in a best-of-three set Davis Cup final in Spain. Can anyone suggest that people aren't going to be into that? Of course, none of this will ever happen. The powers that be don't want to see it become Davis Cup Lite, not at the expense of the event's mystique, not when it has such a rich, continuous body of tradition (Davis Cup has been fought for over 110 years). So each nation and captain has to navigate the problems as best he can.

When we lost our second-round match last year, without Andy, it was to a team that rises to the occasion against the U.S. like no other. The Croatians have it in for us, but that's not a complaint. All's fair in love, war, and tennis. In a way I admire the Croatians, I just wish they wouldn't get so stoked whenever they see the red, white, and blue.

In 2003, Goran Ivanisevic powered them to a solid first-round win at home, forcing us down into the relegation round. In 2005, Croatia shocked us in Los Angeles, even though we fielded two of the best American Davis Cup singles players who ever lived, Roddick and Agassi. That was another first-rounder. And they did it again in 2009, although being without Andy, our team leader, softened that blow. At least this last time it was in the quarterfinals (it sounds more impressive than "second round," which is the reality).

Here's a tennis stat straight out of Ripley's Believe It or Not: Croatia is the *only* nation the U.S. has played but never beaten in Davis Cup.

By far the most painful of those losses to Croatia was the one in 2005, and it came about partly because I'd finally cracked the code and convinced Andre to return to the Davis Cup fold.

Andre Agonistes

Andre was a great Davis Cup player; at 30–6 (all in singles) he ranks a hair behind John (McEnroe) and Andy, and his winning percentage is extremely good. Andre was an interesting guy, a good friend, and a frequent practice partner. Once during tennis's brief off-season I went all the way to Vegas just to practice with him, and he was extremely generous—when you come to his town, he wants to take care of you. He set me up at a hotel, had a car and driver at my disposal, and he gave me a schedule of what we were going to do.

We often practiced at an indoor club, using pressureless balls because of the altitude. One day I beat him, which was really unusual because my game was tailor-made for him. He usually beat me like a drum, which is what made me a good, confidence-boosting practice partner for him.

That night—it was New Year's Eve—he called me, and I asked what time we were going to practice the following day. He said there was no practice—he had all the college football bowl games to watch, and he enjoyed betting on them. So I got a twenty-four-hour reprieve. The following day, he roughed me up something awful. At one point, I complained, "Come on, man, you're hitting a line every time. That's pretty lucky."

He grinned: "That's why they painted them there—for me to hit."

When he was finished pounding me, he said, "You got a set off me the other day, you didn't think I'd let that go by, did you?"

In 1997, just a few months before his marriage to Brooke Shields, Andre hit a low point. He was crushed by Javier Sánchez, 6–3, 6–2, in the first round of the minor tournament in Scottsdale. As his relationship with Brooke moved toward what would be a troubled marriage, he was finding it harder and harder to focus on tennis. His motivation came and went.

I had a wild card into that Scottsdale event, even though I was dealing with serious shoulder problems. I agreed to play in a Pro-Am golf event as part of my wild-card deal, but when I woke up the morning after the golf outing my shoulder hurt so much I couldn't lift it. I had to withdraw, then watch Andre get creamed by Sanchez. We ended up in Andre's room after he suffered that dispiriting loss and had ourselves a regular pity party. At one point, his face clouded over with a very sad look and he impulsively asked: "Do you think the game is passing me by?"

I was stunned, torn between being honest and further depressing Andre. I certainly didn't want to be the guy who convinced Andre that he ought to hang it up. I said, "No . . . But I think the game is improving and now you've got to bust it, work your ass off, just to survive."

Those were tough days for Andre. Underneath it all, he probably sensed that getting married hadn't been the right thing to do (he would say as much, when he published his recent autobiography, *Open*). But he'd decided to make the appropriate sacrifices in order to satisfy Brooke's own career needs. That was the main reason he left his beloved Las Vegas to live in Los Angeles. He comforted himself by buying a vintage 1976 white Cadillac Eldorado, which he called "Lily." He'd cruise all over LA in Lily.

Brooke was pleasant enough. She was an acquaintance of my wife,

Melissa; they had the same voice doctor in New York. We invited Andre and Brooke to our wedding; Andre attended, but Brooke didn't. It was another small sign of what separate lives they led—and where that was leading them.

By midsummer of 1997 Andre was really in the dumps about his tennis. Plus, he was having trouble with his wrist. Brad Gilbert was his coach at the time, and Andre told him he was pulling out of Wimbledon, claiming that he was in "vapor lock." An astonished Gilbert shot back, "What the hell is vapor lock?" It wasn't the wrist—Andre just didn't feel like playing. Instead, he stayed in London for a few days, where Brooke was doing some film work, and hung out with a bunch of actors.

Andre was at the edge of the precipice; soon he would go right over, and plummet to no. 141 in the world.

I lost early at that 1997 Wimbledon, and when I got home I had a message from Andre, who was back in LA, inviting me out to practice. We watched the Wimbledon final that year in Andre's kitchen, just the two of us; it was the year Pete Sampras overpowered Cédric Pioline. Even then, Andre loved to dissect tennis, and he had an unbelievable mind for the Xs and Os of the game.

Watching that final with him, I realized how much he missed tennis. I felt badly for him, thrashing around, trying to be a good husband, questioning the role tennis had played in his life. He was full of conflicting feelings about everyone and everything associated with tennis, including his own father. But at the must fundamental level, tennis was in his blood. Of that I was sure.

It was also in this period that Andre had his dalliance with the dangerous "recreational" drug, crystal meth. When he confessed to it in his 2009 autobiography, it sent shock waves through sports. It wasn't just that Agassi, who emerged later in his career as a paragon of charitable, socially conscious virtue, had fooled around with drugs. He also lied through his teeth to escape punishment, and got away with it.

Agassi, some people suggested, was not just a drug abuser but a liar whose massive celebrity helped him avoid the fate of other drug cheats—and with the apparent compliance of the ATP (it certainly looked as if the ATP wanted nothing more than to make a scandal featuring one of its famous and popular players just go away).

But Andre makes a good point when he says, albeit with a tinge of self-justification, that getting away with his transgression just shows the degree to which the drug-testing procedures were a work in progress, leading to the more transparent and fair system we have today. There's no doubt that we have a stricter, tamper-proof regimen now, because the inmates no longer run the asylum. Drug testing is now in the hands of the World Anti-Doping Agency (WADA)—nobody can get away with pulling a fast one anymore.

However, the disposition of the tennis tours to recreational drugs remains a problem. I support a zero-tolerance policy toward players who get caught using performance-enhancing drugs (which is also the official policy of the ATP and WTA), but the rules governing the abuse of recreational drugs are draconian and maybe even unfair. Martina Hingis had her comeback at age twenty-eight destroyed in early 2008 following a positive test for cocaine (at Wimbledon, in 2007) and the resulting two-year suspension. Just last year, the French player Richard Gasquet appealed a similar conviction, and had his "mandatory" two-year suspension overturned on appeal after he served just a few months.

Hingis denied taking cocaine, although both the A and B samples she submitted turned up positive. Unlike Gasquet, who was just twenty-two when he was busted, Hingis chose not to fight the suspension. Gasquet appealed the decision, claiming that the drug got into his system during a wild night out in Miami, in the course of which he was making out with a girl who had been using cocaine. Whatever the reality, the amount of cocaine in Gasquet's system was miniscule; the equivalent of something like a grain of salt.

Significantly, Rafael Nadal (and some of the other players who would soon criticize Agassi) leaped to Gasquet's defense, even though the drugs in both cases were, if anything, performance inhibitors, not enhancers. The difference was mostly about generational loyalty, kinship, and perhaps how the players in question were perceived by their peers. As the Gasquet incident showed, the players support a strict policy when it comes to PEDs, but they're less likely to condemn behavior that reflects mere bad judgment, or youthful mistakes—so long as they don't give the player who makes them an edge on the playing field. It's a reasonable position, and the one closest to my own.

You have to remember that the players are tested extensively, dozens of times during the year. They must make their whereabouts known to WADA at all times. If your mother or brother falls seriously ill halfway around the world, you have to let the drug testers know you'll be traveling on the spur of the moment, where you'll be going, and where you'll be when you get there. Testers are empowered to come knocking on your door at 6 a.m., or 9 p.m., and demand you take an on-the-spot urine test.

The players get tested during tournaments, and also when they're off the tour, practicing, relaxing, or recovering from injury. The system is incredibly invasive. But a tennis player can't afford to make the kind of simple mistake that has nothing to do with the game, and that any high school or college kid can get away with on a Saturday night on the town.

I'd never encourage anyone to experiment with recreational drugs, but I also believe that those who do shouldn't be held to a uniquely harsh standard. If a player tests positive for any banned substance that isn't performance enhancing, he should get a confidential warning, maybe have to undergo some form of counseling. Bring the problem out into the light, if not necessarily into the public forum. The ATP and WTA are right to have a militant opposition to drug use of any kind, but public censure and a career-threatening or destroying suspension is extreme. It might even push a confused or emotionally distressed player further toward, rather than away from, drugs.

Interestingly, Andre wasn't very clear in his book on when and how he stopped using the highly addictive crystal meth. But he described the failed test as an alarming, soul-shaking wake-up call. We know Andre was confused and depressed; now let's suppose he was still using meth at the time he learned that he'd been caught, and that the ATP took the hard line and threw him out of the game. Would that have made Andre more or less likely to continue using meth?

It's something worth thinking about. Tennis is a game for young people, and they all make mistakes. Exact too high a price for having made one and you can still claim that your sport is morally above reproach and "clean," but you can also destroy a dream and ruin rather than help rehabilitate someone who needs help—or maybe just a good, stern talking to. And if that person tests positive again, throw him or her out.

A Breakthrough with Andre

By 2001, Andre Agassi was done in Davis Cup—he'd won his thirty matches and decided that the unique challenge of the event took too much of a toll on his banged-up body.

To his credit, Andre was also reluctant to parachute in for cameo appearances in ties that would get a lot of media attention. He knew it wasn't fair to the players who had taken the team that far, even though recruiting an Andre or Pete to play a key tie enhanced the team's chance to win.

But I always held out hope, and held the door open. Andre walked through it in 2005; he told us he'd commit to Davis Cup and stick it out—hopefully over the four ties. I believe that Andre, in the waning days of his career, saw that we were building something special with our core players, Andy Roddick, James Blake, Mardy Fish,

Bob and Mike Bryan. . . . Andre had played on some great, winning teams, alongside guys like Jim Courier, Pete Sampras, John McEnroe, Todd Martin, and others. But those "all-star" teams didn't really have the camaraderie and team spirit that can make Davis Cup Special. Those guys were Andre's rivals in Grand Slam competition. They struck an uneasy truce, but none of them was going to yield (or take) leadership of the team.

In Davis Cup, being a celebrity captain doesn't automatically confer leadership, either—as my brother John learned. Great singles players aren't looking for leaders, because they're mostly lone wolves. But occasionally, one of them (like Andy Roddick) *makes* a great leader, if he's surrounded by the right players. Generally top stars are more interested in being understood and catered to than led. A captain has to recognize that his main role is that of manager. If he leads, it's more like a puppeteer than the guy leading the charge up San Juan Hill.

I'm not sure Andre or Pete would enjoy the role of Davis Cup captain. But I think both of them signed up to play when I was captain because they wanted to experience what we'd created.

Lead, Follow, or Get Out of Carson

In his book, *Open*, Andre characterizes his father, Mike, and his first coach as a pro, Nick Bollettieri, as control freaks. For a long time, he resented them for that, but you can't take control yourself if you don't know what you want, and that seemed to be Andre's big problem early in his career. When he did finally figure out who he was and what he wanted, he was off and running . . . controlling. It's a supreme irony, but there it is, another life lesson.

You can see Andre's desire to control in the way he played the game. He loved pulling guys from side-to-side, like a cat playing with a mouse. But also, when you went out to dinner with Andre, he insisted on ordering—for everyone. It would be an unbelievably good meal; he certainly knows his food. But he called the shots. When he asked for prosciutto, he told the waiter he wanted it sliced so thin that if he held it up he could see through it—and he meant that literally.

Andre was into wine, too. He liked this fancy Gaja stuff, which was very expensive, and he was totally into the wine-drinking process, if you know what I mean. It was like, *Let's let the wine sit . . . let's take a sip . . . let's talk about it. . . .* Meanwhile, I'd be sitting there, thinking, *Man, I just want to kick back, drink some wine, and dip the bread into the oil. . . .* But let's remember this obession with "process" played a huge role in Andre's late-career success.

The sure sign that you'd really made it with Andre was when he invited you out to the house for some grilled steaks. He flew those steaks in from some special guy in San Francisco. He marinated them himself for 48 hours, and then grilled them up just so. Meanwhile, he'd mix up a special batch of his famous margaritas—he's always been semiobsessed with the challenge of making the perfect margarita. All this dramatically underscored Andre's transformation from junk food addict and all-around screwup, flying by the seat of his pants, into a hall-of-fame competitor—and a sophisticated man of the world.

When Andre joined our Davis Cup team, I think he also saw the opportunity to help our core group, who had earned an "A" for effort, if not enough "W"s for victory. He qualified as an elder statesman and had developed a big-time Yoda gene late in his career. Andre had earned his spurs in Davis Cup, and we looked forward to having a devastating one-two punch in Agassi and Roddick. Bring on Croatia!

As captain, part of my job is to pick the surface, and that can be a tricky job. Courts are no longer judged merely in terms of relative speed; nuances like height of bounce enter the discussion because of the increased premium on topspin, and the renaissance of the kick serve. Now, you think a lot more about how a surface will—or won't—play into the hands of your opponents, not just how suitable it is for your guys.

For the tie against Croatia, I decided on a fairly slow outdoor hard court for two reasons: It would make life difficult for Croatia's no. 2 singles player, Mario Ančić, and it would help our doubles squad, Mike and Bob Bryan. I thought it critical to win the doubles, because I wanted to lock up the tie without having to beat Croatia's no. 1, Ivan Ljubičić. A tall, strong guy with a big serve and heavy groundies, Ljubičić was already on his way to a career year (he would hit no. 5). And I felt that Agassi and Roddick would be able to handle Ančić.

Things started weird and only got weirder. Our "official" team hotel was in downtown Los Angeles, far from the suburban site in Carson. LA is a big town; no one even seemed to know it was a Davis Cup weekend. And in LA, you're nothing if you don't make people feel like your event is the one everyone who is anyone will attend. We felt a little like a band of traveling salesmen in our first days in LA, coming and going in anonymity as we prepared for a tie that felt more and more like it was going to be played in the Twilight Zone.

The problems began to emerge on our first day of practice. I made one critical mistake before the tie: I'd neglected to personally check out the speed and playing properties of the surface before we gathered in Carson. I don't think the surface was all that bad, but Andre quickly planted seeds of doubt. He always liked to get the ball right in his strike zone, and the gritty, slow surface produced a higher bounce than he liked. So he was missing balls, and soon he was chucking his racket and yelling, "I can't get any progress, I can't get any progress." It's a valuable concept, but on that occasion it became an irritating catchphrase.

Andre had brought along his personal coach, Darren Cahill, a good former player and now an ESPN colleague of mine. After I got burned allowing coaches to attend my first tie as captain, I tightened up my policy. But over the years I relaxed it again and by the time our squad jelled into a tight unit, I'd pretty much abandoned it. Once you get the chain of command and the morale down pat, it's important to be flexible. Make—and keep—your top players relaxed and calm.

Andy Roddick was in the habit of bringing his coach, Brad Gilbert, and I was glad that Brad, a shrewd, seasoned pro in every sense of the word, knew exactly how to handle the delicate situation. But it was different with Darren and Andre. Darren was in Andre's ear, nonstop. Andre wanted it that way. At times, I wanted to yell, *For gosh sakes, guys, give it a rest. It's just a court and a ball, just shut up and figure it out like the rest of the guys. . . .*

But I held onto this hope—in retrospect, it was naïve of me—that if I just deferred to Andre and gave him his head, he'd level out and perform like we knew he could. I allowed myself to become a bystander while Andre and Darren took center stage. Their intentions were good, I knew that. Maybe they were too good, in that Andre probably felt a lot of pressure to set a good example and demonstrate his skill and knowledge of the game to our young turks. Whatever the case, I surrendered too much authority.

At the time, Bob Bryan was dating an actress. Andre, having been divorced from Brooke Shields, was not fond of actresses. He rode Bob all week, telling him repeatedly to not marry "that actress chick." He just kept hammering away at that, day after day. It eventually got to me, too; I'm married to an actress myself. There were lots of issues between Bob and this girl, but our team was close; Bob got plenty of feedback on his personal life from the other guys, friends with whom he had a much deeper bond and friendship, and with whom he'd shared the Davis Cup foxhole on many occasions. But Andre was emotionally tone deaf to all that; he wouldn't stop chewing on Bob's ass.

One night, Andre wanted to take the entire team out to dinner at some great restaurant he knew in Santa Monica. Again, his intentions were good. But we all knew Andre would probably do his control thing. And while the guys respected Andre, they weren't awed by him. Plus, they were just kids—not really interested in how thin the chef sliced the prosciutto, the quality of the wine, or, as Andre might have put it, "the process" of dining. They were just as happy inhaling pizza in sweats.

The rankings positioned Andy as our no. 1 singles player, Andre no. 2. The ITF wants the no. 1 players to meet in the first match on the third day of the tie; it's potentially the clinching match. And because the order of play is written in stone (two singles on Friday, doubles on Saturday, reverse singles on Sunday), you only need to draw one name at the official draw ceremony to set the entire program. It's just a matter of whether your no. 1 or no. 2 guy will play the first match of the tie.

Andre was drawn to open the tie against Croatia's no. 1, Ljubičić. Given Andre's track record and still deadly game, I was hoping that his Davis Cup experience would kick in, especially before a home crowd. And even if Ljubičić won, Andy was the right guy to stop the bleeding and get the momentum swinging back our way.

Once play started, it was clear that Andre was out of sorts. He was still disgruntled with the surface, and looked testy and impatient. It didn't help his cause that the atmosphere was relatively flat, with a poor fan turnout. I was stunned by Andre's apparent lack of self-confidence, and his unacceptably low tolerance for frustration. It almost looked like he was just going through the motions. I kept thinking, *Andre, forget progress and forget the nature of the surface, just find a way to make the guy hit five or six fucking balls. At least make him work. That's what you do best.*

But Andre was in a funk. At one point he turned to Cahill and practically pleaded: "What the fuck is going on here?" He should have known what was going on, and figured out a way to deal with it. He certainly had the experience, as well as the game. But that was Andre, one of the most insecure, moody, and easily rattled of all great players.

Andre went down in straight sets. I had an uncomfortable moment when Andy dropped the first set to Ančić, but he worked his way back into it and basically wore Ančić down on the slow hard court. At least that worked out the way I planned. Although I was disturbed by Andre's performance, my game plan was working as intended. If the Bryans, who liked a slow hard court, won the doubles, we'd need just one singles win. If Andy couldn't handle Ljubičić, I was sure Andre could find a way to lift himself out of his funk in a critical, decisive fifth rubber at home against Ančić.

But by that point, Bob Bryan was like a whipped dog. The pounding he'd taken from Andre over his girlfriend definitely affected the way he played. Bob and Mike, one of the all-time great doubles teams, lost to a very impressive team of Croatia's two singles players. It was a particularly devastating blow, because it took place practically in the Bryans' backyard (they're from Camarillo), in front of their tennis evangelist dad, Wayne. For the first time since they joined the squad, the Bryans lost a doubles. (They've lost one other one since then, but they've also surpassed [John] McEnroe and Fleming as the most successful U.S. doubles team in Davis Cup history.) In the short term, that loss put us in a big hole.

Andy did his best to keep us alive, but Ljubičić was just a little too strong. He clinched the tie for Croatia with a very physical, punishing five-set win over Andy. Davis Cup rarely runs off the rails and fails to provide color and drama, or inspire the players, but this tie was a buzz kill from the get-go. That too played a part in our demise.

Moments after Andy lost, Andre burst into the locker room, congratulated the team, and said, "I'm outta here." He wasn't about to stick around to play his meaningless singles against Ančić. So, to add insult to injury, I had to send poor Bob Bryan out, before a sparse, dispirited crowd and his bummed-out teammates, to play the dead rubber. Andre just hopped in his car and drove back to Vegas.

Here's a footnote: That year, Croatia won its first ever Davis Cup, over Slovakia. It was great for Davis Cup history, but it was also clear that we'd blown a significant opportunity to win it all. I wondered, won't we ever win this thing?

Sweet Home in Alabama

A captain has to be a little lucky to survive a debacle like Carson. I have to give the USTA credit for understanding the tricky nature of that situation and sticking with me. Empathy is a luxury, and it only gets you so far. The consistent, underling mandate is, to quote the famous motto of Oakland Raiders owner Al Davis, "Just Win, Baby."

I did have one powerful hedge against getting fired—the support of my team. Top players from any nation serve at their leisure. It may not seem right, given that playing for your nation is a high honor and, to some, a duty. But that's how it is. The compensation for Davis Cup is pretty good, especially for guys who aren't ranked very high. Top players, though, don't play for the money.

Each nation has a different basic pay scale, but top U.S. singles players are looking at close to a six-figure payday, with a few profit-sharing clauses and expenses thrown in to sweeten the pot. (Highly ranked players earn a larger appearance fee than others.) For doubles players, the nearly $50,000 per man paycheck is sweet. A Roddick or Blake (when he was in the top 10) might pull down comparable money in an exhibition match, and for less work. But he also makes less for winning two matches in a tournament. Plus, there's an ITF prize money bonus pool, doled out at the end of the year.

Davis Cup ties are a schmooze-fest for the ITF and its affiliates, all of which are largely volunteer organizations. Davis Cup allows the USTA to repay some of the people who work in the trenches of the game (running tournaments and recreational leagues, compiling official results and sectional rankings, keeping constituents informed and involved), and for many of them being invited to a Davis Cup tie is a choice perk. The pro game is just the glamorous tip of the tennis iceberg, and all those working below the surface enjoy getting a moment in the bright sun of a big pro event.

The team is well taken care of at a typical tie. The players get first-class travel, and each guy gets a suite, always in a luxury hotel. They can get food at any time they want, at the hotel or in our team room at the arena. And all the incidentals, including stringing, are taken care of by the USTA. Still, by the end of 2009, Andy was growing a little tired of the extraneous demands of Davis Cup. He was pissed by the way the USTA started nitpicking the players' phone bills, or insisting that Mike Bryan's girlfriend take a cab and pay her own way to the airport when she had to leave a tie a day early.

It was petty stuff, easily averted, and a transparent attempt by the USTA to show who's in charge. But the reality is that the USTA (and I include myself) has to be careful not to alienate the top players. There's no law saying they must play Davis Cup, and plenty of players have thumbed their noses at the bureaucrats and executive officers of almost any federation. The support of the team helped me survive Carson, a tie that wasn't by any means representative of our talent.

Carson was a disaster, but hosting is often a powerful advantage. When we traveled to Birmingham for a first-round Davis Cup tie in March of 2009, I was fired up, as I always am for home ties. My go-to guy, Andy Roddick, was poised to eclipse Andre Agassi as the nation's second most prolific Davis Cup singles player. And if I made it through the tie, I'd become the longest-serving captain in U.S. Davis Cup history.

This being Davis Cup, we were presented with a rude surprise when Roger Federer took his sweet old time deciding to pull out of the event (with a bad back). Even that couldn't ruin the occasion for me, because while it killed a lot of the hype and put some additional pressure on us to win, it improved our chances—to say the least.

The one thing I did feel badly about is that the local community, led by the DJs on the Rick and Bubba morning radio show, had done a great deal to promote Federer's visit to Birmingham. They helped sell a lot of tickets, and they were bound to feel let down. I also knew that I was going to be answering questions about Federer's decision all week, which could have a really adverse impact on our team. Even my own brother John, who was supposed to call the match on TV, decided to pull the plug and stay home.

I didn't even dare to think what might happen if the Swiss beat us. And with Stan Wawrinka, a top-ten player on their roster, nothing was impossible. Davis Cup; it's always tricky.

I'd picked a court slightly slower than our two singles players would have liked, but that was based on Federer's participation. It was similar to the situation in Carson. I figured that with Federer in the lineup, the doubles would be absolutely critical, and our outstanding team of Bob and Mike Bryan were most effective when they got a good look at service returns, and could rely on their teamwork and preternatural communication skills to win points (it helps to have played tennis all your life—with your twin brother).

One of the best features of Davis Cup is the importance of doubles. Doubles gets little respect at regular tournaments—it's treated as filler, something you put on to warm up—or cool down—a crowd. But in Davis Cup, doubles gets its own day, Saturday. Every tie is still undecided on Saturday, and doubles is often the critical swing match when the score is a match apiece. Any team going into Sunday down 1–2 is in desperate straits.

If you look at Davis Cup teams that have performed consistently well over a period of time, you'll almost always find a great doubles team at the foundation. It might consist of two great singles players, like John Newcombe and Tony Roche of Australia, a great singles player and a doubles "specialist," like Stan Smith and Erik Van Dillen, or a dedicated team of doubles specialists, like Australia's Mark Woodforde and Todd Woodbridge, or our own Bryan brothers.

Being a solid doubles player myself, I was always sensitive to the crucial role doubles plays in Davis Cup, and appreciated the respect the team game was accorded in Davis Cup. But I still took my time before nominating the Bryan brothers for their first tie, an away match against Slovakia in September of 2003.

One reason I waited so long, even though the Bryans were chomping at the bit, was their relative lack of singles success. If you're going to pick a dedicated doubles team, you've accounted for half your team to win one match and thus surrender your options in singles. It has to be a slam-dunk choice. So I kept telling the Bryans—and their enthusiastic dad, Wayne, who was calling me out in public for ignoring the boys—that I wanted to see them win something before I chose them. Not San Jose, or Barcelona, but something really big. They delivered when they won the French Open in 2003. I was glad I waited; it really helped motivate and inspire the Bryans to become great doubles players as well as great Davis Cup players.

Their first tie, against Slovakia, was a relegation match, so it was more important than a first rounder, even a fairly tough one. The night before the doubles match started, I went to the brothers' room. Although they're entitled to their own rooms, they usually bunk together. And during ties, they always leave the arena before the action on day one is finished. They get too hyped up if they sit there in the arena. They say, "We're going back to the hotel and closing the blinds for the next twenty-four hours." They watch the rest of the singles action in isolation on television, getting each other pumped up in the hotel room.

Anyway, I stopped by their room on the eve of the first tie and laid my cards on the table. I told them that for the past ten, twelve years, including my stint as a player, we almost always rotated our singles players in and out of doubles, or picked one doubles guy and tried to match him up with the best possible partner. We never had a dedicated doubles team. I wanted to change that. I wanted to have a rock solid, bankable doubles team, and decided that they were it. "Okay, tomorrow, get out there and bust it. But I also want you guys to know that whatever happens, you're our team—you're our team for the future, no matter what happens in the short term."

It was like throwing red meat to a couple of lion cubs. They practically jumped up and saluted, and to this day they say that the assurance I gave them that evening really helped. I made that little speech partly because I knew how a doubles player often felt when called to duty. Whenever I played, I always found myself thinking, *If we lose I'm out. . . . I'll never get another chance.* Which is basically what happens. So I wanted to reduce any unnecessary pressure the Bryans might have felt.

So on the morning of their first appearance in their U.S. uniform, Bob and Mike came to the bench after the warm-up and I said, "Okay, guys, let's do it. We can do it."

And one of them replied, "We're ready. We've been waiting twenty-five years for this moment to come."

That's the kind of shit they say all the time; this is one brace of jacked-up, Davis Cup–psycho dudes. I could write a whole chapter about the stuff the Bryans say. Mike will walk into the locker room and say—with a straight face—"Captain, Mike Bryan, reporting for duty." Or Bob will say, "We're gonna die for the flag today!" Mike will chime in, "Yeah! We were *born* for this!" They take the concept of team spirit to a whole other level.

When the draw for 2010 was made late in 2009, and we pulled Serbia, in an away tie, ten minutes didn't go by before I got a text from Mike. "Let's go to war, we're ready to go to fucking Serbia! Zimo (Nenad Zimonjić, Serbia's outstanding doubles player) needs a taste. . . ."

The Bryans know how insanely so many nations want to beat us—bring the mighty U.S. to its knees . . . its knees! And meanwhile I'm thinking, *uh-oh*, the Bryans have their chests all puffed out and they're shouting, "Let's go to war!"

Most players, they do anything they can to take the pressure off. The Bryan brothers seek ways to lay it on. Those are exactly the kinds of guys you want on your Davis Cup squad.

The Insanity of Elevens

Mike and Bob won the doubles title at Delray Beach, Florida, right before our Birmingham tie. They got stuck in Charlotte, North Carolina, because of a freak snowstorm and were forced to stay in some roach motel near the airport. They arrived in Birmingham with bedbug bites. But even though they got in early Monday, they wanted to practice, and we had the court at the convention center from noon to 3:00 p.m.

Early in the week the Bryans like to beat up on our practice partners. In Birmingham, they were Ryan Sweeting and a big, strapping, powerful newcomer, Alex Domijan. A typical Bryan brothers practice must be seen to be believed. They warm each other up, and by the time the sweats come off they've hit a million balls, rapid fire—you can almost see the lump forming in the throats of the practice partners: *What did we get ourselves into?*

When Mike and Bob hit together, they can take one ball and not miss for ten minutes. They'll start, going crosscourt. Then Bob or Mike will drift up to the net and start hitting volleys, while the other practices his down-the-line passing shot. It's all like some elaborately choreographed dance. They don't even talk; it's amazing how much they get done in a very short time, and how instinctively they understand each other.

After the warm-up, the Bryans like two-up, two-back drills, with the practice players as the other team. The Bryans will be at the net; they feed the balls. The receiver can hit the first fed ball as hard as he likes, short of going for a winner. And after that, it's a live point—anything goes. They play that game until either team reaches eleven points. Then they change positions, with the practice guys at the net. The pace is so furious that the Bryans can knock out six games of Elevens in 15 minutes. That's smoking. You get a couple of practice guys who don't volley all that well—and there are plenty of them these days—and the game is over in two minutes: 11–1, to the Bryans. They just pick the guys apart.

On those rare occasions when a practice team does win a game of Elevens against the Bryans, the boys get pissed. They don't even go to the sidelines to sip water. They just say, "Another one, let's go. Rack 'em."

That's what they always say, "Rack 'em," like it's a friendly game of pocket billiards at the local pub.

The Bryans sometimes will finish a two-set practice match, winning something like 6–2, 6–2, and still have 20 minutes of practice time left. They'll decide to kill the time working on service returns. So Jay Berger and I will hit serves to them, from halfway inside the court (to force them to react more quickly). Mike may coldcock nine returns in a row, but if he happens to miss the tenth, he'll plead, "Just a couple more. Just a few."

Early in the week in Birmingham, Mike gave me his wish list—as is his habit. He wanted to sharpen up his serve, get a little more settled in his return. He wanted me to watch for certain things, and issue certain reminders. That's how these guys are—they want that basic stuff that most great players scoff at, or are secretive about. The Bryans are technical, like golfers. Mike likes to have some little thing every week, especially if you can pack it into a neat slogan: *Stay down on the return, like you're sitting in a chair. . . . Racket speed is your friend. . . .* The Bryans love that stuff; they're tennis geeks.

That enthusiasm rubs off, to everyone's benefit. Back in the day, heaven forbid I tried to give Andy Roddick even a little tip on his serve. But partly because of the Bryans, he's more open to it now. He'll ask me to make sure he does this or that little thing; sometimes it's as simple as the placement of his left foot before he serves. Our practices are like lab work, and the Bryans' desire to improve and learn rubs off.

Intense guys often have tics or compulsive habits, and the Bryans are no exception. Most Davis Cup weeks, Mike likes to take a day off. I'd gladly give it to him, too, only he never comes right out and asks. He finds something wrong, something that needs fixing, instead. So he'll skip practice and get a long massage, or ice down his legs. That way, the next day he can get in the team van and say, "Okay, I'm ready. My legs feel like they're going to explode, let's go."

This has become a running joke for us. Birmingham week was no exception; Mike took Thursday morning off. When I met Bob down in the lobby to go to practice, he said, "Mike's taking the morning off. Everything is normal, Cap."

Mike always tries to sneak his girlfriends into the hotel for the week, even though my "official" policy always was no wives or girlfriends until the tie is about to begin. Mike tries to hide his girls, so they end up stuck in his room, watching TV, while we have a good time at our team dinners. Considering what the Bryans have done for us, it would have been insane to lay the hammer down on Mike. But I enjoy putting him on the spot about the girls. Once, knowing he had a girlfriend with him during the week, I asked him on a Friday, "I saw that so-and-so is already here, when did she get in, real late last night?"

Mike averted his eyes and sheepishly muttered, "Yeah, yeah."

What makes it doubly funny is that Andy Roddick, even after all these years, and after getting engaged, still called me before the team dinner on Saturday night in Birmingham and asked, "Is it okay if (my fiancée) Brooklyn comes along?"

Sometimes, my assistant Jay Berger or I practically have to drag the Bryans off the practice court, physically. We worry that they'll leave too much out there. They'll trot over to the bench at the theoretical end of practice like a couple of big yellow Lab puppies, and we'll exchange a fist bump. But a few moments later, while we're just sitting around, Bob will get fidgety if someone else hasn't claimed the court. He'll get up, shake his limbs, and trot out to hit a few more balls, Mike hot on his heels. "Bob, hit me a couple of volleys, just a few."

If Bob's out there, Mike has to be there, too. There's always something to work on, always something that can be dialed in just a little teensy-weensy bit better.

The Old Goat

During Wednesday's official Davis Cup banquet, with both teams present and a swarm of ITF and USTA types in attendance, Alex Domijan delivered the traditional rookie speech. I think he said more words in that speech than he did over the entire practice week. But Andy took a shine to the kid. He liked the way Alex worked in practice. Slowly, Andy has taken on the role of mentor, and he clearly enjoys it.

As soon as possible after dinner, we slipped out of the hall and the boys decided to go looking for a place to eat. We spotted a Waffle House, hard by Interstate I–20. Andy told the driver to head for it.

The place was nearly deserted, and the elderly lady who waited on us wore a name tag that said "the Old Goat."

"What y'all doin' down here, boys," she asked. The guys said they were traveling salesmen. Of course, Andy got right to the point and asked, "What's up with the name tag?"

The waitress explained that it was the nickname of her deceased husband, and she'd adopted it as a memorial gesture. We all talked, one thing led to another. One of the Bryans cued up a popular rap song, "Low," by Flo Rida, on his iPhone (the Bryan brothers are very into their gadgets), and soon the Old Goat started singing and rapping along with the boys. The guys videotaped the Old Goat singing; they were going to put it on YouTube.

I was caught without cash, but Andy was flush—he picked up the check, something like thirty-seven bucks, and left her eighty dollars. On the way home, the guys kept replaying their video and someone said, "Aw, we should have gotten her some tickets or something."

The next morning, I called Anne Marie Martin, our team assistant, and asked her to pull two good seats to the Saturday program and deliver them to the Waffle House by I–20. Just say they're for the Old Goat.

During the first changeover during the doubles match, Andy got up to stretch. He turned around to the exclusive seating area right behind the bench for USTA officials and special guests. His jaw dropped to the floor when he saw the Old Goat sitting right there, among all the USTA bigwigs and their special power-broker guests. The word raced down the bench; the guys loved it. After the match they took the Old Goat into the locker room and loaded her up with all kinds of Davis Cup regalia—official team T-shirts, caps, the works.

Just another Davis Cup moment. We never even learned the Old Goat's real name.

Fortress Blake

Stan Wawrinka's name was pulled out of the hat at the official draw ceremony; the Swiss no. 1, he would play James Blake to open the tie. It was the best draw for the Swiss. Wawrinka was more than capable of beating James. If he did, there was that much more pressure on Andy in the second match, although I saw no way he could lose to the Swiss no. 2, Marco Chiudinelli, a player with little firepower, hovering around no. 50 in the world.

James won the first set, but in the second Wawrinka got better. His rifle-shot backhand started finding the lines, and his serving accuracy improved. As he won the second set and began to build a lead in the third, he took the crowd of 15,000 mostly U.S. fans right out of it.

Wawrinka is a very good player, but he's no ace machine. Unfortunately, James can make guys with medium to good serves look like Goran Ivanisevic. James doesn't really stretch well, he's not what we sometimes call "long," which isn't entirely a function of his wingspan or size. Andre Agassi didn't stretch well either; he was pretty easy to ace. But Andre made up for it with his superb eye-hand coordination, and as one of the all-time great returners, once he got wood on the ball he could hurt you.

Lleyton Hewitt is a good example of a small guy who can return a lot of balls. It's a flexibility and timing issue. He has great reach to either side. If a serve comes in a little short, Hewitt can even nip in and roll it crosscourt. It's a safe shot—a crosscourt ball passes over the lowest part of the net, the middle—and if he gets a good angle, that return can pose problems for the server.

I sank a little lower in the captain's chair as Blake's game degenerated. I sensed that the match was slipping away. I had learned to be extra careful at such times, because in the commentary booth, when one guy really begins to pull away, I can afford to let my feelings be known. I can say, "This is over."

But in Davis Cup matches, you have to expect surprises and plot twists. And no matter how desperate the situation, the captain can't signal a loss of confidence in any way. It's a betrayal of your guy, and it also helps ensure that the worst will indeed come to pass. I was extra careful to mask my feeling that the conclusion was foregone, and I wanted to help James. But that's not always the easiest of things to do.

James is a hard worker and a great guy. He's answered the Davis Cup call consistently. He's a loyal guy, too. For most of his career he's retained the coach who shepherded him through adolescence, Brian Barker (that changed at the end of 2009, when James hired Kelly Jones). When James first came out on tour after his two years at Harvard (a résumé item that earned him a great deal of publicity and support), few would have predicted that he'd make the top 10 and stay there for a long time. Among other things, his backhand was just all over the place. But he proved the doubters wrong.

It isn't easy talking to James, though, or at least it's a chore getting through to him. He's a sensitive, self-protective guy, so I always have to talk in a kind of code; I have to find a positive way to make a point, instead of cutting to the chase and offering a straightforward, constructive criticism or piece of advice. As Wawrinka began to get the measure of James, I wanted to jump up and yell, "Hey James, get your finger out and make a few returns, just get the damned ball in play."

But that wouldn't fly, so I focused on encouraging him at those moments when he showed signs that he might jump-start his best game again. When he made a good return I'd say stuff like, "You're right there, keep going for it."

Part of my dilemma is that James feels he knows his own game better than anyone else, and he's going to stick to his guns. That means he's going to go for his shots, because . . . that's what he's about. He seems convinced that he's going to make the same number of errors whether he goes for the big first serve or takes a little off—if he tries to return big, or just gets the ball into play. His mindset is: *I gotta be aggressive, I have to go for it, that's how I play.* And it's hard to move him off that, because that style has paid off.

One explanation for Brian Barker's longevity is that he rarely told James something he didn't want to hear. I once told Barker that James needed to get a higher percentage of his first serves into play; he's no Ivo Karlović, or Roddick, who can step up and blow the ball by the other guy.

"I can't tell him that," Brian replied.

"Why not?"

"Because he thinks that if he spins it in, he misses just as many."

Huh?

So I have to work around James's stubbornness, without undermining his confidence. And it's unwise trying to crack the code when he's mired in a losing battle and looking sluggish and not confident. While Wawrinka continued to hurt James with his serve, and James was unable to find the service box with his own, I just kept my own counsel. When he hit a good serve, wide, I'd tell him, "That serve works. That's a great serve. Keep swinging him wide."

But what I was really trying to convey was, "Take a little bit off." Because that's just what you have to do in order to get that good angle on the wide serve.

The contrast between my two big guns in singles, James and Andy, is profound. I've had to figure out psychological strategies for handling each of them, but that hasn't really been a burden. It's actually been fun—most of the time. Here you have Andy, who's pretty open, even though he can be a wiseass and a know-it-all. Andy is less guarded about his game than he once was, but that's an outgrowth of the way he's always looked to get better. And there you have James, quiet, polite, but not very good at communicating or taking criticism or advice. James has been more prone to look for ways to do the same things over and over, only better.

On a typical changeover, Andy might flop into the chair and mutter, "Hey, this guy is looking for my serve every time, he's kind of got it figured out." What he expects mostly is confirmation of his observation; but he's also opening the door for my input—asking without having to ask. So I'll suggest, "Go to his body a little more," or "Take a little off the first serve and move it around more." Little things like that.

One of the things Andy's learned to do, but James hasn't mastered, is play two or three different styles—sometimes within the same game. If an opponent is serving at 15–30, second serve, that's a good time to step in and go for it. But even a Pete Sampras would take a serve at 30–all and just chip it back nice and low, just to keep the ball in play. Sometimes you go for it, sometimes you try to make the other guy miss. You have to adjust to the score, the situation, and the opponent.

By the time Wawrinka won the third set in Birmingham, it was looking bleak for James. Early in the fourth set, I couldn't bite my tongue any longer. I said what I should have, many games earlier: "Take a couple of steps back on the return, give the guy a different look." It was hard to judge James's reaction, because he's not outwardly emotional. I know at times he's pissed at me, but he won't say anything, where Andy's more likely to challenge me if I say something he doesn't like. So I just kept my fingers crossed.

For once, James seemed to listen. He took my advice, battled back, and pushed the fourth set to a tiebreaker. That's not a bad setup for Blake, who's capable of electric shotmaking that can save an entire set with two or three swings of the racket. But he lost the tiebreaker, because his own serve was a mess. How does a top 10 player register a first serve percentage of under 50 percent in ideal indoor conditions? I wondered. It's one thing if the guy has an unbelievable second serve to fall back on, so he's unloading on every first serve. But James has no such luck, yet he still unloads on every first ball. So he went down the tubes.

Later, I sat next to him at the press conference as per Davis Cup tradition. I knew James would say the same shit as always: *Yeah, it's a great week, I'm going to do my best, the team will lift me up, I've got Indian Wells coming up, I hope to do well. . . .*

I sat there reading the minds of the reporters: *Come on, gimme something I can chew on.* But you're more likely to get that out of the Bryans, or Andy. They'll show you what a loss, or win, really means to them, in a more heartfelt way. James has this self-protective thing going on, some thick walls he's built up around himself.

It can be tough get into the fortress. But it will be worth the effort.

The Last Match of Their Lives

I knew there was no way on earth Andy would lose to Chiudinelli, who just kind of brushes over the ball. That doesn't work against Andy, especially not when his all-business attitude, summed up in that ridiculously effective serve, brings a Davis Cup crowd to life. He won the first two sets easily, and controlled the third-set tiebreaker to set up the Bryan brothers to break the 1–1 tie the following day.

The first thing I heard Mike Bryan say on Saturday morning before we had our warm-up hit was: "I got eight. I woke up at three, but then went back down and got a good six. Man, my legs, they're ready to explode!"

That was in response to a simple question: "How'd you sleep?"

In the locker room a little later, Mike said, "This is all that matters—this and Grand Slams. Let's play like this is the last match of our lives."

Andy looked at him, kind of sideways, and cryptically said: "You never know. . . ."

While the boys warmed up, I couldn't resist playing along. I said, "Mike, man, you're moving great. Your legs—they're like . . . exploding!"

"Yeah. I'm feelin' it."

Mike told me to remind him that he has to drink; he gets so jacked up on court that he forgets that he needs to hydrate on the changeover. And during the match, the boys eat these power gel things, I think they're aptly called "Gu." They gobble those things nonstop, starting in the warm-up. Any normal human being that eats that many of those gooey supplements drops dead of toxic sugar shock or puts on twenty pounds overnight.

I patted my pocket as the boys went out to start the match, just to make sure I had the Tums that Mike also makes me carry around. He takes Tums during every match. Sometimes I need them, too, but this was not going to be one of those days—I hoped.

The Bryans got off to a great start, but after three games Mike started complaining about his foot. On the changeover, he looked grim: "Tell Doug (Spreen, our trainer) to get something ready. Quick. Get some pads ready."

I was like, "What is it, what's wrong?" I saw no sign of any problem, and it was too early in the match for blisters to be an issue. Still, I was worried. I went to Doug and told him that Mike was complaining about his foot, and asked for some pads to put in his shoes.

"What the hell was he talking about?" Doug looked baffled.

"Never mind. Just get something ready. Cut up some squares of moleskin or something."

The boys took the first set from Wawrinka and Yves Allegro, 6–3. On the changeover, Doug trotted out with his little kit, ready to minister to Mike. He had cut up eight pads. Mike began to take off his shoe and suddenly Bob cried, "What are you doing? We've got the momentum. This is no time to take an injury time-out!"

I'd followed Davis Cup protocol and told the chair umpire that we'd be taking the three-minute injury time-out, and he'd informed the Swiss captain, Severin Luthi. So when Mike started jamming his foot back in his shoe, with Bob jumping around and telling him to hurry up, Luthi leaped out of his own chair and protested to the umpire. He thought we were trying to pull a fast one on his squad, and I could hardly blame him.

"It's always something," Doug muttered, clearly disgusted, as he packed his kit back up. "Mike always has to have something."

I settled back into my chair. It was still pretty early in the match—who knew what might happen next?

What happened was that Bob started going off about the tension in his racket. The brothers are meticulous about their string tension. On the first day of practice, having moved from the outdoor courts of Delray Beach to this indoor arena, I'd heard Mike ask: "Bob, whatcha got?"

"Fifty-four," Bob replied, meaning pounds of tension.

"I think I'd better take it up to five-five, maybe five-four and a half."

The next day, Bob asked Mike how the new tension felt. "Good, good. I think I'm locked in."

Bob is usually the calmer Bryan, but there he was, unhappy. So I sent one of his rackets out to our stringer, Roman, with instructions to make the tension a precise fifty-four pounds on the nose. Two changeovers later, with the boys still well ahead, Bob went off: "Where the fuck's my racket, it's been forty minutes!"

Actually, it was only fifteen. But I turned around to Jay Berger and said, "We'd better get that racket back. These two guys are strung a lot more tightly than fifty-four and I don't want them to snap."

But I wouldn't have it any other way, because the Bryans play best when they're all wound up. It only becomes a liability when they get in a tight spot, because then all the potential distractions can play havoc with their confidence and focus. They're classic front-runners, better at steamrolling people than navigating tight spots that call for a greater measure of sangfroid.

When they were up two sets to none and 2–1 on serve in the third, Mike turned and looked at the clock. "Bob, Bob. Fourteen more minutes. Let's go, give me fourteen and we're out of here." They've done that kind of thing before, closed the deal exactly the way they wanted, almost to the minute. They take comfort in precision.

But it didn't go like that. Allegro had been conspicuously the weakest player on the court, to the extent that I found myself feeling badly for the poor guy. But he managed to lift his game, and in no time, it was four-all in the third. *Uh-oh,* I thought. *Don't let this set get away from you. The last thing we need is some kind of dogfight.* After all, Wawrinka had been a doubles gold medalist at the 2008 Olympic Games (with Roger Federer for a partner), and he was capable of carrying Allegro.

Thankfully, the boys played a great tiebreaker and closed it out neatly, in straight sets, to put us up 2–1. In his on-court interview, Mike couldn't contain himself: He guaranteed the crowd that "the Closer"—that's his nickname for Roddick—would finish the job in the first match the following day.

Andy was in the locker room, watching on television. He winced and shook his head when Mike guaranteed the coin. When the Bryans tumbled in, Andy said, "Thanks, Mike. Nothing like putting a little extra pressure on me."

"I know," Mike said contritely. "I'm sorry. It just kind of slipped out."

Andy rolled his eyes. Mike has a habit of putting his foot in his mouth; sometimes it's funny, sometimes it requires a little cleaning up after him. I knew how Andy felt; Wawrinka was playing the best tennis of his life—and could beat anyone on a given tennis day.

But I also knew that "the Closer" did a good job cleaning up. What I love about coaching Andy is that you know he's always going to give you everything he's got. Luckily, his all wasn't required the following day. He came out firing on all cylinders, and Wawrinka saw the handwriting on the wall, in addition to feeling the fatigue of two tense matches in his legs. Andy won easily, and by that night we were all drifting off, going our separate ways. There's always another stop on the tennis caravan.

TALENT FINDERS, PLAYER SHAPERS, AND CHAMPION MAKERS

The phone rang in my hotel room in Mason, Ohio, on the morning of the 2007 final at Cincinnati, the biggest of the hardcourt events played in the U.S. and Canada as a prelude to the US Open. Cincinnati isn't really played in Cincinnati, but in the far outlying, semideveloped flatland of Mason, near the King's Island amusement park.

No matter. These hardcourt tournaments, now promoted as the US Open Series, once marked an annual high point for American players. It was our home turf, we played best on the hard, cement-based surfaces the U.S. introduced to tennis. But many once-fine tournaments on the summer circuit, clay or hard, have been dying out. The globalization of the game and the burgeoning prize money (and budgets) have been death on tournaments in secondary-market cities like Stratton, Vermont, Louisville, and Indianapolis. Cincinnati has hung in there mainly because civic and local business forces take extreme pride in the event, and throw their considerable weight behind it.

Cincinnati, now the Western and Southern Financial Group Masters, is one of the elite "Masters 1000" events that rank right below the four Grand Slams. The ATP makes them obligatory; if you qualify for direct acceptance, you're expected to play. Both the

ATP and WTA operate a tier system of tournaments, with an elite, top level of nine Masters 1000 (ATP) events and a similar number of Premium Mandatory events for the women. The prize money at these events is currently in the $5 million range for both tours, and they offer the most number of ranking points (after majors). That Cincinnati can compete on a level playing field and attract as high quality a field as tournaments that take place in metropolises like Madrid, Toronto, or Rome is a tribute to the men and women who created and grew the event.

The atmosphere in Cincinnati is still a cross between the US Open and a county fair. Players from foreign countries have always found the surroundings in Mason somewhat weird ("There's nothing there" would be a standard description), and in some ways the sleepy developments, Walmarts, and strip malls amid all that empty midwestern space can look bleak and uninviting. Europeans don't understand what a big country this is, how much we rely on cars, how little we think of driving ninety minutes or two hours to go somewhere for the day—or how we actually like a plain, comfortable life even if it lacks many cultural amenities.

Yet tennis's cast of international, worldly characters, seasoned travelers who feel at home in Rome, Moscow, Tokyo, and Bangkok, still make the annual pilgrimage to Mason and a few similar places where there may not be anyone within a 100-mile radius who speaks anything but English, or who's traveled farther from home than Nashville or Branson, Missouri.

Roger Federer and James Blake met in the Cincy final in 2007; I was on site as a commentator for ESPN and CBS. As U.S. Davis Cup captain, I was really pleased with James's great performance; to that point he had yet to win a tournament of the elite Masters grade. A Masters event presents a daunting challenge. You play best-of-five set tennis at a major, and play seven matches to win, but you get a day off between matches. A seven-day Masters demands that you win five matches on consecutive days, against a field unsurpassed even at the majors.

I was there to help James if he needed it in Cincy, but when I picked up the phone I was surprised to hear the voice of Roger's agent, Tony Godsick. He told me Roger didn't have anyone to warm up with for the final. Would I mind hitting with him?

Ordinarily, it would have been a pleasure. But what would James think if he happened to show up on an adjacent court at roughly the same time, and saw me, his Davis Cup captain, running around getting Federer ready for their match—even if it was just a hitting session? Roger's a classy guy, I never for a moment suspected that he was trying to play mind games with James; he doesn't need to play mind games with anyone (by the final, most everyone is pretty much gone; you take what you can get in the way of a hitting partner). But it still might be a distraction for Blake.

That wasn't the first time that the multiple roles I play in the game have overlapped, or created a real or imagined conflict. One of the most frequent criticisms I get is that I "go easy" on our Davis Cup squad members when I'm doing my TV commentary. Such conflicts are inevitable, and they've always been part of tennis, because our core community remains pretty small and insular, no matter how big the game gets. There's a lot of cross-pollination.

Trust me, Andy Roddick, James Blake, the Bryan brothers, etc., don't think I go easy on them at all. Andy is an up-front guy who doesn't shy away from saying what he thinks, or listening to what you have to say. And we've had our share of blowups over critical things I've said about the Davis Cup on the air. Sometimes, he didn't even hear them firsthand, but things always get back to the players.

Early in my Davis Cup captaincy, I said during a broadcast that it was time for our team to step up and win a few matches. Andy sought me out afterward to let me know he wasn't pleased. He suggested that people listened to what I said and took it to the bank—and to Andy, who would then have to address the criticism. That's how controversies are created, and how dissension can develop and, with the enthusiastic participation of the media, put strains even on a harmonious group.

"I understand," I told Andy, "but I've got to be honest."

We agreed to disagree, but after the conversation the truth—and implications—of what he said sank in. I decided to play my cards a little closer to the vest from that point on. I've worked out pretty basic guidelines for how I handle situations when guys I coach, either as Davis Cup captain or as the head of the USTA player development program, are my subjects on the air. I talk about what I see happening on the court, and leave it at that. I'm also careful not to divulge any sensitive information that comes to me confidentially in my other activities. And I refrain from making the broadcast chair my bully pulpit.

There It Is, the Bender!

My first turn in the broadcast booth was during a US Open in the mid-1990s, when the USA network had all but the prime weekend broadcasting rights to the tournament. The late Vitas Gerulaitis, a friend of the family, was one of USA's talking heads, and he invited me on to comment on one of John's matches. I joined Vitas and Ted Robinson for a set. At one point, one of them asked me about John's hands—he had an extremely good "feel" for the ball. I said something to the effect that he had "hands of gold," and that went over big with the producer. Moreover, I felt relaxed and natural. From then on, TV guys kept an eye on me as a potential broadcaster.

It was a logical thing for me to dabble in, because I was comfortable with the press and had a pretty good understanding of its workings. Being John's brother was great preparation, because ever since the age of twelve, the media guys often went after me; I was a natural story for them. John sometimes likes to give me crap about following him in everything he does, but I always remind him that I preceded him to the broadcast booth.

In the mid-1990s, the growing cable-television industry always needed content, so stations would send a guy to tennis events to provide a few days of coverage. If I happened to be playing a tournament, the Eurosport network sometimes asked if I'd join Bill Threlfall in the booth, which I was happy to do. He was well-mannered, very intelligent, blessed with a dry wit, and simultaneously kind and witheringly critical. He blew me away; I felt like a kid, wet behind the ears. The players all loved the guy, so the bar was set pretty high for me.

I got my real start, though, at the Key Biscayne tournament in 1996, working for ESPN. The budding network at that point had Cliff Drysdale and Fred Stolle, both highly accomplished former players. But Cliff, who's from South Africa, and Fred, an Aussie, were already middle-aged guys with accents. A whole new generation of tennis fans didn't know much about them. Although the ESPN folks never said anything to me about it, I think they were looking for some new, young blood—preferably without the exotic accent, to strike a greater balance. One accent per booth was enough for them.

I had shoulder surgery that pretty much killed my year (and career) soon after that Key Biscayne tournament, and ESPN hired me to work the Rome tournament. I was to be their main "color" guy for the week. That meant I was supposed to bring special insight into the game or the players when I was in the booth (as opposed to the play-by-play guy, who just describes the action), and do some inventive, colorful things outside of it. I worked with Joel Myers, who's gone on to be (among other things) the play-by-play man for the NBA's Los Angeles Lakers.

I wanted to impress the higher-ups, so I did all that crap a color guy is supposed to do. I waded into a crush of fans waiting for the gates to open and hammed it up, with a faux Italian accent, as I interviewed people. I did the obligatory pizza, prosciutto, and espresso stories—stuff like that.

For the matches, we sat in this tiny booth surrounded by those massive marble statues for which the Foro Italico (the site of the tournament) is famous, and Joel would sit there, showing a remarkable ability to call the match while holding a pair of binoculars and scanning the crowd, smitten and amused by the stylish and glamorous fans all around the ancient stadium. There I was, at my first real broadcasting gig, all gung ho and nervous, with all my notes and reminders, and Joel would be calling the matches with his field glasses in one hand, scouting talent of a different kind.

Joel christened the wide, slice serve "the bender." One moment he was on the mic, shouting, "There it is, the bender!" and the next he was on his field glasses again. One day Joel told me, "You're good at this, Pat. Just stick around the booth, you don't have to do all that shit, walking around in the crowd or interviewing the gelato vendors." When we went off the air, Joel and I would go out to the fan area and sit there on a grassy spot under a big old cypress tree with a piece of pizza and a glass of wine. Joel would just sit back, forgetting even his binoculars, and take it all in. At some point, he always said, "Is this great, or what?"

Off to a good start, I was soon working quite a bit with Cliff and Fred. I quickly became the official "courtside" guy, conducting quick interviews during matches with coaches, or giving my impressions from court level. I was content, and respectful toward Cliff and Fred. I knew my place and I had a sense that if I just bided my time, everything would work out. Besides, I hadn't fully retired. I still tried to play now and then, singles or doubles or both, and ESPN was very understanding about it. They were bringing me along.

Over time, the situation between the network and Fred Stolle deteriorated. They were clearly shunting him aside. I felt bad because Fred's a great guy and he always treated me really well. The handwriting was on the wall, though, and it didn't end very well. ESPN began to cut Fred loose. We sensed that it wasn't going to end well, and wished the situation could be handled more delicately. It's tough in TV that way, though: you almost never get a chance to say good-bye on your own terms.

With Fred gone, Cliff and I became regular road warriors for a number of years. We covered all the summer hardcourt events. We did Indianapolis or Washington, D.C., and went straight into a seventeen-day run, starting in Canada. The morning after the Toronto or Montreal final we flew straight to Cincinnati, followed by New Haven, Connecticut, and the US Open. Most days, we were on the air from 1:00 to 5:00 p.m., took a two-hour break to eat, and returned to the booth for the evening shift, seven to ten in the evening. As you can imagine, Cliff and I got to know each other pretty well.

One year at the Miami/Key Biscayne Masters tournament, I got in the elevator just a few minutes before we were to go on the air, knowing that Cliff was already in the booth, getting ready for his play-by-play role. Mary Jo Fernandez, our fellow ESPN commentator, was with me. The elevator started to crawl up (Miami has the slowest elevator of any tournament), then it just locked up. Stuck. Mary Jo and I were captive with a bunch of fans, it was sweltering, and the seconds ticked toward air time.

I called Cliff on my cell phone and told him what happened. He started to broadcast solo, and he still likes to tell people it was the best show we ever did. That was classic Cliff. He was a mentor at the start, but the relationship quickly evolved into one of equals, despite our age difference of twenty-plus years. Cliff was very relaxed; we had a ball. He used to say, "I've never had this much fun. This is great. We just talk—we're just two guys talking tennis."

I joined the CBS US Open team in 1995, replacing Vitas Gerulaitis, who died in a freak accident in a friend's pool house right after the 1994 US Open. Over the years, I worked for the studio show that would set the table for the day, run features, and wrap up the day's action with a late-night report.

In my time, the show was hosted by Pat O'Brien, Rich Eisen, Michelle Tafoya, Bobby Bernstein, Andrea Joyce, and Mary Carillo. But CBS never gave me a shot at the host slot. In 2006, they began to scale back the studio time, and pretty soon there was no studio at all. So Bill McAtee (who was in the same boat) and I would be stranded out on the grandstand, twiddling our thumbs and watching a match—just in case things didn't go as planned at Arthur Ashe Stadium and the producers decided to throw us on the air. By 2008 I was sick of going nowhere with the network and I quit. They had no real commitment to tennis anyway; they were just interested in the US Open as a broadcast commodity.

ESPN started taking tennis more seriously in the past decade, recognizing the value of a truly international game, as well as the prestige value of its top events. NBC and CBS, two giants of traditional television, would continue to do weekend broadcasts at three of the majors (they left the Australian Open entirely to us), but ESPN gradually locked down the rights to everything that NBC and CBS disdained—almost the entire first week of play, and a good portion of the second, at those other three majors (although Tennis Channel is the primary rights holder at the French Open).

ESPN has become the Grand Slam network, although the financial commitment required also led ESPN to cut out the kind of week-in, week-out coverage that Cliff and I once provided. It's all part of the drift in recent years to bigness, and smaller tournaments have paid a heavy price. The ATP has been a culprit in this, too. One guy who learned that the hard way was the innovative promoter Jim Westhall, who took what started as a small, four-man, all-Aussie exhibition at bucolic Bretton Woods, New Hampshire, and turned it into the Volvo International (at nearby North Conway), which at one time was dubbed the "Wimbledon of the Woods."

That was a great tournament that drew from a huge regional base in New England (much like the NFL's New England Patriots). But the increasing pay-to-play policies of the ATP made the economics difficult for Westhall. He realized he had to have separate night sessions if he were to sell enough tickets to meet the ATP's various fees and prize money demands. A combination of circumstances, including local resistance to after-dark noise and traffic, forced Westhall to find a new home at Stratton Mountain, Vermont. And from there, he eventually migrated to New Haven, Connecticut, in an attempt to establish his event as a major US Open tune-up. The event lost its charming identity, and over time his tournament simply went under.

Westhall may have tried to grow too big, but the ATP also forced him to think in those terms. Variations of his story have been told numerous times, although I'll be the first to admit that market forces are still the best drivers of the game. The advent of Tennis Channel, which broadcasts numerous smaller events, has provided the smaller tournaments with some relief. I especially appreciate this development, because it's important to have some kind of continuity between the majors, and the diversity of tournament locations and surfaces is part of our game's appeal.

Davis Cup took our broadcasting team to some strange places, thanks to the choice-of-ground rule. The most bizarre of them all was the first-round tie the U.S. played against Brazil in 1997, at a small club in the resort town of Ribeirão Preto. It was a perfect setup for a Davis Cup ambush. Brazil's Gustavo Kuerten was on the cusp of greatness (he would win the French Open for the first of three times just months later), and their no. 2, Fernando Meligini, was a solid tour player, especially good on clay.

The U.S. team was led by Jim Courier; Mal Washington was the other singles player, with Richey Reneberg and Alex O'Brien on the doubles team. Our visiting team ESPN crew consisted of just three people: Cliff, producer Steve Mayer, and me. The U.S. team traveled to the remote resort town by private plane. We had to drive from the airport in São Paulo. It was a five-hour trip over horrible roads in a beat-up van. On the whole, flying first-class as Davis Cup captain is preferable.

We finally got on site on Thursday, the day they made the draw. We checked out the towering broadcast booth. It had been built two days before, and if you put your hand on the framework the whole thing shook. A rope ladder would have been more fitting than the shaky stairs that led us up to the small space where we'd have to call the matches—standing up. If we sat down, we couldn't see the court.

Things were shaky in more ways than one. Mal had the temerity to go up two sets to one on Kuerten, and the vocal Brazilian fans taunted him mercilessly. They hurled the "N" word and other racial insults, which was weird because Brazil is known for its diversity and embrace of mixed races. At one point, a small plane buzzed the stadium; it flew so close to the ground that as it approached, Cliff and I turned to each other, looking horrified, and we both actually ducked to avoid being hit.

The equipment we rented was so dated that Mayer had to station himself in the booth with us, and work this old-fashioned sound level mixing board right there. Mal produced a gutsy performance, though, winning in four tough sets, including two tiebreakers. Courier, our no. 1, had a tougher time of it against Fernando Meligini. Midway through the match, somebody pulled the plug—literally—on our broadcast. Everything in the booth and our lone, small, production truck went dark.

Mayer went nuts; what the hell is going on? Apparently, the promoters had willfully or accidentally sold the "exclusive" rights to a Brazilian station as well as ESPN, but somehow we ended up on televison in Brazil (something we didn't care about). Someone on their team decided to do something about it, and the result was chaos. Eventually we negotiated our way back onto the airwaves, but not in Brazil, which was just fine by us.

Meanwhile, Courier was struggling in the oppressive heat and humidity. This was a guy who, in his time on the tour, set a new standard for fitness and hard work. Jim would often win a match, even in a major, and then go for a long run. In fact, Jim was so fit that he burned out a little faster and earlier than anyone expected.

I know how hard Jim worked. I was a doubles player in a tie hosted by India in 1994, when Jim was still near the peak of his career. We beat India on grass, in awful heat and humidity. After Richey Reneberg and I won the doubles to lock up the sweep, we all breathed a sigh of relief; we were going to celebrate, maybe come out the next morning to hit for twenty minutes and then play the dead rubbers.

Not Jim. After we clinched it, Courier took our two practice guys out and he made them drill with him, doing two-on-ones for two full hours. And this is in stifling heat, on grass, even though Jim's next tournament would be on clay. That was Jim's mentality, and he's the first to admit that his appetite for work hurt him, longevitywise. He trained until he hit the wall, and he eventually lost the desire to go out and kill himself to stay in the hunt near the top.

At his peak Jim never stopped to smell the roses and take some downtime. He felt that if he let up, he'd lose that edge. But his philosophy sure paid off in the short term, and it made him remarkably tough. He was different from everyone else. He was a monster. Jim entered the top 10 in the spring of 1991, and won his four majors (two each at the Australian and French Opens) in the span of just over one year. He spent 58 weeks at no. 1, but by the fall of 1994 he was out of the top 10, although he continued to win a tournament now and then for a few years after that.

Jim was still a warrior during that tie against Brazil; he sucked it up and beat Meligini in five grueling sets in the tropical heat, and had to take IV fluids to rehydrate when he collapsed in a heap right after the match.

Brazil won the doubles, so the tie was still live on Sunday. Like an idiot, I decided to wear a nice blue shirt to work. Within minutes of arriving on site and just as I was about to go on air, I started to get those black sweat stains on my shirt. I put on my jacket, tugged it this way and that, but it was no use; I couldn't disguise the stains. Mayer told me he could still plainly see them on camera.

Suddenly, I had a brainstorm. I asked for a bottle of water. I took my jacket off, unscrewed the cap, and dumped the water all down the front of my shirt. Now the whole shirt was dark. Problem solved.

Courier recovered sufficiently to take out Kuerten in four close sets to clinch the tie for the U.S. Problem solved.

Roger and Me

Knowing that James Blake is a good guy and a gentleman, I welcomed that opportunity to hit with Federer in Cincinnati in 2007. The guy needed a hand and who's going to turn down a living legend—and great guy? I grew up hitting with my brother John and his cohorts. I practiced often with Andre Agassi and Jim Courier. I knew the kind of ball Pete Sampras hit. I often hit with our Davis Cup team members. But Roger Federer in 2007 was playing a brand of tennis rarely, if ever, seen before.

I was eager to "feel" what his shots were like. It may be hard for a spectator to tell, but every player's game is like a fingerprint; no two are exactly alike. I wanted to touch his genius, even if it was at racket's length. Roger was at the peak of his powers at the time, and intensely focused on his mission to break Pete Sampras's Grand Slam singles title record.

On match days, pros like to prepare with a light hit just to get the blood flowing, and to get a sense for how they're feeling the ball. But every player is different; Jimmy Connors went at it with brio in a fast, furious warm-up to whet his appetite, abruptly cutting off the workout while he was still hungry for more. Others, like Pete Sampras, preferred to go easy, more or less limbering up like they just got out of bed and want to stretch out. The funny thing is that your warm-up isn't a reliable predictor for how you'll play two, three hours later. You just never know what's going to happen when that chair umpire finally says, "Linesmen, ready? Players, ready? Play."

I arrived at the Player Reception Center in Cincy before Roger. When he showed up, he was alone, carrying two rackets. We exchanged pleasantries and he went over to the sign-in desk and asked for a couple of cans of balls. We went out this little tunnel, heading for the court, making small talk. No minders to protect him, no lackeys to fetch the balls, no adviser to whisper in his ear about other obligations. Roger asked about my broadcasting and Davis Cup duties with sincere interest.

Finally, the security guards seemed to realize that Roger Federer was out there on the grounds, walking around like any other mortal on this finals day. They ran after us. By that time, the savvy fans who show up early, hoping for just such an opportunity, were clustered around us. Roger signed a few autographs as we walked, moving the scrum. He was utterly at ease, chatting with the fans.

When it comes to his workouts, Roger is in that casual Sampras mold; the thing that struck me about the way he hit was his ease. He expended minimal energy; when I put a ball into play he'd roll to it, the ball would disappear into his racket face, and then it would come flying back. He doesn't hit a particularly heavy ball, like a Rafael Nadal. But the ball always seemed to come off the bounce faster than I expected, and the action on it reminded me of that first good look I'd had at Roger, back in my first Davis Cup tie as captain. He works the ball; it's like the thing has different properties every time he addresses it. One moment, it's shaped like an egg, from topspin; the next, it's got so much backspin that you can almost hear it purring.

What I felt, mostly, was his control; the ball seemed to follow a different command with each shot, like a well-trained dog. Roger's pace was impressive, but by no means overwhelming. But I still had to hustle because he uses so much of the court. It felt like my side of the court was twice the size of his; he found so many places to put the ball. Keeping the ball deep is standard operating procedure on the tour, but that reduces the amount of court in play. With his gift for using all the available space, including the short angles, Roger is like a guy playing three-dimensional chess while everyone else is still playing the regular way.

Roger has successfully married an old-school mentality—an

all-court game, the willingness to use slice, a visible degree of self-control and modulation—with the advantages of modern equipment (he uses a blend of Luxilon polyester strings and the much more elastic, old-school gut). You know he's grooved when he's cracking those one-handed backhand topspin shots down the line, but most of the time, his backhand serves other purposes, mainly setting up his forehand. And once during our warm-up, Roger hit a shot he pulls off pretty often, but I've never seen anyone else use.

He took a short ball (around the service line on his side) on the forehand side, got under it, and ripped it crosscourt with heavy top, landing the ball inside the service line on my side—but so close to the sideline that I had no chance to do anything with it. It just flew by, a winner. It was a little like the experience of walking toward someone in a narrow corridor and the next thing you know, he's gone by you and you never bumped shoulders.

Roger doesn't have an overpowering serve, although he regularly clocks in that respectable 115 to 125 mph category. He doesn't look to hit aces even though only two men—Ivo Karlović and Joachim Johansson—have hit more in one match than the 50 he blasted in the 2009 Wimbledon Final. But Roger often uses his serve to set up a killing follow-up, or to take command of a rally. Likewise, Federer isn't heralded for his return. Yet he's very difficult to ace. And instead of gambling on a return winner, he's content to make a return that eliminates the server's advantage. Once the playing field is level, who's going to match him, stroke for stroke?

Roger hit a few low backhand slices down the line, to my forehand. I wasn't about to try to put any of them away with a crosscourt winner, not in a warm-up. But I recognized it as a shot he used often, and understood how the shot was a dare. Under match conditions, I would almost have to try for a big forehand—opening up the court for Roger to retaliate with his big forehand down-the-line. It's a trick straight out of the Pete Sampras playbook.

When your opponent can determine what kind of shot you must hit in order to remain reasonably aggressive (and you'll never survive Federer if you aren't), that's pressure. And it forces you to try to beat him to the punch, which is like the strategy the Polish cavalry tried when they attacked German tanks on horseback at the start of World War II. You may look gallant doing it, but it doesn't usually end well. Still, what choice do you have, if you have just a horse, and he's got a tank?

After hitting with Roger, I also had a better understanding of why the guys capable of giving him the most trouble are leftys, or guys with special powers on the (right-hander's) backhand side, like David Nalbandian or Marat Safin. They're capable of dealing with his cross-court backhand, as well as the powerful forehand down-the-line.

Even though our hit was a mere warm-up for Roger's match, it left me with a firsthand impression of how hard you have to work to beat the guy. He moves you around the court as effectively as an Agassi, only it doesn't look that way because he doesn't really make you run sideline-to-sideline sprints. He jerks you around, pulling you up and pushing you back and stretching you this way and that, always finding places to put the ball where you're least comfortable hitting it.

After I showered and settled into the broadcast booth to call the match, I had time to reflect on just how tough a task James Blake faced that afternoon.

The Palace of the Deluded

If you didn't know better, you might assume that Roger Federer is the most well-coached player on the tour. Ironically, he's one of the very few top players who's rarely traveled with a coach. Peter Carter, an Australian, did more for Federer's game than anyone. (Roger himself has said that while Carter wasn't his only coach, he was his "real" coach.) Carter died in a tragic car crash in Africa while on holiday; a year later, Roger won his first major, Wimbledon, and cried afterward, remembering Carter. People pretty much forgot all that in the ensuing years, as Roger rewrote the tennis record books. But maybe losing Carter at such a tender age (Roger was twenty) kept him from ever wanting to rely heavily on a coach again.

Roger has worked with Jose Higueras and Tony Roche; Severin Luthi, the Swiss Davis Cup captain, helps him out, and Roger has a somewhat mysterious fitness trainer, the dramatically named Pierre Paganinni as well as a Swiss banker friend who seems to have played some sort of coaching role. Among them, Roche lasted the longest as a serious influence and day-to-day presence, but the aging Aussie veteran was so loath to travel the tour with Roger that the relationship became a bit of a farce. Roger didn't need a coach who couldn't be bothered making the trip to New York for the U.S. Open, or to Roger's adopted home of Dubai.

As a matter of fact, Roger Federer didn't need a coach, period. He proved that conclusively in the summer of 2009, at just the moment when the off-and-on-again "Roger Needs a Coach!" movement reached fever pitch. I have to confess to being part of that chorus. At the time, Roger had gone seven months without a title; even the blind loyalists were beginning to question his stubborn independence. Roger invited my colleague Darren Cahill to Dubai for a consultation and a few days of training, but nothing came of it. Just when it looked as if Roger might be guilty of hubris, he won the French Open and Wimbledon back-to-back. So much for the theory that Roger needed a full-time coach.

Coaching tennis is an opaque enterprise, a game in which passionate, dedicated, principled students of the game operate side by side with dreamers and schemers of every kind, including parents who barely rise above the description charlatan. It's hardly surprising that tennis players themselves aren't always the most grounded individuals. Nothing in their life experience of athletes demands that of them. Tennis can be a palace for the deluded.

In tennis, you don't need anyone else to survive. You can be the biggest prick, or a sorry misfit, and if you've got game, everyone can just shut his pie hole. It's hard to get away with anything like that in team sports, where you need to function in a social context. You screw around too much, you get kicked off the team. Or the coach will lose faith in you. At some stage, even a Michael Jordan or a Drew Brees, as a college freshman, had to find a way to fit into the fabric of his team. Not in tennis, and it's a real problem, sociologically.

Many of the guys I came up with in the pros, including Richey Reneberg, have become successful later in life; some who showed promise but failed painfully as pros have done extremely well in the "real world" they probably never thought they'd have to inhabit. Tommy Ho, once a dazzlingly successful junior, was a washout as a pro—seemingly a real cautionary tale. Today, he's a hard-charging executive with Korn/Ferry International, an elite head-hunting firm, and he's a USTA director at large.

In my role as head of USTA player development, I run into dozens of guys who were good players, even name players; a number of them were so talented it could take your breath away. And now they're working at clubs, feeding balls to little kids, looking for a way to get back into the action. Some of them are now living with their parents. They hit me up for jobs, and it hurts a little to say no to them. I played alongside some of these guys, and had fun times with them. Some stayed at my home, or I at theirs, as juniors. It probably pains them at some level to call me, always on some awkward pretense, just to ask for a job.

So many of these guys have managed to remain clueless about how the world works, but still hope they'll make a big score someday. One journeyman player of my era came to me recently and, despite having a very thin résumé as a coach, brazenly told me all about his needs (never mind ours) and asked for an annual salary of $250,000—over twice the amount most of my coaches in the field make.

And famous coaches can be just as unrealistic, for roughly the same reason—because they can get away with it. If you're an NBA or NFL coach, you still have to answer to your boss, the team general manager or owner. There's still someone else signing your checks, and you're working within a system. But you don't really have to live within the tennis system to make it in tennis. If you're tough and determined and stubborn enough, you can make it on your own terms—if you're lucky enough to find that one gifted kid to whom you can hitch your wagon. Sometimes, that kid is your own offspring.

The better the player, the fewer coaches he or she is likely to have had in a career. When a player is winning, big, and in a comfort zone with his coach, there's not much reason to change until the relationship goes stale, or the player hits a bad patch. It may not be the coach's fault, but he's the one who gets thrown under the bus as the player tries to reinvent himself. When a top player changes coaches, it's often a warning shot fired across the bow of his rivals. *Watch out, I'm making changes and on the move.*

The very top players have had just a couple of coaches associated with their glory days: Andre Agassi had Nick Bollettieri, Brad Gilbert, and Darren Cahill. Pete Sampras had Tim Gullikson and Paul Annacone. Jim Courier had Jose Higueras and Brad Stine. Björn Borg had Lennart Bergelin, and Stefan Edberg had Tony Pickard . . . and so on.

Tennis coaches can be divided into, roughly, two categories: developmental and elite-player coaches. The developmental coaches do the grunt work of shaping a young player's game. Robert Lansdorp's fingerprints are all over a number of champions, from Tracy Austin, Pete Sampras, Eliot Teltscher, and Lindsay Davenport to Maria Sharapova. Yet he never took a successful step up to the next level, coaching a pro on a day-to-day basis.

Sampras was an interesting case, because he was developed in committee, with his father, Sam, very quietly overseeing the process. The guy who decided that Pete should learn his forehand from Lansdorp, and his footwork from Del Canty, and various other parts of his game from different individuals, was Pete Fischer. He was like the general contractor for a guy who builds a house. Sampras parted ways with Fischer not long after he won his first major. Sometimes, you need a certain kind of person to take you to a given point, and then you have to move on as your needs change—or conflicts emerge, as they did in Pete's relationship with Fischer, who tried to cash in when Pete catapulted to fame as a (barely) 19-year-old at the US Open in 1990. In addition to taking a healthy cut of Pete's tournament winnings, Fischer wanted Sampras to buy him a car. (It was a Ferrari; Fischer can't be accused of thinking small.) He wrote his demands down on a paper plate while making one of his routine supper visits to the Sampras household.

Like literally hundreds of other coaches, Fischer had more or less volunteered his services, trusting that he'd be taken care of—if and when Pete made it big. When that day came, according to Sampras, Fischer freaked out and got greedy. They never trusted him again.

Coaches are notorious for failing to formalize their relationships with players and then getting screwed, but in some ways it's their own fault. They fall in love with these kids, because they worship talent. They fall all over themselves to ingratiate themselves with a talented prospect's parents, and the parents often shrug when offered free help and think, *Why not?* Plus, the parents often think their kids are god's gift, so why shouldn't a coach feel honored just to be associated with him?

The better-known developmental coaches include guys like Rick Macci, who helped shape the games of the Williams sisters (without ever getting appropriate credit), and Nick Bollettieri—although Nick also enjoyed success as a pro tour coach, and even worked with some players he had no hand in developing, like Boris Becker. These developmental coaches—and there are almost as many out there as there are players—are talent finders and game shapers; the elite-player coaches are the champion makers.

The champion makers include familiar names like Brad Gilbert (coach of Andre Agassi and the two Andys, Murray and Roddick), Larry Stefanki (John McEnroe, Yevgeny Kafelnikov, Fernando Gonzalez, Roddick), Paul Annacone (Pete Sampras and Tim Henman),

Ion Tiriac (Ilie Năstase, Guillermo Vilas, Boris Becker, Henri Leconte, Goran Ivanisevic), and Bob Brett (Andrés Gómez, Boris Becker, Goran Ivanisevic, and Marin Čilić). Then there's the host of parents whose MOs are mysterious (although "nonexistent" may be a better word), and whose success is so deeply rooted in their complex emotional relations with their kids that you can't make heads or tails of it. I know for sure that some of them know nothing about tennis and succeed in spite of it because they've made some sort of Faustian bargain with their kids.

The number of great players who insist that one or another parent is his or her only "true" coach, while everyone knows they owe their games, if not their success, to others, is staggering. And they're mostly women. Girls like to please their daddies, right? Venus and Serena Williams (Macci), Maria Sharapova (Lansdorp and Bollettieri), Monica Seles (Bollettieri), and Jennifer Capriati all gave their parents almost exclusive credit.

Sometimes, families take that tack in order to protect themselves from financial claims after they've achieved success. Sometimes, a parent wants to justify his parasitic existence, and enjoys all the perks that go with coaching, including face time on television. But they don't fool anyone. I've seen male players and coaches laughing out loud as they've watched one or another top female star being "coached" by her dad on a practice court at Wimbledon—years after some poor schmo shaped the girl's game. But you know what? Winning justifies everything. You win, and you can laugh in the face of the world and all its opinions and prejudices.

By the time an elite-player coach gets into the picture, a player's game is very close to fully formed. That doesn't mean the coach can't find things to nitpick, improve, or correct—the best ones do that. And top coaches can have a profound impact in the areas of tactics and strategy. Pete Sampras struggled mightily against lefthanders early in his career, but when Tim Gullickson convinced him to take a few steps over toward his backhand side when he was receiving, tempting the server to try to slip the ball by his forehand (and allowing him to hit a more solid backhand), Pete won his next 13 straight matches with leftys.

An elite coach is mostly a manager of the player's psyche, a sounding board, and—perhaps most important—a scout. It's pure gold when a guy as observant as Paul Annacone can go back to Sampras and tell him that so-and-so uses his kicker to set up his forehand rally shot; get to his backhand with the return and the guy doesn't know what to do.

Like many other enterprises, coaching isn't rocket science; it's mostly about observation, the ability to pick up habits and tendencies (in your own guy, as well as his opponents), and knowing what to say to your player, and when to say it. For example, the better the player, the less likely it is that he responds to blunt, direct suggestions. Coaches operate on the horse-to-water model; you can't make him drink, but you can lead him to the spring. A top coach often gets his player to implement an idea by figuring out how to plant it in his mind. Then he sits back, lets it take root, and eventually the player, convinced it's his idea, will try it.

Players a few links down the food chain, like I was, often work with a variety of people for all kinds of reasons starting with economics. You run out of money, you stop paying for coaching. You find a way to make some more, and you hire one again. Besides, there's only so much a coach can do for a player who's no threat to set the game on fire. It doesn't take long for a coach to download 90 percent of his most valuable insight; after that, it's fine-tuning and a quality-of-relationship issue. For a top player, a little improvement translates to a huge gain in income; for a journeyman or middle-of-the-pack player, getting a little better doesn't carry nearly the same reward.

The motivation to continue a coaching relationship is fueled by a player's degree of success, although sometimes a player and coach stick together simply out of mutual respect, trust, and friendship. It's lonely on the pro-tour trail; having someone along to share the ride is a pleasure. But unless you form a tight bond or continue to build on your success, you will inevitably want to move on, try something different. And the coach will be looking for a different and, hopefully, better player.

After Tony Palafox put the finishing touch on my game, my first real coach was an old friend from the Port Washington Tennis Academy, a guy who had also helped John and Peter Fleming, Carlos Goffi. Carlos really believed in me as a kid, and he had a knack for firing me up. He left Port Washington and, hooking up with Nike, set up a bunch of tennis camps in Florida. I trained with him off and on down there; he was very into doing drills, particularly up-and-back ones, baseline to net. We worked hard, so when I decided to try making it as a singles player, I asked him to come along as my coach.

The old axiom says that a coach gets too much credit when a team wins, and too much blame when it loses. That's not entirely true in tennis; too much of the game is on the player's shoulders. Poor execution often means that even if your coach comes up with a brilliant plan, you're nowhere if you can't execute it.

Carlos, like Nick Bollettieri, was an outstanding motivator. He was big on being tough, he even wrote a book, *Tournament Tough*. But when we formed a formal partnership I was pretty mature, and looking less for motivation—I had plenty of that—than for concrete, game-based advice and suggestions. We never got much traction as a team, because Carlos's whole thing was, *You gotta tough them out, man. Show them who you are. You gotta be tough*. That only went so far. I quickly got to the point where I was thinking, *Enough already*. Tell me something I don't know.

It didn't take that long for the tensions to develop. I wasn't slashing my way through draws; I was thinking, *Shit, am I ever going to make it?* Beyond that, I wasn't really fit. Carlos knew that and it accounted for the way he tried to get me to play a more aggressive attacking style. And at one of these qualifying or Challenger-level tournaments, I remember glancing over to where Carlos was sitting and feeling the pressure. I was paying his way, but I wasn't making any money; worse yet, I was struggling in the qualifying rounds. So I blamed it on him, because when you're a tennis player, that's what you do. I finally told him, "Look you're really freaking me out, I think you should go back home."

No sooner did he leave than I took advantage of a wild card and got to the semifinals at the Copenhagen Challenger, where I lost a tough three-setter to Marc Rosset, who would go on to win a singles-gold medal at the Barcelona Olympic Games. I'm convinced I did well in that period because suddenly I felt liberated. I had no one to answer to but myself, and no one to support. And I could justify cutting Carlos loose because I did better on my own. In certain ways, I suppose I was already tournament tough enough.

My next coach, and first tour-level one, was Larry Stefanki, who's gone on to become one of the top elite coaches of this era. I often bring this up when we're talking about Larry on the air, and my booth mates invariably say, "Yeah, and then he went on to coach your brother John, right, Patrick?"

I turn the conversation back, "Yeah, but he coached *me* first. It didn't take much to coach John, but you know he's a good coach because he got me to win some matches."

I'm only half-joking about that. I was one of Larry's first forays into coaching, back in 1993. He signed on to work with me and my doubles partner of the time, Jonathan Stark. We were in no position to hire private coaches, but splitting the expense of one made sense, since we played doubles together. The experiment went so-so, because Jon and I had two totally different games, which meant that Larry had to throw switches in his head from hour to hour, depending on the player in need.

We called Jon "Starky" or, often, "Wild Thing." He was a big, tall, blond-haired stud from Oregon, a real lumberjack. He had a huge serve and a horrible game. His game plan was to rely on his big serve and then try to bluff has way in to the net. His technique was terrible, but he was a good athlete. The combination of big serve and outstanding athleticism can take you pretty far.

Given that my own game was based on good returns, counter punching, and moving the ball around, we made a good team. And for all the complexities of coaching two wildly different guys, Larry did a great job. He knew his Xs and Os, and he was a great motivator.

The number one thing about coaching is that you really have to be passionate, you've got to love doing it. Otherwise, you won't have the patience, or the desire to always put your player first. You'll be tempted to hold back what you're really thinking, especially if it's critical. It isn't easy to dress down the guy who's signing your weekly check.

What I liked about Larry was that there was no bullshit about him—he was an absolute straight shooter. Maybe I was more responsive to that tack than others, but I liked the way he just looked you in the eye, told you what you needed to do on a daily basis, and what you needed to do to get better. He was realistic, let the chips fall where they may. A good coach must be a good communicator, although there are different ways to accomplish that; some players like to take their medicine straight, others prefer it diluted.

Eventually, Larry and I ended up kind of coaching Starky together, because Jon and I would watch each other's matches. Starky might be out there, battling out a tough match, and I'd say to Larry: "Why is Starky staying back? He can't fucking rally."

Larry would roll his eyes and mutter, "I know."

Starky had a two-handed backhand as well as a wristy one-hander. We tried to get him to chip and charge a lot more, but the wristy backhand prevented him from hitting an adequately penetrating, firm ball. The experiment was a failure, but we tried.

Larry's never confused coaching with babysitting, or being buddy-buddy with his player, which is another thing I like about him. When practice was over in the afternoon, he would go off and do his own thing, saying little more than, "See you at practice tomorrow at ten."

A lot of these guys, they need to spend every minute with their coach. I saw that in Andy Roddick earlier in his career. He needed to be glued to his coach, whether it was his first coach as a pro, Tarik Benhabiles, or Brad Gilbert, or Jimmy Connors. A relationship like that quickly becomes like a marriage, but worse, because it takes place in the workplace. You start with the coach up on a pedestal, and if you're not careful pretty soon you're irritated by the way he eats his cereal, or you don't like the way he's always talking about baseball, or the financial markets. That kind of closeness makes it much easier to blame the coach when things aren't working out.

Larry was good at setting the appropriate bounds for a relationship, but in reality Starky and I were treading water, locked into a certain level of success we were destined never to surpass. Larry, though, was on a pretty fast track; he wanted to be a big-time coach, so it was inevitable that he would move on to greener pastures. We were stepping-stones, and we helped lead him to my brother John. And when Larry hooked up with John, Yevgeny Kafelnikov, and others, his methodology changed. Because of how lonely it is at the top, those big guns had greater need for a coach who was also like a best buddy.

Wiener Schnitzel, Wind Sprints, and Magic Bullets

The next guy I worked with in any meaningful sense was an Austrian protégé of Bob Brett, Gunther Bresnick. He'd worked with a lot of people, including Boris Becker. He was an interesting guy—a real character—and he was big on fitness. He asked me lots of questions, he wanted me to really think. He told me I should study

German and try to use my brain. I was like, *Why the fuck should I study German? How is that gonna help my tennis?*

What can I say, I was a tennis player.

I think my instincts in hiring Bresnick were good. He saw the physical, baseline-based game that was coming down the pike, which explained his interest in fitness. As far as the Xs and Os went, he basically wanted me to tee off on every shot—like some of the successful guys of today. That sounded crazy to me—we even joked around about it. I was more into finesse, working and setting up points. Just hit the crap out of the ball? I thought the guy was kidding. Actually, he was prescient.

The thing that originally made Gunther attractive to me was that focus on extra-technical stuff, especially running and agility. I knew that a relative lack of mobility was one of my liabilities. Gunther was into all these exercises that involved skipping, jumping, and rolling around on the ground—stuff I had never done. And he used to make me run a lot. I used to go for a half-hour run before practice; he kept a chart for all the different runs I would do. At Wimbledon, he would make me go running with him in Wimbledon Commons, the huge park that butts up against the village on top of the hill.

Gunther's approach to training was systematic and multifaceted. It was about how you prepared and train your whole body and mind for tennis. It made me wonder if I might have been a better player had I gone that route earlier, instead of focusing so heavily on stroke production or strategy. The closest thing I did to off-court training on any regular basis as a kid was being an obedient son when my dad said, "Hey, do you think you should go for a run?" I'd answer, "Sure." Then I'd go running through the streets of Douglaston. It was the same for John. Stretching, off-court training? We never did any of that.

The Europeans, I learned, were ahead of the Americans, and maybe that played a part in breaking the game wide open internationally. The American guys followed the Australian model. They'd just go out there and do two-on-one tennis drills and kill themselves. Or run a few 400-meter sprints and then collapse, gasping.

That was training. The Europeans looked beyond that; they started looking at the science, trying to see the big picture and the connections. How does using your brain interface with using your body? How can you help the muscles you use for tennis in ways that have nothing to do with tennis?

I also enjoyed having an Austrian coach for cultural reasons, even if it wasn't entirely about eating Wiener schnitzel and drinking good Austrian beer. I liked spending time in Europe, to me that was kind of cool. Gunther was based in Vienna, and at the time he was single. He lived with his mom, who was an old but very sweet lady. She would make us these huge breakfasts every day before we went out to train.

Some of my American buddies, like Richey Reneberg, thought this was kind of weird and gave me shit about having an Austrian coach. Richey would sometimes wryly ask me, "What are you doing with your forehand now? What's the stroke du jour?"

He had a point. Once I found a comfort zone with Gunther, I started tweaking things in my game. What the hell, the clock on my career was ticking (I was twenty-six); I hoped to wring out every ounce of my potential. I tinkered with my forehand incessantly—I'd try keeping my elbow up, to get a little more loop into my swing. I kept it down, to drive a flatter ball. It got to the point with my forehand where I was like Guillermo Vilas with his serve—every time you saw me, I hit it a different way without ever finding the magic bullet.

But I kept looking. Gunther made some progress, too. He made a few tweaks in my forehand that enabled me to get more stick on the ball—if I followed his prescription and just shut my eyes and teed off. He achieved the same things as today's polyester strings do, enabling me to have more control the harder I hit. For a while things were great.

One of the few times I questioned Gunther was when he took on another protégé, a fairly hopeless, left-handed German kid who was basically a terrible player. You could tell he would never amount to much. Gunther used to make this kid go on a long run, an hour or so, before he played, and after his matches. I watched this going on, silently, and started to put two and two together. He was using this guy as a guinea pig, testing out his training theories on him.

This kid wanted to be good; he went out and did anything Gunther asked—so much so that by the end of a typical training session, he'd be fried. One day, I couldn't take it anymore. I pulled Gunther aside and asked, "Why are you doing this? You're just using this fucking guy to test your theories, like some kind of mad scientist."

Gunther just smiled at me, saying nothing.

"Well, don't pull that shit on me," I warned him. "I'm not here to be a guinea pig. I think I can still go out and actually win a few matches."

After about a year, the magic wore off. I lost at Queens in 1994 to an unknown kid, Brent Larkham, 7–5, 6–1. Then Martin Damm put me out of Wimbledon in the first round, 6–2 in the fourth. It was official: I was playing like shit. I realized that part of it was that I had been working on all this stuff, all this technical stuff, on the practice court. My head was full of it. Most of it had to do with my two weaknesses, my serve and forehand. And it was all I could think about on the court, when the only thing on your mind then should be trying to win the match.

There is no magic bullet. I was learning that, quickly.

I felt low after that loss to Damm at Wimbledon, but when I saw Gunther he was emotionally tone deaf. He started right in with the questions: *So what did you do wrong? Why did your forehand let you down?* I finally got so pissed off that I snapped: "Why don't *you* tell me what you think I did wrong? You're the coach. Stop asking me questions. All I'm doing is thinking about this shit on the court, when I should be thinking about how to win."

Those were tough times. My chance to make a big move again in the rankings was diminishing. It was the beginning of the end for me and Gunther, and our relationship just petered out soon thereafter. I'd catch up with him again and have a laugh about old times after the wounds healed, and we later found ourselves battling it out as captains of our respective Davis Cup squads.

Dickie Herbst was my last coach. He was a great guy and a thoroughly professional coach. He was an American who operated before the tennis world was remade on a European model, so he was less into the big picture than things like patterns of play—how I could use my forehand, with the spin I needed to increase my margin for error, to set up my best shot, the backhand.

In some ways, Dickie merely articulated things I was trying to do already, albeit half-consciously, but when you actually understand what's happening and why, it's much easier to hone strategies. We worked a lot on things that could get me set up to hit a backhand from the middle of the court—when I was able to rip that shot, I could hurt a guy, but it was also a pretty safe shot because of my court position. Dickie liked the idea of taking the ball early and hitting it aggressively, without necessarily going for the outright winner. That could win you a lot of points; it might tease out an error, apply pressure, or set you up for a winning placement.

I was with Dickie when I had my best year, 1995. I won my first main tour title in Sydney, and finished no. 35 in the world, after reaching my career-high singles ranking of no. 28. My Grand Slam season ended with a strong quarterfinal showing in the tournament that means the most to me, the US Open.

I had high hopes for 1996, and I started well, winning a few matches on the Australian swing. But by then the chronic shoulder pain I'd been living with became unbearable. I couldn't see playing out the entire year in my condition, so I pulled the plug in March. If I had to undergo surgery, so be it. But coming off my best-ever US

Open, with my career entering its twilight, I wanted to be able to return for at least another go before I capitulated and put down the racket and reached for the headset.

The Ball Boy from Basel

Almost exactly a decade after I made that painful decision, I was wearing those headphones in Cincinnati after warming up Roger Federer, and calling a match that was a testament to how quickly the geopolitics of tennis had changed. Roger took one of America's brightest hopes, James Blake, and manhandled him. He gave James just five games in two sets in a command performance that he would repeat, at tournament after tournament, on surface after surface, in those heady months and years of his supremacy.

Immediately after the match, I conducted my first on-air, post-match interview with Roger. He slumped back in his courtside chair, relaxed and a little relieved. He slipped on the headphones, and I said, "Hi Roger, Patrick McEnroe here . . ."

Before I could comment on his outstanding performance or ask a question, he said, "Patrick. Do you remember playing the tournament in Basel (Federer's home town) in 1994?"

I said, "Sure."

Basel had been a highlight of my singles career; I'd reached the final there.

Roger grinned: "You know, I was a ball kid for you in that match."

I laughed. Why hadn't he told me that when we'd hit earlier in the day? I guess he was saving it, as a surprise. I said, "Well, I hope you were rooting for me."

"Well, that's why I didn't want to tell you before," Roger said. "I'm afraid I was for Wayne Ferreira [who beat me in that final], of course. He's a South African [as is Roger's mother, Lynette]."

This was a typical moment in contemporary tennis—an American from Queens, New York, chitchatting with a Swiss who probably took up the game instead of soccer because his mother was from tennis-mad South Africa. Tennis players and their camp followers comprise a coterie of international tennis nuts. National identities and borders mean less and less all the time. The once mighty American tennis empire has collapsed (although one of my jobs entails trying to restore it to its accustomed place), but globally the game is on fire—and getting better all the time.

I hope the fire keeps burning, but the flames shoot a little higher again at home.

THE US OPEN: THE CURSE OF THE McENROES

It's a mixed blessing to be from one of the four Grand Slam nations, especially if you also grew up, as I did, in the city where it's played. As a kid, you dream about doing well in the event, but it can be pretty daunting to go out on the stadium court, take a look around, and realize that countless pairs of eyes belong to people you know, or knew at some point. That girl you asked out in eighth grade, who said no. The guy who sold your dad life insurance. The kid who used to take your lunch money. That creates a kind of pressure that you simply don't feel when you're playing in a foreign land halfway around the world.

It's even worse for an American from New York, because among all the Grand Slams, the US Open is the least likely to produce a surprise matchup in the final. There's a lot of crap written about how the French Open calls for the most stamina, Wimbledon calls for the most mental toughness, the Australian Open calls for the most fitness. Those things come into play at *every* major, and in more or less equal degrees. The real keys to the different tournaments is surface.

Every male winner of the US Open was, or would become, the no. 1 player in the world (we'll see if the 2009 champ, Juan Martin del Potro, will continue the streak). No one comes out of nowhere, the way Albert Costa popped up to win at Roland Garros, or Tomas

Johannson won the Australian Open. Chris Lewis was a finalist at Wimbledon; Arnaud Clément made the Australian final, and Alberto Berasategui was just one of many unlikely French Open finalists. Those guys could all play, no doubt about it. But guys like that have rarely penetrated the final rounds in New York, and that's because of the surface. The US Open provides the truest test of all-around play.

Once the USTA adopted hard courts as the official surface at the Open (after a long history on grass and a brief flirtation with green Har-Tru clay, which is a little faster than the red *terre battue*), the playing field was leveled. You can't win the Open just being aggressive. You can't win it just by playing great defense and grinding. You may get the occasional surprise semifinalist, but almost every US Open finalist had won, or was destined to play, a final in at least one other major. Greg Rusedski, who lost the 1997 final to Pat Rafter, is one of the very few exceptions, but for a period there he was a legitimate top five player.

Although the surface speed at the US Open can change from year to year (it depends on the amount of sand they put into the cement and elastic paint on top of it), it's usually a relatively quick hard court. I always felt I had my best chance to do well on that surface, because it made my counter-punching game pretty effective, it helped my relatively weak serve, and gave my forehand a little more sting.

I played decently at the Open, too. I usually lost to quality guys like Jimmy Connors, Boris Becker, Michael Chang, or Thomas Muster. I lost to only three guys who weren't Grand Slam champions: Christo van Rensberg, Byron Black, and Richard Fromberg. Every one of those guys was considered more dangerous on fast courts than his ranking or reputation suggested.

Still, the home-court pressure was significant because the tournament was such a big deal in the McEnroe household. I had only one beef with it. While watching the final on the Sunday after Labor Day I often thought, *Wow, this is great but aw, crap . . . school starts tomorrow. . . .*

Our family tradition at the Open went all the way back to when my brother John was just fifteen, and played in the main draw of the doubles with his coach, Tony Palafox. As a youngster, back when the tournament was still played on grass at Forest Hills, I used to run from court to court, like a kid in a candy store.

When the tournament moved to its new home in Flushing Meadows, I cooked up a great scam. I really liked the Italian ices that were served on site, but at a buck-fifty a pop for a small cup, I couldn't afford too many of them. I found out that the owners of the concession monitored sales by how many cups were used. I figured out that if I bought an ice and then kept the cup, I could go back and have it refilled any number of times during the day—as long as I gave the ice cream guy a "tip." He pocketed the money, and I got my ice. By the end of a typical day at the Open, my paper cup would be a soggy, disintegrating mess, but my belly would be full of Italian ice.

Our home in Douglaston was on Manor Road. The informal, family entrance was at the back, through a lower-level garage where we had a Ping-Pong table set up. We would stage these tournaments, and it got so heated that we'd throw the paddles against the wall and then have to tape them up to continue playing. Countless times I remember my dad coming to the top of the stairs and hollering down, "Hey you kids, shut up down there!"

I vividly remember the day John came home from that controversial, terrible loss in the last round of qualifying to Zan Guerrey. We were all upstairs on the first floor. We heard the garage door open and John's footsteps on the stairs. He said nothing. He looked utterly devastated. No one else dared speak. The mood in the house the rest of that day was funereal.

I lost a comparable qualifying match myself, just weeks before I went off to college in 1985. For my money, one of the toughest matches to win in all of tennis is that last round of qualifying for a major. The guys in a Grand Slam final have already enjoyed an enormously successful two weeks; it's all gravy to them. Journeymen players good enough for direct entry at majors know they'll get a good draw here, a bad draw there. But the difference between winning and losing in that last round of qualifying is enormous. You walk off the court with nothing to show for all the work you did, including the matches you won to get to the last round. It all goes down the drain and you're left feeling like you're just one of the other 73 billion people who isn't playing at the US Open.

In 1985, I was in the final round against Lloyd Bourne, a guy who had been at Stanford with John. For some reason, John couldn't stand the guy. He showed up at the court to watch, maybe just to tick off Bourne. I gave it my all, but lost in gut-wrenching fashion, 7–6 in the third. John and I commiserated later; clearly, the McEnroes were cursed in the US Open qualifying events. (As a point of interest, John never had another chance to qualify after that Guerrey match, because he skyrocketed to stardom the following summer at Wimbledon.) I played the Open many times, but not once did I get in as a qualifier.

When we lived in our family compound in Cove Neck, I often drove John to Flushing Meadows to play his US Open matches. I'd warm him up on our private court, then we'd hop into his little Mercedes 450SL. It was the first car John ever bought, early in his career (he kept it for about twenty years). John would often fall asleep in the passenger seat minutes after starting on the 45-minute drive to the National Tennis Center. Here he was, sleeping like a baby, shortly before he'd have to go out and play a Lendl or Connors in the American slam.

In 1980, Jack Nicholson was a special US Open guest of John's. I sat with Jack during John's brutal battle with Connors in the semifinals. At the time, the player-guest box was right on the court, in the corner across from and to the left of the umpire's chair. John had also given a ticket to a relatively unknown actor pal named David Keith, who sat in the row right behind us.

David didn't know much about tennis etiquette, and he sometimes cheered or clapped at inappropriate times. Jimbo was not very pleased about that; he kept looking over, trying to stare down David.

At a crucial point in the match, David started applauding after a Connors error. Jimmy was on our end of the court, and he slowly walked all the way over from the other side, right toward us. He stopped a few feet from the box, and hawked up a real nasty lougie. He spit it right at us, just short of the box. He snarled at David, "Hey, why don't you pick that up?"

There was a brief moment of utter silence, whereupon Jack Nicholson, totally unruffled, drawled in that unmistakable voice of his: "Sure . . . *tomorrah*."

The memory of that painful five-set loss to Jimmy Connors in 1991, a devastating blow at the start of my career, remained with me through the years, and I hoped for a chance to atone for it. That finally happened at the US Open in 1995, when I found myself down by two sets to love in my third-round match with a solid Russian player who was no. 32 in the world, Alexander Volkov.

At that point in the match, I remember telling myself that I had to change my game—the same-old, same-old just wasn't working. Volkov played a similar game, clean and fairly flat, and he was just a little quicker and sharper than me that night. Dickie Herbst, my coach, had been in my ear about varying my game for some time, trying to convince me that I should show a few different looks, change things up and keep opponents guessing, even if it took me out of my comfort zone. It was time to put his advice to use. I started throwing in all kinds of junk shots, like soft slices and moonballs. I got Volkov out of his rhythm and ended up winning an exciting match in five sets in the cozy confines of that Grandstand Court.

I actually won many matches from two sets down in my career, but no one remembers them except me. This was one of the better ones.

I had Daniel Vacek next—a great draw in the fourth round. They scheduled us to play the night match on Labor Day. I was playing the night match at the US Open on Labor Day! It doesn't get any better than that. I would learn later in my broadcasting career that it's the one match TV programmers *don't* want; they'll pick some throwaway match to broadcast because everyone is driving home from their three-day weekend at the beach, or returning home half-fried after the big barbecue.

Playing well, I rolled through Vacek in straight sets. Finally, I'd made the second week at the Open. That it was in my home town meant everything. It mattered even more than my semi in Australia, and by chance I'd be facing the same guy—Boris Becker.

Boris and I were third match on the stadium, so it was one of those twilight specials that started in daylight and ended at night. I had lots of chances in the first set, but couldn't convert on any of them. I lost the second set in a tiebreaker, after having set points. On the changeover, I was thinking: *You're two sets down, but playing about as well as you can. Just keep it up.*

Dickie Herbst had a line he liked to use on me: "Just cut loose." I didn't have a lot of power at my disposal and played a pretty conservative game, and Dickie felt I had to take a few more chances, especially when I was feeling good, playing a superior opponent, or both. I said to myself, What the hell, what do I have to lose? I'm down two sets and playing Boris Becker on the center court. I'm not going to get a prize if I just play pretty tennis and melt away in straights. Fuck it—just cut loose.

The average spectator may not have noticed—I'm a tennis player, not a miracle worker. But I suddenly felt I was hitting the ball like Andre Agassi—and that can make a huge difference in your own mind. I dialed it up, little by little. I started going for that little extra that was just beyond the perimeter of my comfort zone. And I was finding it.

I won the third set, and the crowd started really getting into it. The next thing I knew, I was in the fourth-set tiebreaker—looking at taking this thing to five sets. And I was very confident in my fitness at that point.

Boris was a great player, and he was famous for a few of his quips, including this pretty dumb one: "In the fifth set, it's all about guts." Sure, you need to play with courage in a fifth set, but it's really more about fitness than anything else. I don't care how much guts you have, if your tongue is hanging out and your feet are dragging, chances are slim that your intestines are going to win you the match. I was strong enough, all right, and I was playing well. But I was also up against a multiple Wimbledon champion with a monstrous serve on a pretty fast court. I lost the fourth set, and the match, in a tiebreaker.

At the end of the day, though, I took real satisfaction out of having played my absolute best for a spell. I found that extra little level to go to, which won me the third set and almost got me the fourth. I'd finally put in the performance I hoped to put together one day at my home Grand Slam.

But I was still Pat McEnroe and he was Boris Becker, and there was only so much I could do about that.

Actually, Let's Not *Talk About It*

Love Means Nothing to a Tennis Player. I remember seeing a picture of Björn Borg in a T-shirt bearing that message, and cheesy as it sounds in some ways it's true. If mamas shouldn't let their babies grow up to be cowboys, then papas shouldn't let their babies grow up to be tennis-player girlfriends. At least not until said tennis players are about thirty years old and starting to recognize that maybe it's worth the effort that goes into a serious, committed relationship.

Tennis players are, by definition, footloose. The profession is right up there with "rock star" for a guy who just wants to date a lot, because he knows how easy it is to end a relationship—even a long one. A tennis player always has this foolproof fallback: *Sorry, girl, I can't deal with this now, I've got to catch a plane to Kuala Lumpur—we'll talk about it when I get back from the Asian swing in three months.*

That basically means you never have to talk about it. The tennis way of life is a drama killer.

It's a little trickier dating a tennis player, simply because it's hard to avoid each other or go your separate ways when it's over. And being in the same business, it can be tough to decide whose needs take priority. As much as tennis is an international sport, it's also an insular society. It's a little like being in the circus. You may travel the world, but you're always living in the Big Top, seeing and mingling with the same people wherever you go. The scenery outside the flap is different, that's all. While I was coached by Gunther Bresnick, I dated an Austrian player, Petra Ritter. She was having a good time in her youth, but looking forward to a traditional family life. And I knew that she had a guy from home in the background; like many Europeans, it was more or less understood that when the time was right, they would get married. I was probably a last fling for her, and we had a great time. She made me feel at home in Europe, as if I had some connections beyond the tennis court.

When I went to Vienna, I trained with Bresnick, and then I'd go out with Petra, or just have dinner at her place, often with her family. They were very nice people, but they didn't speak a word of English. And I never got much beyond *guten tag* in German. Petra tried to teach me, and Bresnick encouraged me to learn the language, but I wasn't very responsive. Those family dinners were pretty long, but as a fellow player Petra understood my priorities, and the way of life. I dated a few other players over the years, but none of those situations developed into anything serious.

Not long after my relationship with Petra ran its course, I started dating a French girl, an actress, whom I met through the French player Guy Forget. Amelie and I were together for a little over a year, a pretty long time for a tennis player, and she was with me during that satisfying US Open of 1995.

By then, Amelie had her heart set on a future with me. She traveled with me in the summer, and between tournaments we stayed at the apartment I'd bought in Manhattan on tony Central Park West with my earnings from a single tournament where I never even got past the second round. That was the same Grand Slam Cup (I qualified for it twice) in which Pete Sampras had beaten me in the first round and quit the tournament after he qualified for his $750,000 bonus. In 1991, I was luckier—I drew Thierry Champion as my first opponent, and the win netted me an astonishing $300,000.

Granted, Amelie traveled with me at my invitation. But it felt like one day I blinked and there was all her stuff in my apartment. By the end of the 1995 Open, I was contemplating an exit strategy; she was pushing too hard and too fast. I didn't really want her to come along to Asia that fall, but she assumed she was going and I didn't have the guts to tell her to stay at home, or to hash things out. It was a little tense on the flight over, because she kept wanting to talk about "us," and I kept dodging the issue. Finally, when we were pushing our luggage through the airport in Malaysia, she put her cards on the table: *Are we going to be together, are we going to get married?*

What? Uh-no. How do I say this nicely? I wondered.

I didn't really find a way. Before we even made it out of the terminal, she turned around and caught the next plane home to Paris.

I didn't know it at the time, but soon I'd meet my future wife in my hometown of New York.

My right shoulder had been troublesome for some time, but it started to bother me seriously in the spring of 1996. The diagnosis was impingement of the acromioclavicular joint. The corrective was surgery. I took a deep breath and decided to go under the knife, hoping that I could be sufficiently recovered to build on the momentum I'd gained in the 1995 US Open and do well in the next one. The surgeon went in and shaved my shoulder bone, and expressed confidence that I could play pain-free in New York come August.

I had a deal with Dickie, and I wanted to keep my commitment to him. Dickie, a loyal, principled guy, was eager to help me with the long, slow process of rehab. A few months after the surgery, I had the green light to start hitting—left-handed. Dickie came and stayed at my place in Manhattan, and we'd go hit on Har-Tru clay at a ramshackle club that had somehow survived right on Columbus Avenue and 96th Street in Manhattan, an easy walk from my apartment.

We started slowly, but I seemed to be on track. Yet after weeks and weeks of rehab, I noticed that not only did my shoulder ache from the surgery, every time I moved my arm to a certain point I felt that original pain, undiminished. It was like I had just doubled my problems. I still held out hope that all the pain was still part of the recovery process.

I gritted my teeth and kept working. Soon I was hitting balls regularly again, but the pain was still there. About six or seven months after my surgery, I was back to square one; my shoulder killed me when I tried to serve; I could barely lift my right arm to shoulder height. The US Open came and went; I was in too much pain to play, and really bummed out about it.

Shortly after the Open, I took part in a tennis charity event where I met this guy, Slobodan (his last name escapes me, because we fell out of touch a long time ago). He was from the nation formerly known as Yugoslavia. He was interested in the story of my shoulder, and claimed to have some sort of medical expertise. He told me he could help. I was at the end of my rope. He seemed a nice enough guy, he lived in the same city, so I figured what the hell, give it a shot.

Slobodan was like a sketchy, cool dude in a movie; he lived pretty well, in a nice apartment in Battery Park City, and he had this bimbo girlfriend who dressed and looked like a hooker. I'm not sure I even wanted to know what Slobodan really did for a living. He told me he owned some kind of nightclub in Miami. Slobodan talked a good game, medically, and he did all these crazy tests on my shoulder. He then worked up a regimen of unconventional but intriguing exercises. Some of them involved swinging around a great big pole; others had to be performed in the water, in a pool (he was ahead of the curve on that).

Eventually, he talked me into renting an apartment in north Miami where he could still supervise my rehab. Dickie Herbst agreed to come along to live with me for a few months. While there, Jim Courier and I got together frequently to practice. Nineteen ninety-six was rapidly slipping way; I was already thinking ahead to 1997.

I have to hand it to Slobodan, he was dedicated to helping me, and he was persistent. His special exercises were tailored to take pressure off my shoulder while making it better at the same time. But none of it seemed to be working. However, I worked so hard—on everything—that I ended up in the best shape of my life.

Dickie helped me whittle down my service motion until I was basically starting my serve with the racket already dangling in the "backscratcher" position, but it did little to alleviate my pain. Meanwhile, I was hitting the ball from the baseline as well as ever, so I finally decided, to hell with it. I was going to play. I entered the tournament in Doha, Qatar, which began on December 30, 1996.

I drew Paul Harhuis in the first round. I was familiar with his game, and had beaten him one year at the US Open. Paul was also an excellent doubles player, so our paths had often crossed. Any hopes I had to gut it out, to overcome the pain and loss of strength by putting myself on the tournament firing line, quickly vanished. My serve was pathetic, clocking as low as eighty-five, ninety mph. And on top of that, Harhuis was giving me shit about it all the way. He kept making remarks, in a stage whisper: *This guy can't fucking serve.*

I guess he was frustrated because, thanks to my baseline game, I was actually winning; maybe the very weakness of my serve was throwing him off. Maybe he thought I was messing with his mind. Finally, I got tired of it. I got into it a little bit with him. I called across the net, "Hey Paul—I'm winning. I'm beating you so it must be your fault—don't blame it on my serve."

I got the win, 6–3 in the third, and it was one of the most satisfying of my career. I played a hell of a match in the next round as well, against Hicham Arazi, although I went down, 7–5 in the third.

Just hours after the loss to Arazi, I was due on the doubles court with my speedy, mercurial Czech partner, Petr Korda. I gave it a shot. But I could barely roll the ball into the court, and our opponents took turns having target practice at poor Korda, up at the net. He finally turned and asked me, "What the hell are you doing?"

I just hung my head and said, "Listen, man, this is pretty much all I got."

I still didn't know it, but I'd soon learn that my surgeon had performed an operation I didn't need for a problem I didn't have, and which had no effect on the real source of my discomfort. It could have been worse; he could have operated on the wrong shoulder, too.

A Penny for Your Thoughts

Just a few weeks after my surgery in 1996, while my arm was still in a sling, I was sitting around in my Manhattan apartment, feeling sorry for myself. For some reason, I was going through my drawers and I found a postcard from Mike Errico, who was my best friend through all of grade school. Mike had a kid sister, Melissa, who used to tag along with us—their mother still has a picture of the three of us as kids, at a Yale vs. Harvard game at the Yale Bowl. Melissa was always cute, and I had a secret, innocent crush on her—insofar as a seventh grader can have a crush on a third grader.

In the ensuing years my mother would sometimes say, "Oh, you should really meet Melissa Errico again. She's really beautiful, and she's a star on Broadway." Yadda, yadda, yadda . . .

I looked at that postcard. It was an announcement for some dates Mike, who had become a singer-songwriter, had lined up. I dialed a number on the card and found out he had a show the following night in a small club in Greenwich Village. What the hell, I thought, I may as well go. In the back of my mind, I also thought I might run into Melissa there, and it would be fun to check out what she'd become.

The club was small, and there were only a couple of dozen people there. I sat at the bar, feeling a little self-conscious with my arm in a sling and seeing no one I knew. I checked out the room carefully, and saw a girl I thought might have been Melissa. But I was wrong. Melissa at that same time was in a taxi, coming straight to the club off a flight from Mexico. She was recovering from a dead-end affair with Howard Davies, a well-known British guy who had directed her on Broadway in a revival of *My Fair Lady.* He was thirty-five years her senior.

Anyway, she'd gone to Mexico with a close friend from their Yale days, Rachel. On that trip, I came to learn, Melissa had told Rachel that she was sick of dating these brainy, intellectual types. Rachel very sensibly suggested she get something going with a hunky, hot soccer player, and by coincidence an entire soccer *team* got on their plane just before it left Mexico for New York. Melissa flirted with a few of the guys on the flight, but she decided she wasn't interested in soccer stars. Rachel then floated the idea of a tennis player, saying, "They're kind of stylish, you know, and some of them even went to college."

Melissa got off the plane and went straight to Mike's show, and found just what Rachel thought she should be looking for: me. I don't know about stylish, but I'd gone to college. And I was a tennis player—kind of.

After the show, everyone was kind of mingling and Mike was gathering up his equipment when I went over and said, "Mike. Hey, Mike. It's Pat."

Mike's face lit up and he greeted me warmly. We started chatting and that's when Melissa walked in. She had this crazy, long, curly brown hair, and she was tan. She looked gorgeous. Mike reminded her who I was, and we all went out for a few beers. Melissa was talking a mile a minute and I sat there quietly; I'm basically pretty shy. Besides, what career I had was quickly going down the toilet, and she was basking in the glow of success on Broadway and television. I knew no more about that than she knew about tennis.

We did have one thing in common: Melissa had recently undergone vocal surgery, and here I was in a sling. We were able to commiserate about our respective "injuries."

I was smitten. Mike was done in, but Melissa was still energized from her trip. She suggested we go and get a burger in a local bistro, and it was close to dawn by the time I dropped her off at her West Village apartment. I think I waited all of twelve hours before I called her and took her out on our first date, to the popular downtown art-house movie theater the Angelika.

We knew little about each other's lives, but we connected, probably because she was regularly dealing with all this angst (it comes with the territory for an actress), and I struck her as a calm, stable, and positive person. I liked the fact that I came to represent some form of solidity and support for her, and she inspired me to work extra hard on my rehab. Later, after we'd been dating a while and she came down to visit me in Florida, she thought I was nuts when she saw the kinds of exercises and fitness training I was doing.

Sure I was nuts; I was in love.

Despite my frustrating experience in Doha, I insisted on playing the Australian Open in 1997. Melissa wanted to go, mainly because she was in the habit of taking interesting vacations with her mom. Her mom loved the idea; neither of them had ever been to Australia. She also remembered me as a little boy; she'd been fond of me and had remained in touch with my parents.

So the Errico girls showed up in Melbourne two days before the tournament started, knowing jack about tennis. I was inspired, and won my first round. I would have to play an emerging young talent next, Spain's Carlos Moya. The match was scheduled for the Margaret Court Arena, which at the time was second only to the Rod Laver Arena as a show court. I knew nothing about Moya, other than hearsay, but when they called our match and I stood next to him and covertly took in that rangy, well-sculpted 6–3 frame, it hit me. The game is changing, and fast. I thought, *This kid is just nineteen and look at him. Man, these guys are getting big.*

Of course, the crowd was for Moya—he was hot, young, Spanish. Girls were practically keeling over in the aisles. But I had Melissa, in her big, floppy hat, and her mom; I didn't want to disappoint them.

I went right after Moya from the start. I was fit and hitting the ball well off the ground, so I tried to take everything really early to keep Moya from dictating with his huge forehand and solid backhand. It worked—for a set. Moya seemed baffled, maybe a little rattled, until he finally realized that I couldn't serve at all; I was barely moving the needle past the 90 mph mark. That emboldened him and he started whaling on me, winning the next set, 6–0, and the third, 6–3.

It was pure misery. I was getting crushed, in front of my new girlfriend and her mother. Meanwhile, you would have thought Moya was Mick Jagger or someone, the women in the stand were so gaga for him. As if all that wasn't bad enough, I started having trouble with my knee. I couldn't serve, and soon I was also hobbling on one leg. I quickly went down a break in the fourth, and it was just about over. But I managed to play a good point at 4–1, and suddenly this lone voice rang out, loud and clear, in the still, crowded stadium: *Come on, baby, you can do it!*

I reflexively turned to Melissa and went "Shushhhhhh!" As in, "Shut up!"

Then I felt guilty about that, because even though she had called out at an inappropriate time, and every soul in the stadium, including Moya, knew there was no way in hell I could "do it," it was very sweet. Of course, it didn't help. Limping, aching in the shoulder, feeling guilty about having chided the one real fan I had in the crowd, I went down without much more of a fight.

When I got home from Australia, I went to see a doctor about my bad knee. This was another guy who seemed eager to put me under the knife, but I'd learned to be wary of surgeons. I wanted to get a second opinion, and I ended up seeing Dr. David Altchek, a well-known orthopedic surgeon who'd worked on a score of top pro athletes.

He diagnosed my knee problem and felt confident that a few

weeks in a knee brace would make it better. And he was right. I sucked it up and played some of the winter indoor events, and found myself back in Scottsdale, a wild-card entry. That's where I played that ill-advised golf pro-am, and when I tried to practice the next morning for my Monday night match with Mal Washington, the pain was so fierce I had to quit.

I went to see the legendary ATP Tour trainer Bill Norris. He asked a few questions, examined my arm, and said: "You're fucked. Go home. Now."

When I returned to New York, I went back to Dr. Altchek and asked him to look at my shoulder. He decided on surgery, using an arthroscope. When he moved my arm to a certain position, he was finally able to see a well-hidden bone spur that had escaped all other detection, including an MRI. Dr. Altchek performed the surgery almost exactly a year to the day after my first, superfluous operation.

The injury kept me sidelined until the midsummer, and I struggled when I returned. I won exactly one singles match in 1997—that first one in Melbourne. I would win just one more, in 1998, before basically pulling the plug on my singles career. (I believe I'm the only man in tennis history to turn down a main draw wild card. The USTA offered me one into the US Open in '97, but I told them it would be a wasted gift.) But at least my girlfriend's career was flourishing; she was getting all kinds of offers to do different Broadway shows, and she ended up, among other things, starring in a revival of *High Society*.

By the end of 1997, Melissa and I were on the marriage track, although we had decided not to move in together until we closed the deal. I broached the subject late in 1997, but she kind of blew it off, saying she wasn't "ready." I let the matter drop, and played it cool. I think that made her a little nervous. New Year's Eve came and went. So did Valentine's Day. So did a safari we took in South Africa. In February, I took her around, looking at some apartments in New York. Not long after, we went on a cross-country skiing trip in Vermont. We hadn't been in our cozy condo long when Melissa finally ran out of patience. "Looking at apartments, going on these trips, what does all this . . . mean?"

I had to bite my tongue and fly through the flack; I already had the engagement ring in my pocket. The tiff ran its course, and I knew I just had to hang on for another day. The next morning, I hid a bottle of champagne in the snowbank outside our door, and we went off skiing. I could tell she was distracted. Maybe she finally was ready.

It was a frigid but gorgeous, utterly still day, with blue skies overhead. As we skied along, I let her get ahead of me, down a mild incline, and I pretended to fall over and hurt my ankle. I cried out for her. She came tramping back up the hill to help me.

When we started dating, I often found a penny in the street. I got in the habit of picking up the coin and giving it to her with some little saying: "I love you," or "This is for good luck." I had a penny with me, and as she came up the hill I quickly buried the ring, in its box, and just lay the penny on top in the snow. When she reached me, I said, "Oh, look what I found!"

As soon as she looked and saw the penny, she knew. We were married before the year was out. The middle name of our first-born daughter, Victoria, is Penny.

Pistol-Packin' Imus

My dad has a relentlessly active mind. He's a stickler for detail, a compulsive t-crosser and i-dotter, and as good a copy editor as anyone who ever hefted the blue pencil. He's always got ideas, some of them pretty crazy, and he's not afraid to pursue them. He drives all of us kids (and my poor mom) nuts sometimes. He may think "outside the box," but he's also a hard-nosed realist, with the hide of a rhino. That single child from a poor Irish family, determined to make his way in a world full of elites and big shots, has lived on in him.

Dad was a huge fan of that pioneer of talk radio, Don Imus. Back in the 1990s, Imus and his show, *Imus in the Morning*, was huge (he still is, having rebounded successfully from an unsavory, race-based controversy). One morning near the end of 1999, Imus mentioned on the air that he needed a replacement on the sports desk for Mike Breen, who was sharing the duties with that old hero of mine, Warner Wolf. It was like a casting call he just threw out there. When my dad heard it, he immediately said he wanted to call Imus and suggest me for the job.

The idea seemed off the wall, but then I was interested in trying something beyond the realm of tennis, and I was interested in journalism. This was more realistic than trying to become a news correspondent. So I figured, what the hell. Dad called Imus, who referred him to the program director for *Imus in the Morning*, Mark Chernoff. He suggested that I call and set an appointment to come in for an audition.

There was only one problem. When my brother John got wind of the idea, he blew his stack. "Why didn't you throw *my* name out there," he complained.

Dad was smart. He said, "John. The job pays something like two hundred bucks a day. Do you really want to establish that as your market value?"

"Maybe you're right. Maybe it would be a good thing for Patrick."

Now there's brotherly confidence for you.

I was preparing to go to Australia for the beginning of the 2000 season, and I knew I'd be gone for a month. Anything could happen back in New York during that time, so I decided that if I wanted the job, I ought to hustle after it. So I went to audition at Imus's studio in Astoria, Queens, just days after we floated the idea. I had to get up at four in the morning to be there by 5:30. On the way over I wondered, *What did I just get myself into?*

I'd prepared some material, and I knew it would be a mistake to be intimidated, or obsequious, with a guy who thrived on controversy, confrontation, and free-form radio drama. I had to be comfortable, confident, irreverent—and get right in Imus's face, if it came down to that. You just can't let a guy like that railroad you.

The audition went well, but I was still slightly surprised to get a job sharing the sports desk duties with Warner Wolf. The pay was as lousy as Dad predicted, but at least they had a car and driver to take me on those pre-dawn runs to Astoria every morning. I'd show up at my little desk in the "bullpen" portion of the studio, and I'd huddle with a guy who had already prepared a variety of sound bites to use from various players and coaches. I wrote some material riffing off them, then I'd play the audio and rip the guy, praise him, or add some commentary.

The show started at 6:00 a.m. Imus always strolled in right at 6:01 on the dot, just as his sidekick Charles started reading the news. Imus has a firearms carry permit, and he always had his gun right on his hip. He inevitably made some crack when he saw me: "McEnroe, what the fuck are *you* laughing about?"

Imus, I'm laughing because you look like a tool with that six-shooter on your belt, I might think, but I'd just say something like, "You gotta relax, Imus. I'm just in a good mood this morning."

I had a lot of fun at that job. There was a frat-house spirit about the studio, as there was about the Imus show; it was strictly guy humor, and often off-color. Having been an athlete all my life, I was comfortable with that. Melissa, who's artistic and intellectual, thought it was all pretty mortifying, but she knew I enjoyed it and that the experience was valuable.

Getting up at four every morning wasn't my dream schedule, but I didn't mind that either. As I got my teeth into the job, I started hoping that they would make me the regular guy. I loved Warner Wolf; he's still a great broadcaster. But I sensed that they were easing him out of the picture, and I hoped that left me as the sole sports guy. Maybe I could even get a raise.

In the fall of 2000, after I'd been doing the Imus show for about a year, Melissa and I relocated temporarily to Los Angeles, mainly for the sake of her career. We rented a nice little house in Laurel Canyon.

I was able to continue with Imus, because by then he was on the MSNBC network, and they had a television studio in nearby Burbank. But because of the time difference, I had to wake up shortly after 1:30 a.m. and be ready to go on the air in Burbank by 3:00.

It was surreal: Every night, I would sit down in the middle of this big, empty newsroom, at the same desk as the guy who had anchored the big evening news show a few hours earlier. It was just me and a cameraman and the sound guy. They loved it, though, because unlike me they were pulling down big overtime bucks. And all they had to do each day was come on the air for brief periods at 40 minutes past the hour. On the way to work, I'd often stop and get a box of Krispy Kreme donuts and coffee for us to share.

Melissa was cool about it all; she kept her own days full. But we were a young, newlywed couple, on the schedule of senior citizens. We'd try to be in bed by 9:30 at night, and I had to get up a few hours later, stealing out of the house where she'd sleep the rest of the night alone.

Some days it was hard, because I didn't know if I'd be on for thirty seconds or five minutes. It all depended on Imus's mood, and how his show was going that day. I'd hear him in my earpiece: "So, what've you got for me today, Patrick?" I'd start to say something and he might cut in and say, "I don't have time for this today, see ya!" And that would be it. That was the nature of the beast, and it was frustrating on days when I felt good about the material I'd prepared.

Mostly, though, it was fun. I've always been interested in politics and current events, which were the meat and potatoes of the show. I tried to work those things into my reports. I was down in Australia (Imus loved it when I called in from foreign places) when Howard Dean made that famous "The Scream" speech. It happened right after I got the job as Davis Cup captain. So I did an imitation of Dean, but using Davis Cup nations: *Imus, We're going to Switzerland . . . and then we're going to Italy . . . and we're going to France . . . ayyeeeeeeeee!!!!!!!*

That kind of thing really worked for Imus and he seemed content. But I was quickly running out of steam. My ESPN work was ramping up, and I was in the running to become the new Davis Captain. The USTA is a pretty conservative outfit, and an easy target for anyone who has it in for the establishment. If Imus, who's made a living being a contrarian and a self-styled rebel, really wanted to push the envelope and put me on the spot by going off on the USTA, it could really damage my Davis Cup aspirations, and nothing in tennis meant more to me than that captaincy. My two jobs added up to a volatile combination.

And that schedule, it was brutal. I was tired of getting home from the show at 7:00 a.m., to crawl back into bed next to my wife, hoping to get two, three hours of sleep. Over time, I started to feel really run down. But I was still doing the Imus show when we went to Switzerland for my first tie as Davis Cup captain. When we returned, Imus fell back on his usual shtick and started to rip me. *You lost to Switzerland? How can the USA lose to tiny Switzerland, a country full of long-haired hippie dudes?*

Not long after that, I was sitting alone in Burbank in the middle of yet another night, staring at the camera. I was doing the sports, and Imus was on some tangent, something about his son not liking toast or something . . .

And I found myself thinking, *Enough already.*

So I called Imus's producer, Bernard McGuirk, a brilliant, tough, funny Irish guy who's been with Imus forever. Bernard is really the ringleader of the show—the guy who sets the wheels of chaos into motion. (Bernard was the driving force behind the ugly incident that got Imus fired for referring to the Rutgers women's basketball team in racially insensitive terms.)

I asked Bernard, "What am I doing, sitting here? Imus is just blowing off sports and I'm sitting on my hands. This is killing me."

"No kidding," he said. "This is brutal."

"Why don't you do something about it. Talk to Imus."

"What do you want me to do? I work here full time. I deal with this shit every day. You're the one flying off to fucking France every week, you're the one with the cushy life."

Excuse me? I could hardly believe my ears. "Well, I've had it, I'm gonna say something."

In the back of my mind, though, I knew this was just what Bernard was dying for—he wanted me to lose it on the air and get into a pissing contest with Imus. It was shaping up as a great radio moment.

I waited, calmly. Finally, Imus said, "Now, on to sports and here's Patrick McEnroe."

Often, when I started to do the sports, Imus would take off the headset and leave the room for a break, letting the other guys on the show chime in. He started to do that and I said something, right off the bat: "Hey Imus, what's going on here?"

He stopped in his tracks. "What are you talking about?"

We were on the air, but I didn't care. I said, "Look, do you want to do sports in your program or not?"

He replied, "Well, no, not really."

"Okay, fair enough. It's your show." (Imus could afford to be pure as the driven snow back then, because he didn't have a sponsor for the sports slot, the way he does now.) I went on, "I took this job a year and a half ago, Imus. You took a chance on me because I'd never done anything like this, and what have I done for you?"

"You've sucked," Imus said.

I knew the fix was in; I was being set up. But at that point it was still pretty good-natured, we were just a couple of buddies, trash talking.

"No," I said calmly. "I delivered. I've given you what you wanted. Some laughs, some insight, some inside stuff."

Without even thinking about it, I said, "Well, you know, I've had it. I really . . . I don't need this anymore."

I started to take out my earpiece; I was going to walk right out. But the MSNBC producer chimed in: "Patrick, wait a minute—Imus's wife is on the line."

He meant Deirdre, a former track athlete who's about thirty years younger than Imus. She would call in from time to time to stir the pot. She got on the line and basically ripped me. She went on and on: "*That McEnroe, he's a joke anyway. You don't need him.*"

Of course, Imus was loving it. He's like, "Patrick, can you hear this?"

"Yeah, I hear it. Deirdre, why don't you take that pacifier that you have there for (your son) Wyatt and stick it in your mouth? No one wants to hear from you."

No one on the show had the nerve to go after Deirdre—even on Imus, there were limits, especially when your paycheck was concerned. But I think even Imus knew, in his own way, that she was a pain in the ass.

Imus started playing off my exchange with Deirdre, bringing her back on the line. It was getting ugly, which meant that Imus was very happy.

So Deirdre went on about me being a has-been, a professional brother, trying to push all the buttons. It didn't cut very deep, and I found myself resigned, thinking, a little sadly, *Who needs this?* I said, "Imus, I've had it. I'm done. Call Warner. He's in Thursday and I'm out of here."

I took out my earpiece and yanked the microphone off my shirt and threw it aside. All this was on camera. I grabbed some papers I wanted to keep and just walked out of the studio—trailed all the way by the camera.

Imus reveled in it. But when I got in my car, I called Bernard again. I told him, "Just so you know, I really am done. I'm serious. You'd better get Warner."

I turned on the radio. It was bizarre. I sat there listening as Imus asked Bernard, "What just happened there?"

"Well, I think Patrick just quit."

"Was he serious?"

"Yeah, he just called me, off the air. I think he was serious."

When I got home and climbed into bed, Melissa rolled over. "How did the show go?"

"Great," I answered. "I just quit."

She smiled, and reached out to take me in her arms.

THE GENIUS AND THE PLUGGER

Dad had always pushed hard for John and me to play doubles together. Part of it was that family pride, but his hope was grounded in sound logic, too. I was a solid doubles guy, and it was Peter Fleming who had famously said, upon being asked to name the best doubles team he'd ever seen, "John McEnroe and *anyone*." So why not me, John's flesh and blood?

Well, there were a few good reasons for John and me to resist playing together, starting with the fact that in some places it was bound to be interpreted as a form of nepotism; some people inevitably would snicker and suggest that John was carrying me, as a blood favor. Neither John nor I needed that. And brothers, with a few exceptions, don't always make the best doubles partners because of the familiar sibling rivalry issues.

It was even more awkward in our case, because John and I were doing the same thing, careerwise, and at the same level if not with the same degree of success. We always had to navigate around that, and it did create problems between us from time to time, going all the way back. But there was pressure, and not just to play together. If Dad thought I wasn't representing the McEnroe name adequately, he'd remind me that other people are always watching extra hard. For my part, I learned to tell early on whether people judged or related to me as John McEnroe's brother rather than as an individual who happened to be a brother of tennis's most notorious hellion.

At times, though, the situation bordered on the absurd. Dad would say, "You've got to act like you're proud to be a McEnroe," and I would roll my eyes and think, *Did you see what John just did at this or that tournament? That wasn't very cool. Is that what it means to be a . . . McEnroe?* But on the whole, none of this was really a burden for me; it was more like an occasional irritant.

John also felt unwanted pressure thanks to Dad's lobbying. He bridled against the implication that he *had* to play with me, and he always did worry about overshadowing me. He almost went too far in the other direction, he was going to beat me as soundly as he could, just to prove that he was giving nothing away. No one was going to even suspect that there was nepotism or empathy in play.

But . . . overshadowing? I was used to it. What tennis player wouldn't be overshadowed by John? Undue credit? I knew in my heart that I'd earned every W on my record. In tennis, you always do. Nepotism? Any player in his right mind would give his eye teeth for a chance to call John his doubles partner. Winning is a powerful pleasure that makes it pretty easy not to sweat the details, or gossip.

Once in a while, just to keep Dad off our backs, we played as a team. It wasn't always pretty. We played the US Open in 1991 and got cold-cocked by the illustrious Swedish team of Ronnie Bathman and Rikard Bergh. Who was I going to blame, my useless partner, and hold a press conference to say Peter Fleming was full of it?

Of course playing against John was no picnic for either of us. He took no joy out of beating me, even if he refused to let up. I only played John in singles three times, and lost each match; the good news for me was that one of those matches (Chicago) was a tournament final—a big week for me, no matter what happened in the championship match.

But I had pretty good success against John in doubles. We had some good matches that went either way. One of the more memorable matches we played was in Madrid, which at the time—spring of

1992—was outdoors on clay. I was partnered with Patrick Galbraith, and in the quarters we met John and Javier Frana, an Argentinian lefty who really ripped the ball.

Altitude is an issue in Madrid, so the conditions were pretty quick. Galby was similar to me, in terms of strengths and weaknesses, but a lefty. He needed a solid power player for a partner to put his skills to best use. He was a very good returner, but his serve was shaky. His lack of power kept him from exploiting the natural advantage of a lefty. Galby basically had one serve—he'd kind of slide the ball into your body. It was effective, as such things go, but even back then you could rarely get away with being a one-trick pony.

In our match, Frana kept teeing off on Galby's serve from his deuce court post, setting up John with break point after break point. In one game there must have been six, seven ad-points for them. I'd ask Galby, "Where are you going with the serve?" and he'd hiss, time and again, "Body . . . the body."

The altitude helped the ball hop around, and it made Galby's serve better than it was. Whatever the case, John had a lot of trouble returning and closing the deal in the ad-court. It was driving him nuts, but Galby kept sliding in that serve, and we kept dodging bullets until we won that match.

John was livid; this guy Galby (he might have been thinking of me, too, for all I know), who from a talent standpoint shouldn't even have been on the same court, had put up a W at his expense. John wouldn't even talk to me after that match. He held a grudge about it for a couple of weeks. Not that I cared about any of that; after beating those guys, Galby and I knew we might win the tournament, and that's just what we did.

John and I also faced each other in the doubles final of Basel in 1991. His partner was the mercurial Czech Petr Korda. I played with Jakob Hlasek of Switzerland. We had some success as a team, and we both had been coached at different times by Gunther Bresnick. Jakob and I had no illusions about what we were in for that day, because just hours before the doubles final, Jakob had beaten John in a thrilling five-set singles final. The big question was which of those two singles finalists would have more gas left in his tank.

As it turned out, both of them had plenty. Jakob and I lost the first set, 6–3. We won the second in a tiebreaker. The third and final set also went the distance. Jakob and I reached match point at 5–6 in the 'breaker, with Korda serving to me.

Korda had a slick lefty slider, but he couldn't really hit it too well up the T. Knowing he'd still try to squeeze it in there to my forehand, I slid over a little—just enough to allow me to step around and hit the return with my backhand. The return went straight down the middle, between them. Game, set, match, Hlasek and Patrick McEnroe. John was disgusted—totally pissed. But on that occasion he didn't sulk. After a few hours, his sense of humor returned. He laughed as he told me the exact words he had spoken to Korda in their mini-conference at the baseline, right before Korda served that match ball.

"Whatever you do," John had said, "make sure you keep it away from Pat's backhand."

If you look up the last singles title John won on the main tour you'll see it was in Chicago, in February of 1991, and the guy he beat, 6–4, in the third was me. John played with his usual intensity that night; the only thing that made it different from the two previous times we'd played was that it was no beatdown. It was a match I could have won. I can only imagine how John would have reacted had that happened.

John was near the end of his career, and I was playing as well as ever. If ever I had a chance to win a big singles match from him, this was it. But I remember thinking, *Shit, if I win this match, he'll never talk to me again.* I knew that losing the match would hurt him a lot more than it hurt me. At one point early in the match, I glanced at the courtside boxes, and there sat our father, proud as a peacock. He had flown in from New York, just to be part of this great family event—life as it should be for the McEnroes, the first family of men's tennis. If he only knew—really knew—that it was never quite as joyous an event for us as it was for him.

I took my foot off the gas in that match, just that little bit that made all the difference in the world. I'm not saying I would have won it had I been playing without inhibitions. I can't claim that I should have won it, on form, either. I just know I was thinking, *Do I really want to win this? It would be such a hard pill for John to swallow. . . .*

I don't begrudge John for beating me that night, or spanking the tar out of me in our other two singles matches, at Stratton Mountain, Vermont, and Basel, Switzerland. You play tennis to win; you owe it to yourself, and you also owe it to the paying customers, as well as your support team. John *always* played to win, and there's a beautiful kind of integrity in that—it's honest. I just didn't have the same degree of ruthless, blind drive. Down deep, I knew I didn't want to beat my brother.

I also learned that night that if I lacked anything in my career as a singles player, it was that extra dose of desire, or maybe it's need. John wanted and needed to win every match. If he lost, it was never because he went soft, or let anything undermine his desire. That night, he flew back to Los Angeles, into a marriage that was beginning to unravel. I flew in the other direction, back to New York, seated next to my dad, who was still feeling euphoric about that great day for the McEnroes.

On the way, we flew through one of the worst storms I ever experienced on an airplane. The plane was pitching and wallowing through the night. I clutched the armrests with both hands, hoping that we'd make it home.

Down and Out in Paris (Bercy)

The middle of 1992 was a very tough, turbulent period for John. He was isolated; his marriage with Tatum O'Neal was on the rocks, and our father was too busy managing the industry called John

McEnroe to be emotionally useful to him. At one point, John asked Dad to back off a little bit. He told him, "I need you to be a father, not my lawyer or manager."

Our family circled the wagons and tried to help John work through his difficulties, although that McEnroe ineptness at communication hampered the effort. I offered to fly out to Los Angeles to spend some time with John, but he wasn't the type to unburden himself to anyone. We all knew that the greatest source of his anxiety was the custody of the two children he had with Tatum. Knowing her personality and family history of substance abuse, John feared for the safety of the kids in the event that the courts determined that they ought to be with Tatum.

I got along fine with Tatum, although I knew she had issues. When I brought home my college girlfriend one time, Tatum treated her like shit. Here was someone young, pleasant, eager to please, beautiful, and smart—a coed at Stanford. I guess that was the problem, because Tatum reacted like a child who feels threatened. I guess down deep she *was* like a child.

I met Tatum's dad, Ryan O'Neal, a few times. I thought he was a son of a bitch but he could be really friendly, too. He seemed very unstable, a real up-and-down guy. One time Ryan and Farrah Fawcett stayed with us in Cove Neck. I walked in to find Ryan in our little TV room. He was watching some news report about suffering children in Africa, and he started crying. He certainly had a tender side, but he also was into boxing and had a temper that made you give him a lot of leeway.

It was probably hard for Tatum to join our family; it's hard for any wife to marry an entire family. We were tight and bound together by tennis, something about which she knew nothing and couldn't care less. I don't think Tatum liked my parents very much. Because of her own family, she knew a lot about alcoholism; I think she felt that our family had that problem as well, but was in denial about it. And she was volatile, much like John.

When John married Tatum, he was seduced by that whole LA thing. It got him away from tennis, and into that celebrity sphere that was Tatum's world. In all fairness, I'm not sure she led him into it by the nose. It was just her life, and he'd fallen in love and started a family with her. It wasn't that different from what Andre Agassi went through when he married Brooke Shields. It's probably a lot more sensible, and certainly a lot easier, for a big-name player to marry a woman who didn't have competing ambitions.

John was a wreck by the fall of 1992, and he expressed what desire he had to connect with his family at a tough time. That meant tennis. He declared that he wanted to play doubles with me in the big Paris Indoors tournament in early November. It started just days after John and Tatum made their final decision to divorce, and he was so devastated that he was barely functioning.

John lost early in the singles in Paris, a particularly cruel blow for someone who always found haven in the game. But he still had doubles, and I was surprised by how well he performed despite his anxieties. Maybe feeling like he was taking care of his little brother took his mind off his own problems. Whatever the case, he took me under his wing to an unusual degree. One night early in the tournament he took me along on a night out with his buddy, the French tennis and pop music superstar Yannick Noah. "Take care of my kid brother," he told Yannick. The next thing, poof, I was surrounded by gorgeous girls, including a *Sports Illustrated* swimsuit model. She and I hit it off and had a great time in Paris; it was certainly good incentive to keep winning that week. The doubles were played at night, so we'd be out until three or four in the morning, I'd sleep until one or two in the afternoon, and then John and I would play our matches at night.

Not bad, I thought, *a swimsuit model, Paris, John McEnroe for a doubles partner. Life may suck for John, but at the moment it sure is good for me. . . .*

On paper, John and I had the makings of a good doubles team. It was a natural fit: a lefty and a righty, a shotmaker (him) and efficient server with a steady partner who could set him up for the kill with precise returns. But the pressure was too great, because the shadow of our father loomed over the enterprise, no matter how much he tried to downplay the pride he took in seeing us as a team or his expectations.

We did have one significant technical problem. John and I both preferred to play the ad (left) court. Although the steady player usually takes the deuce (right) side to set up opportunities (most of the break points are played in the left, ad court), I preferred the ad side because of my excellent return, especially with the backhand. It was hard to get that wide serve by me, and rule no. 1 on break points is: Make sure you get the return back into play.

John groused about my desire to play the ad court, but he grudgingly agreed to move over to play the deuce side on the grounds of his superiority and experience. He was more likely to adapt successfully if forced out of his comfort zone. The alignment worked out well.

We played all of our matches at night, before huge crowds. In the quarterfinals, we played a good French team, Arnaud Boetsch and Olivier Delaître. It was a very tight match that came down to a third-set tiebreaker. At five-all we got the benefit of a truly bad call against the French. The cavernous arena at Bercy was packed and it just erupted. It was pure chaos. The French team was hopping mad, arguing with the umpire. The fans were booing and jeering us. I got a taste of what it was like to be John, for whom this kind of anarchy was business as usual.

John was patiently waiting to serve the next ball, but the scene was out of control. He stood there with his hands on his hips: What's the problem with all you whiners? After a few moments, he called me back to the baseline where he stood. He paddled the ball against the court. He grinned slyly and said, "Don't worry about it. We've got this thing in the bag."

Don't worry about it? The arena was full of hostile fans. The

French team was motivated by righteous outrage and egged on by their countrymen, and support from a home crowd can make you capable of nearly superhuman feats. The way I saw it, these guys wanted to be heroes, the scene was set for them, and John and I were in deep doo-doo.

Finally, some semblance of order was restored. As a hush descended on the arena, John stepped up to the line. He went through all the familiar shirt-tugging and lip-licking rituals. I could almost feel the perverse pleasure he took at that moment—the feeling Pete Sampras has described as the intoxicating, exhilarating pleasure of being in the position to give a stadium full of fans the equivalent of a big, fat, middle finger.

John went into his signature, radical service stance with his back almost to the net, coiled up like a cobra as he tossed the ball, and snapped around to hit an unreturnable serve.

Game, set, match, John and Patrick McEnroe.

As we walked off the court, John had this evil little smile on his face. He was flat out loving it. He shook his head in disbelief and started laughing. It was the happiest he looked all week.

We went all the way to the final, where we won the first set easily and broke our opponents in the second. I remember thinking at that point, Wow, this is easy. We've got this in the bag. But John wasn't about to let me relax. He was hyped up, and he kept saying things like, "Come on, we gotta get a break here . . . We gotta bury these guys. . . . Don't let up."

It really hit me then, how his intensity level was just always so insanely high. Sure I was trying my hardest, but it was like playing with house money and I felt a little complacent, a little satisfied. I was enjoying myself, thinking, Great, we got another break, let's just cruise on through.

Not John. He wasn't buying into that. Maybe he remembered that long-ago US Open qualifying match with Zan Guerrey; maybe he thought of that French Open disaster with Ivan Lendl. This was a final. He wanted to demolish and bury those guys, and that's just what we did, winning 6–3, 6–1.

We never played doubles together again.

Larger—and Smaller—Than Life

When the job as general manager of the USTA's player development program came open, I felt I was a good candidate. You could substitute the words "parent management" for "player development," because the road to success with a promising player, especially in more recent times, runs through parents. Tennis was in many ways the glue that kept our family close, although my dad might, with some justification, flip that and claim that family was the bonding agent that enabled our success in tennis. Either way, we'd lived a typical tennis family's life, and stood out mostly because of John's extreme talent.

My job as a television commentator also seemed an asset. Some of the lifer coaches, especially formerly high-ranked players, are a little out of touch with the game and how it's changed. They're going to impose a dated template, which is fine for some of the foundational stuff, if not good enough to keep pace with change. I'm pretty sure that some of the iconic names in tennis haven't even hit balls with a racquet strung with today's newer polyester strings.

But being relatively young and a broadcaster, I'm in touch with the day-to-day changes, issues, and controversies in the game, sometimes in a way that puts me in a conflicted or uncomfortable position, as was the case after the ladies' doubles final of the US Open of 2009.

The 2009 US Open ended with a Monday final because of rain. And anyone who watched the event, or even read about it in the media, knew what happened on Saturday night. Serena Williams, taking umbrage at a foot fault called against her while match point down, went medieval on the foot-fault judge (whose main job is to call the baseline at her end). Serena totally lost her cool and threatened the woman in an expletive-laced tirade. The linesperson followed the rules and reported the menacing abuse to the umpire. The violation called for a point penalty.

The tournament referee, Brian Earley, came on court during the heated discussions that followed Serena's outburst. Serena had already used up her one allotted warning when she smashed her racket up after losing the first set. This next infraction automatically meant a point penalty, ending the match. As big a deal as it was, Earley and the USTA were lucky. I can only imagine how the crowd would have reacted had Serena gone gonzo at 3–all in the third set, long before that highly competitive and entertaining match was close to finished.

The controversy intensified when Serena issued an official statement the following day through a public relations firm, admitting that she "handled the situation poorly." It was a self-serving statement, and while various officials were still trying to decide what further punishment to dole out, critics jumped all over the fact that nowhere in her statement did Serena actually apologize to anyone. On Monday morning, Serena released an "amended" statement, in which she did apologize, after, unbeknownst to most, her arm had been sufficiently twisted by interested and influential parties.

Darren Cahill and I were scheduled to call the Monday men's final between Roger Federer and Juan Martin del Potro for ESPN, in case the network wanted to rebroadcast it almost immediately. I also had a long-standing commitment to speak at a charity luncheon put on by the Eastern Tennis Association earlier in the day. As the men's final was scheduled to start at around 4:30, I was in pretty good shape—until US Open tournament director Jim Curley's assistant Cindy called and asked me to host the women's doubles awards ceremony, preceding the men's final.

It was a pretty standard request—the USTA likes to have its own people serve as award presenters, and two of my jobs are USTA positions. I had already backed out of one such commitment earlier in the tournament, owing to my obligations as a commentator. So I agreed to do it, but as I rushed down from the luncheon in

Westchester County to do my turn, the wheels started turning in my head. Venus and Serena were almost certain to win the doubles. And I was a familiar face on live television, and to everyone in the stadium, as an ESPN journalist.

The way I saw it, I was duty bound to ask Serena about the repercussions of the Saturday night incident and its aftermath. If I didn't, it would impugn my integrity as a journalist. The awkwardness of my situation dawned on me.

I called Jamie Reynolds, our ESPN coordinating producer, and explained my misgivings. If I were to go on live television to present the trophies and ask two or three questions, I would have to ask about the Saturday incident and its aftermath. Normally, my colleague Mary Jo Fernandez would have done the on-court interview and presentation, but she wanted no part of it. Mary Jo is the Fed Cup captain, and she wasn't willing to risk damaging her relationship with Serena by putting her on the spot—not with Serena having agreed to play the Fed Cup in a final against Italy later in the year.

I couldn't blame Mary Jo; if it had been Andy Roddick in the midst of a similar mess, I would have felt equal reluctance. Furthermore, ESPN was aware that some of us in tennis wear multiple hats, but they didn't want one of their people out there if the relevant questions were *not* going to be asked.

So at the morning meeting between various stakeholders, including the USTA and ESPN, it was agreed that the subject would be avoided altogether. And then I came into the picture. Jamie Reynolds understood my bind; if anything, he was ticked at this apparent back-door move that got me mixed up in it. He also agreed that if I were doing the on-court interview holding an ESPN mic, I just had to ask about the incident and the apology controversy.

Next, I called Jim Curley. I told him I'd be happy to go out and present the trophy, but if I were to do the on-court interview as well, I was going to ask the uncomfortable question. I had to do it, for the sake of my credibility as a journalist. Jim said, fine, do what you think is best. I then called Gordon Smith, the executive director and

COO of the USTA, and told him the same thing. He had a great attitude, and said, "Fine, it's a great opportunity for Serena to apologize in a more public way, on television."

On my way into the stadium, I was lucky enough to bump into ESPN producer and behind-the-scenes reporter Willie Weinbaum. He's a pro; he would understand my bind. He suggested that after I congratulated the women, I should ask a nice, soft question about the incident to give Serena an opportunity to talk about it. But I should have a good, tough backup question ready to go, in the event that she stonewalled.

When the time came, I was ready. After rendering kudos, I acknowledged that it had been a tough forty-eight hours for Serena, and asked if she had anything to say to her fans. Willie was right on; she ducked the questions like a boxer ducking a jab.

I followed up by asking if anything had clicked in her head in the past twenty-four hours, to make her amend her original statement and add an apology. No sooner were the words out of my mouth than the crowd started booing and jeering. Venus and Serena both broke out their familiar smiles, the ones that basically say "fuck you." And Venus patronizingly interjected: "I think the crowd is saying, 'Patrick, I think we're all ready to move on.' "

Well, I tried.

Over the next few hours, I received an incredible number of emails lauding me for asking the questions that had to be asked. And it was especially satisfying that so many of the messages were from frontline, respected, fair journalists. They praised me for not letting Serena off the hook so easily. Given some of the inherent, inevitable conflicts in my job, I felt really good about getting the thumbs-up from what can be a very tough crowd. Next to it, the boos from the spectators meant nothing.

Venus and Serena Williams are astonishingly talented, enormously successful players—that they're sisters and have both been ranked at the top and won multiple Grand Slams is one of the greatest sports stories of all time. We've lived it, so we're accustomed to it. I know firsthand how unlikely their history has been, and how exceptional they must be in some way I can't even fathom to have come so far and achieved so much.

None of us can really know what they went through as outsiders in tennis, successfully crashing a game that could hardly have been called popular on the mean streets of Compton, Los Angeles, where they grew up.

But I also know that the sisters didn't go from those legendary cracked courts with the holey nets straight to the victory podium at Grand Slam events. They had an enormous amount of help along the way, some of it from people who hoped to cash in as they became famous, others who just fell in love with their talent, or wanted to help because they thought the girls could write a truly inspirational tale for others, particularly among minorities that tennis has a hard time reaching.

I sometimes wish the sisters were a little more conscious of what the game has actually given them in the way of opportunities, material rewards, a platform for their ideas and opinions, and even relationships. But they've been sucked into that shallow narrative that encourages them to think that they doublehandedly conquered a world that was intrinsically hostile to them. The truth is that tennis was dying to have someone like the Williams sisters come along, and not entirely for selfish reasons. Most people love to see the underdog or the disadvantaged succeed, and among those who do, the ones who fare the best are the ones who realize they had a lot of help along the way—that they're part of a pretty good, well-intentioned community.

But let's stop right here for a moment to do something we sometimes neglect because of how close Venus and Serena are, and the extraordinary way their careers have proeeded, like parallel train tracks. Venus and Serena are two very different individuals—as different personally as they are as tennis stylists.

Venus is more diplomatic, as befitting an older sister (and one who's often tried to shield and protect Serena). In recent years, she's become more of a spokesperson for the WTA Tour and stepped to the forefront on a number of gender-related issues (including equal prize money). It's fitting that she's had all of her Grand Slam successes in recent years at Wimbledon; she has a clear appreciation for the traditions and society of tennis.

Serena has brought a lot to tennis, no doubt about it. But she doesn't seem to recognize that tennis has brought a lot to her, too. Serena has the star power and name recognition to be a female Andre Agassi. She could win big events for many years, and she's at the age when maturity and self-awareness might transform her into a comparably iconic figure.

Like Andre, Serena at one stage longed to be "more than a tennis player." She thought she wanted to be an actress, and took her best shot. It went nowhere. But she hasn't yet connected the dots the way Andre eventually did, and come to accept that life can be pretty good if you recognize that tennis is your destiny, and on the whole that isn't all that bad. It offers some enormous advantages and power to do some good, or at least make people feel really good about, if nothing else, being tennis fans.

At this point, Serena still isn't really tuned in to the power she could wield. She's got a deep instinct for showmanship; has anyone else so thrived on drama, and so often proved critics and detractors of her game, or fitness, wrong? She did it once again at the 2010 Australian Open, laying to rest the notion that she was number 1 only because Justine Henin of Belgium had taken a surprise leave of absence in the spring of 2008. By surviving a few serious threats, and weathering a patch of brilliant play by Henin to end her comeback dreams in the final in Melbourne, Serena showed that nobody could claim that the best female player on the planet had taken a break.

Serena has a big, big game—she takes the WTA game to another level with her serve, bold returns, and steely nerves. And she has a personality as big as that game. She's like the young Muhammad

Ali, convinced that she's "the greatest" and happy to let the world know.

But Serena is no folk hero, like Ali was for the baby boomers of the 1960s. And she's a tennis player, not a prize fighter; she's held to a different standard in a sport that still values grace and good manners. Serena often rubbed people the wrong way after suffering a loss, because her typical reaction precluded giving her opponent any credit. It was all about how badly Serena had played, how lucky the winner was, yadda-yadda-yadda. She's gotten a lot better about that lately; you can see her making an effort to be a gracious loser, so maybe she's figuring it out.

The Fed Cup is the women's version of Davis Cup, and while it isn't nearly as popular, especially in the U.S., it's still an important event to most nations, and playing for your nation is always an honor. At the end of 2009, a surprisingly feisty U.S. team led by Mary Jo Fernandez clawed its way to the final with no help from Venus or Serena. Serena had agreed to play if the U.S. made the final; in fact, she said that Fed Cup was terribly important to her. Serena is especially prone to pledging her undying devotion to Fed Cup, and then reneging when it comes time to play.

The lucrative and prestigious WTA year-end championships were played in Doha, Qatar, the week before the Fed Cup final. Not long before Doha, Jill Smoller, Serena's agent, called and asked if we would send a coach to the championships to work with Serena. She specifically requested Mike Szell, who worked mostly with our boys but had once been coach to Monica Seles.

Our USTA policy is to help any American player, male or female, famous or down on his luck, if it makes sense. I was happy to send Mike to work with Serena, with just one caveat: He would only go if his full services were needed. If Serena just wanted a hitting partner (many women hire male players with whom to hit), I didn't want to waste Mike's time or our resources.

Jill agreed, and Mike went with Serena. She had a great tournament, ultimately winning the title. The USTA and the Fed Cup team had been holding its collective breath, hoping that Serena would indeed make the trip to Italy as promised. But after her semifinal match in Doha, she abruptly announced that she wasn't going to travel to Italy to play Fed Cup. She was too banged up.

Serena's abrupt about-face was a severe disappointment, particularly for the U.S. team, which had accorded her special treatment (and rightly so). Serena was scheduled to do a photo shoot in London right after Doha, meaning she didn't even have to join the team until a day or two before the balls started flying in earnest. It was a tough schedule, for sure; on the other hand, the travel wasn't horrific and the tie was, after all, a weekend affair against Italy, a nation that isn't exactly an international powerhouse, played on a forgiving outdoor clay surface.

I thought it particularly galling that Serena pulled out of Fed Cup before she had even finished playing in Doha. I wrote Jill an email and said Serena certainly didn't look very hurt to me. Jill wrote back that I should see what bad shape Serena was in, how much treatment she needed, just to keep going. But I wasn't buying it. I knew Serena wasn't at death's door, and was certain she'd make her photo shoot. She just didn't want to go to Italy.

At some level, I have no problem with those who choose not to play Fed or Davis Cup. But at least have the decency and honesty to come right out and say it doesn't work for me, I'm not interested. Instead, Serena kept everyone waiting, including the captain and teammates who were counting on her presence. And then she just bailed.

I wrote back to Jill: I guess that's the thanks we get for sending Mike over there.

She fired back haughtily: I didn't know there was reciprocity involved.

I replied, That's the point, there wasn't. We just did it on good faith, knowing that Serena had also committed to Fed cup. And this is what we get. . . .

But it was pointless to nag the issue to death. If you don't want to play, say so. Don't yank everyone's chain. The thing that bothered me is that I had a suspicion that she had no intention of going, from the get-go. And it occurred to me that maybe she had said all those nice things about going to Italy to suck up to the USTA at the moment when the organization was part of the group debating what further punishment was appropriate for Serena's transgressions in that semifinal US Open match with Clijsters.

When the Grand Slam Committee finally did act on Serena's actions at the US Open, fining her $82,500 and placing her on a two-year Grand Slam probation, her reaction was that the decision was somehow "sexist." That if a male player had done such a thing, he would have gotten off with a slap on the wrist. But I'm still waiting for the incident in which a male player gets off lightly for physically menacing and threatening an official; there's an order of magnitude issue here, and it was discouraging to see Serena reach for that sexist card. Her outburst at the Open wasn't unforgivable, and it could have been resolved and forgotten if only Serena took ownership of her actions. It would have made it easier, to borrow an expression from Venus Williams, to "move on."

Instead, the whole episode only served to make Serena look worse and worse, which is too bad. She has a riveting, charismatic personality, and an enormous platform in the public arena. She has a great deal to give, if only she could forget about the taking.

The Era of Heresies

My role as Davis Cup captain adds to my credibility as the head of the national development effort. Young players are focused on the here and now; as familiar as the names Sampras, Evert, or Connors might be, they're names from the past. Kids don't connect any more immediately or naturally with them than they do with Willie Mays, Ronald Reagan, or B. B. King. But it probably helps when they see me high fiving with a James Blake, or huddling with Andy Roddick during a Davis Cup match.

I learned many valuable things growing up with and playing alongside and against John, but great training was not one of them. One time while I was still on the tour John asked to join Jared Palmer and me in one of our regular practice sessions. I told him we had an indoor court booked at 10 in the morning, and he said he'd come an hour later. That was fine, it would give Jared and me time to do our drills and get in a good hit.

John showed up a little on the early side, and stood watching us through the big glass window overlooking the courts. When he came down to play, he was shaking his head: "What the hell were you guys doing?"

He warmed up for five minutes, max, and suggested that we get it going. We took turns playing points, sometimes going two-on-one. After John had enough, he showered up, took up his place by the window again, and watched us doing various drills. Finally he came back down to the court and said, "Let's get out of here, man."

"What?" I said.

"This is the biggest waste of time."

"What do you mean?"

"Tell me, when are you ever gonna hit balls like that in a match?"

He was right, at least partially. You never play a match in which you assume that the next twenty balls you hit will all be crosscourt backhands. But John was like a genius of improvisational jazz denigrating musicians who spent a lot of time rehearsing published scores. And the art of drilling has changed, dramatically, in the span of a few years. I'd seen and learned things in Europe that I thought we in the U.S. could really incorporate into our plan to get back up to speed as a tennis power.

Jim Courier, one member of that golden Sampras generation, understood what I wanted to do, because he knew the man I had quietly sized up as the right person to lead the charge, Jose Higueras. Jim's decision to hire Higueras as his coach early in his career was prescient. It came about almost by accident, when Jim realized that he couldn't get the support he needed from his coach at the time, Nick Bollettieri. Nick was too wrapped up in another of his protégés, Andre Agassi.

The wisdom of Jim's decision was manifest in the French Open final of 1991. Andre was the odds-on favorite to win Roland Garros; he had beaten Jim en route to the final the previous year, which Andre then lost in a shocking upset to thirty-year-old veteran Andrés Gómez of Ecuador, a first-time Grand Slam finalist.

A year later, Andre raced to a 6–3, 3–1 lead over Jim in the final, blistering the ball. He had a break point that was a de facto set point when rain stopped the match. In the locker room, Agassi would later reveal, Bollettieri said absolutely nothing to him. Higueras, huddling with Jim, advised him to take a few steps back, especially on his service return, to buy a little more time and make Andre play more shots. He boosted Jim's confidence with his faith and advice. Jim went on to win that match, which launched him on the three most prolific years of his career.

Jose was one of the notorious "clay-court specialists" of an era awash with them. He was legendary for his work ethic, setting standards that a fleet of Spanish stars would soon emulate. I felt that the New World desperately needed a dose of his Old World work ethic.

Cross-cultural projects easily go awry, but Jose had immigrated to the U.S. near the end of his career, settling near Palm Springs with his American wife. They ran horses—and the occasional tennis player, like Jim. When I got the job as head of player development for the USTA in the spring of 2008, Jose was the first man I wanted to call and the last one I *did* call after interviewing other candidates and half-a-dozen long talks with Jose himself. He agreed to be my Director of Coaching.

Jose was such a grinder in his heyday in the top 10 that some people thought he was just a "pusher," and would teach our kids to wage dull wars of attrition from the baseline. Nothing can be further from the truth. First of all, there's a big difference between a defensive pusher whose only real weapons are consistency and stamina (the species is now extinct) and a grinder, willing to do whatever it takes, all day, to get the job done. Second, Jose had limitations as a player, but to me he's shown none as a coach. If anything, his own shortcomings as a player left him keenly aware of how much more you need than the ability and willingness to grind.

But I still like to get Jose going by saying stuff like: "Just remember, we're still Americans. We still want to pound the fucking ball." Put more politely, I'm telling him that I want to retain that basic American tradition of playing aggressively—playing to finish the point rather than prolong it, playing aggressively to create opportunity.

Jose's vision could be called Spanish, although guys like Jimmy Arias and Jim Courier, both out of the Bollettieri Academy, were also pioneers of the aggressive baseline game and violent racket-head acceleration. On a broad, institutional level, the Spanish were the first to pick up on that trend, and they were flexible and wise enough to give their budding players intensive training on hard courts. The technological advances in strings and rackets also enable players to take huge cuts, and the Spanish emphasis on topspin, especially on the forehand side, ensured that the players got sufficient clearance over the net to have a built-in margin of safety no matter how viciously they attacked a ball.

The contemporary player who best represents the ruling style is Rafael Nadal, even though his technique is stylized to the point of seeming radical. You know the guy is no ordinary baseline grinder because of his success on all surfaces, including grass. Granted, Rafa is a rare individual talent. But Jose saw that much of what he did was based on general ideas that could be taught.

Jose has a long-standing friendship with Rafa and his coach, mentor, and uncle, Toni Nadal. He knows Toni's philosophy of the game, and what he did to express it through Rafa. Jose has this one drill he puts kids through that consists of a series of forehands, the last of which calls for the youngster to take a ball that's very low and close to the net. He has to dig the ball out and fire it back over the net, but with enough topspin to make it fall within the court. It's a drill that Rafa did relentlessly, since the time he was about ten.

Many of our top private, developmental coaches, like Robert Lansdorp, are big on penetration—hit flat and clean and try to get an opponent back on his or her heels. The main problem with that approach is that when you get pushed behind your own baseline, you're out of options. I've watched Andre Agassi in slow motion, and could see that the further back he was pushed, the more spin he applied, to give him a more forgiving margin of error as well as to buy time. But that's a very defensive approach.

In our program, we like to develop an ability we call going "in and out." A player needs to know what to do when he's moving in aggressively, or finds himself getting pushed back, or out. It applies to moving and hitting side-to-side as well. The idea is that you play tennis in a circle, and you need to develop sound technique for this 360-degree job. Today's players have to know how to turn the tables and seize the initiative from all points on the court. Net clearance is a big issue for Jose: the farther back you are on the court, the more height you want on the ball crossing the net. The closer you are to the net, the less clearance you want.

We also emphasize decision making under duress. When you're playing in a circle, you need to decide if you're on defense or offense, if you ought to play high or low over the net, if you're better off volleying short, or punching the ball deep. Hit the volley deep and there's a chance the other guy will be able to make his passing shot dip low over the net, forcing you to hit a defensive volley. But if you play the volley short, your opponent has to come up with the ball but still hit it with enough pace and spin to pass you and drop it into your court.

Jose also does these "progression" drills. He'll take a young kid, stand on the same side of the net, and hand-feed him balls. He literally takes the kid—and he did this even with Roger Federer, whom Jose briefly coached shortly before coming on board with the USTA—and tosses a variety of balls in succession. The kid, or superstar, can hit any shot he wants, as hard or gently as he likes.

Jose makes the player run up, or go back. Go to this side or that. What do you do with any given ball? It's all based on decision making and footwork. Sometimes Jose will toss the ball very close to the player, so he has to move away from it before he hits. And because it's a hand feed, you have to make your own pace for whatever shot you choose. That's where racket acceleration enters the picture.

Later, Jose will do the same drill, but this time he'll be on the other side of the net and feed off his racket. He does the same thing, only this time it's tougher because the ball is coming at the student faster. That makes it easier to create pace, an important factor, but it also makes it imperative to know how to receive pace—and we're very big on that. Watch Nadal and you'll see that he's exceptional at hitting a great, hard shot while moving backward.

Some of the kids in our program were already taught what might be called the American way, and it was amazing to see their reaction. They would try to step in, or forward, to meet the ball during a progression drill and of course they would miss it. That traditional and once useful notion of trying to take every ball on the rise isn't as effective as it once was; it represented playing tennis in a straight line, rather than a circle.

Back in the day, the idea of actually teaching someone how to hit an aggressive shot while backing up would have been considered heresy—if the very idea could even have been conceived.

But this is the era of heresy; teaching American kids the Spanish way to play, but with a greater emphasis on finishing points, is just part of it. And while things in the near term look a little shaky for our mature juniors, we're very encouraged by the performance of the kids in our sixteen and fourteen-and-under age divisions.

. . . .

My job as head of player development is mostly about management; in some ways, I'm a bureaucrat, reviewing salaries, or trying to figure out what to do about lousy food at our training camps. Meanwhile, guys like Jose Higueras and his two top aides, Jay Berger (head of men's tennis) and Ola Malmqvist (head of women's tennis), are out doing the fieldwork.

As a manager, I'm in charge of budgets and hiring. I know how the USTA is perceived in the coaching community. Everyone criticizes the organization, but everyone also wants its stamp of approval. Everyone thinks the USTA has a huge checkbook, and hopes to collect a big check. The same people criticize the USTA for spending money. And everyone thinks he can help turn the American game around and restore our former glory, but almost every one of them wants to do it on his terms.

That impulse is especially strong among well-known coaches and former players, especially great ones, including my own brother John. The hearts of most of these guys are in the right place. Nick Bollettieri, Rick Macci, Robert Lansdorp—guys like that have an unbelievable passion for the game. Many of them have been critical in the development of players who went on to be great champions. And almost all of them have at some point or another gotten screwed for their efforts—written out of history by a fame-hogging parent who suddenly turns out to be his daughter's only "real coach," or sometimes just because the advisers of the new star are terrified that the coach who invested so much in the player is going to want a cut of the action.

When these prominent names, former top players as well as coaches known wide and far, are asked by the press, they often say they're ready and eager to help the USTA but the organization never calls. That's an easy story to write, and a large institution like the USTA is a high-value target. Robert Lansdorp, who's had a hand in shaping some of the best players of three generations, once complained, "How come you guys (player development) never call me?"

"Robert," I answered. "My guys have called you four times. I kept on top of that. And as I understand it, you never returned their calls."

Great players and top coaches like to be wooed and cajoled. They act and probably feel they have the key to success, and maybe they do. But they only want to reveal it at a price. They don't want to call, they want to be called, and not by just anyone. When the organization does reach out and makes the call, the results can sometimes be bizarre.

I approached one Grand Slam legend about helping us out, partly because I'd read about this player's willingness to help the program if the USTA would only reach out. Well, I reached out, with realistic expectations. I suggested that the player commit to showing up a certain number of days at one or another of our practice facilities. I wouldn't even ask the player to fly or spend a night or two away from his family. Eventually, we got around to talking about money. When I suggested that we'd pay the player $75,000 for a pretty modest commitment of time, staggered throughout the year, the player promised to get back to me.

The response was this terse text message: "Add a zero."

Like I said, on *their* terms . . . either financially or in some other fashion. Few of the iconic figures in the American game have stepped forward and said, "Listen, I want to help. Tell me how I can be of most use to you, and maybe we can work it out." Maybe I'm nuts, but that seems like the way it ought to work. But everyone wants to be the chief, not the Indian. I lose interest quickly when a big-name player says he or she wants to help, but only if his name is on a tennis stadium somewhere, or on a big check that I could never justify cutting—not even in my own mind.

One exception to this trend is the former two-time US Open champion Tracy Austin. I approached her cautiously, wondering whether she'd buy into the philosophy of our program. Tracy was one of Robert Lansdorp's first great success stories. She hit incredibly clean, precise, flat strokes—all Lansdorp trademarks. And unlike many of Robert's other protégés, Tracy remained loyal to him, partly because they were in some ways kindred spirits: frank, outspoken, tough. What if we hired Tracy, because of her background and status, and she went rogue there and told the kids something entirely at odds with what they'd been hearing every other day of the week from our full-time coaches?

And there was the ever-present compensation issue. What if we couldn't afford her? What if we went through our discussions and she came back with, "Add a zero."

My concerns were unfounded, and it made me realize it wasn't me who was out of step. Tracy listened, asked all the right questions, and decided that she could endorse our approach and help promote it—and she quickly developed into one of our most valued assets, bringing enthusiasm and passion to the job. Tracy wanted to be paid, but it was mainly because she knew that you get what you pay for—getting a check would take her sense of responsibility to the next level.

We quickly agreed on a reasonable amount, after which I had to go back to telling high-profile coaches and former players (many of whom couldn't carry her racket as competitors *or* coaches) that no, I wasn't interested in paying them $250,000 a year for sharing their wisdom and experience. And certainly not when I have great coaches out there, busting their asses for these kids on a 24/7 basis for less than half of that. Those coaches are the ones who have the biggest impact on these kids; if I'm going to take care of anyone first, it's them.

If some of Tracy's mental strength and determination rub off on the youngsters, we'll be in good shape. But that's even tougher, in some cases, than teaching someone to play tennis in a circle.

I was also open to bringing Tracy's mentor Robert Lansdorp into our tent, but anyone can tell you he's a tough nut to crack. Robert has a history and well-earned reputation as a lone wolf; he's the classic guy who's got a basket of balls in the trunk of his car and a résumé that enables him to ask whatever price he wants for a half-hour or 60-minute lesson. You can do pretty well for yourself, getting two or three hundred bucks for an hour lesson.

Also, the prototypical Lansdorp product is a vanishing breed on the tennis landscape; it's about topspin and fitness these days. Robert is a very smart guy, and he's made some adjustments to keep up with the times. But he was by no means an automatic fit with the program I conceived.

Some of Robert's ideas are original and provocative, great starting points for debate, even if they run counter to our own view. Among other things, Lansdorp believes that the only way to create champions is on a one-on-one basis. A great player, he believes, needs someone to serve in a hybrid role as coach-manager-authority figure. For Jimmy Connors, it was his own mother, Gloria. For Bjorn Borg it was Lennart Bergelin. For Rafael Nadal, it's Toni Nadal. And the women's tour is awash with parents, almost all of them fathers, whose control over their daughters is comprehensive.

But a strong protégé/mentor relationship, while common, is by no means the only path to success. As valuable as Tony Palafox was to my brother John, he wasn't a towering figure in his life. Nor was my dad, at least not in a tennis context. Many of the fine French players bubbled up out of a state development program, while Roger Federer didn't have an omnipresent coach-manager—nor did Lindsay Davenport, despite the critical role Lansdorp played in shaping her game.

We don't want to get into the business of these intense one-on-one relationships, although we'll support them as a third party in any way that makes sense. And we don't write checks under the assumption that the money will be well spent by a kid's mentor. That's like plonking down your money, squeezing your eyes shut, and rolling the dice. But you'd be surprised to know how many parents or coaches come to us for help and pretty soon make it perfectly clear that the only thing they really want is cold, hard cash. Often, there's a streak of paranoia under the surface—the coach or parent is afraid that we want to steal the kid and get all the credit for his or her subsequent glory. So they try to keep us at arm's length, while appealing to us for help.

While we aren't trying to buy champions or create a tennis welfare program, we'll help anyone. Lansdorp's right when he says that intense mentor-protégé relationships can pay off. If a talented kid chooses not to live and train under our supervision at one of our main training centers, we'll look for some other way to help him out. It may mean financing his or her trip to Europe, where the player can compete in minor league events; it may mean sending one of our coaches on the road with the kid, or underwriting a two-week training session at camp in Spain, so the youngster can get a taste of a different culture, and immerse himself in clay-court tennis.

Ryan Harrison, one of the U.S.A.'s outstanding prospects, is affiliated with the IMG Nick Bollettieri Tennis Academy; his father, Pat, is a teaching pro there. That's just fine with us. The last thing we want is to go into competition with successful private academies or pros. And we still want to do whatever we can for Ryan and others like him.

Our approach is very disappointing to parents and coaches who just want to tap into our financial resources. Then they go and complain to the press, and the story becomes one about our institutional indifference, or alleged refusal to help this poor, starving tennis player. Most people would be shocked to know the extent to which the USTA helped some players who never uttered a public word of thanks, even after they became very successful.

With us, it's not a matter of "our way or the highway." It's more like, "We're willing to spring for a tank of gas, but we want to know where the bus is going."

THE SPEEDOMETER STOPS AT 50

My wife, Melissa, doesn't just do a really nice job when she sings the National Anthem to start a sporting event. She kills it. She's sung it at the US Open, Madison Square Garden, and many times at Davis Cup ties; it's something she really enjoys indoors or under an open sky. She does the anthem in a pure, elegant, traditional way. I love it—and so do most of the team members.

In 2007, team USA finally made it into the Davis Cup final, and we chose to stage it on a fast indoor court in Portland, Oregon. The USTA asked if Melissa wanted to sing the anthem. When she's asked to do it, she's thoroughly professional; it's a whole day and a half of preparation—her own Davis Cup final. She gets nervous, she needs to plan her schedule and do a warm-up, get all that wild hair just right, all of which requires a little bit of love and encouragement from me.

Melissa was scheduled to fly from our home in New York to Portland on Thursday for the Friday start, bringing along our eighteen-month-old daughter, Victoria. If she sang the anthem, it would further complicate things, because now she'd have performance anxieties and logistics to figure out as well. I had so much on my plate that the last thing I needed was an extra layer of responsibility.

So I told the USTA that she was coming as a spectator, supporter, and mommy, and to relax and enjoy the great occasion.

I called home on Tuesday, just three days before our first day of reckoning.

"What's the story with the anthem?" she asked. "Am I doing it?"

"You know what, baby? I don't think you should. Forget it. I don't want you to have to worry about it."

"Okay," she said. "But you know, Andy's going to ask about it."

"No, I don't know."

"Haven't you noticed? He always likes when I sing the anthem."

I rolled my eyes, even though it was true enough. She and Andy Roddick get along great and he was always enthusiastic about the way she sings the anthem.

"I don't know," I said, not wanting to offend her. "This is the Davis Cup final; I think he's got other things on his mind."

"Sure. I just needed to know."

The next morning, our team piled into the van. Andy jumped right into the front passenger seat—the captain's seat. My seat, riding shotgun. No one else would ever do that, but I let Andy get away with it now and then because of his contribution to the team. Why try to stop the big dog from peeing on the fire hydrant?

We pulled away and Andy said, "Hey, capt'n? Are the girls coming out?"

"Thursday night."

"Cool. Melissa is doing the anthem, right?"

"Ah . . . I think so."

"She's gotta do it. We *need* her to do it."

"Oh yeah. Don't worry. She's doing it."

So as soon as we got back from practice, I flew up to my room and called home. "Guess what, baby? You're doing the anthem."

The single elimination concept, whether it's at a big tournament or in a competition like the Davis Cup, is a beautiful organism that takes on a life of its own the moment the first ball in a tournament is struck. Remember when Pete Sampras shattered Roy Emerson's all-time singles Grand Slam title mark, at the 2000 Wimbledon? At a time when Andre Agassi, Lleyton Hewitt, Richard Krajicek, Mark Philippoussis, Tim Henman, and a handful of other very dangerous grass-court players were around, the men Pete beat to complete his historic feat were, in order: Jiri Vanek, Karol Kučera, Justin Gimelstob, Jonas Björkman, Jan-Michael Gambill, Alexander Voltchkov, and—finally, the only one of those guys who'd previously played a Grand Slam singles—Pat Rafter.

The Davis Cup can be like that, too. A few things break your way and you find yourself facing an Israel or Belarus in a semi, with a home tie in the final. In our case, we got two nice breaks in 2007. We were able to host mighty Spain (and thus avoid having to play them on red clay) in the second round, and we got game but starless Sweden in the semis. Although Sweden was one of the Open-era Davis Cup powerhouse nations, it had fallen far and fast. We played at their place, but the Swedes had to go with a surface that helped their roster the most and that was a fast indoor hard court, the kind we also like. We punched through to the final, although with a few more anxious moments than we expected.

But there we were, in Portland. After seven long years—seven years of diligent team building and unwavering commitment from our American players—we were on the cusp of adding to our nation's distinguished Davis Cup history. But the final was no slam-dunk. We were hosting Russia, which had a deep stable of talented players and a shrewd, roll-the-dice captain who loves to pull surprises, Shamil Tarpischev.

Marat Safin, a multiple Grand Slam titlist, was a free spirit, but when he was on his game he swung the racket as well as any man, ever. He'd earned his two majors with wins over Pete Sampras (US Open, 2000) and Lleyton Hewitt in Australia (after a 9–7 in the fifth win over Roger Federer in the semis). Dmitry Tursunov was a moody guy, but as electrifying at his best as our own James Blake.

Nikolay Davydenko had spent most of his career in top five territory and Mikael Youzhny was a versatile guy who could play clean, efficient tennis on all surfaces.

If the Russians were clay courters, surface choice might have been a routine decision. But their best guys were hard-court bangers, much like ours. So while I knew we were going with a fast indoor court, I wanted to tailor it as specifically as I could to suit our players. I'd certainly learned from my experience at that debacle in Carson. Getting the surface right meant taking a trip to Premier Services, a company in Baltimore that fabricates cement-based tennis courts. It would be my second trip there in six months.

Premier Services makes your basic hard court in sections and ships it out, for installation at the actual site. They can control the speed and height of the bounce by adding more or less sand to the paint they use on top of the court. When you want to speed up a court, you just cut back on the sand and put on a few more layers of paint.

A month before we played Spain in Winston-Salem, North Carolina, in the quarters of Davis Cup in 2007, Rafael Nadal had torn apart Andy Roddick in straight sets at Indian Wells on a high-bouncing hard court. I knew we had to try to get that bounce down before we met Spain, and gave my specs to my contact at Premier, Chris Rossi. He made the court, and it worked beautifully for us in Carolina, even though Rafa surprised us by pulling out of the tie with injury. (Did I mention that it helps to have a few breaks go your way?)

I was pleased that Premier really nailed it. When you hit a slice, the ball skidded away instead of sitting up. The tuning worked so well that I was loath to leave well enough alone, especially with a big final coming up. I decided to push the envelope to see just how far we could go, speedwise, although there was a point of diminishing returns because returning serve was a bit of an Achilles' heel for everyone on the team. Also, I had to be aware of the ITF's "common-use" clause.

The definition of common use is a bit hazy, but it basically prohibits a nation from using a surface that isn't reasonably well known. The Slovak Republic once hosted Spain on a court so fast that the Spanish filed an official complaint, and the ITF censured Slovakia. Wood, like the kind used in bowling alleys, was once a common indoor surface (this is going back decades now), but today it would be disallowed.

It was hard to draw clear lines on this issue, so the ITF came up with a formula that rated court speed on a numerical scale, going up to an arbitrary no. 50 (the fastest the ITF would allow). The court Premier made for Winston-Salem was rated 46. Premier still had that court at one of their warehouses, and I asked them to make it even quicker and reduce the bounce even further. For the final with Russia, I wanted it bumped up to 48. (By the time we faced France in the second round the following year, 2008, I would nudge it up to 49—close enough to the edge that the French team complained, and we received a stern letter of warning from the ITF: *You guys are getting very close to the line here, watch out. . . .*)

One noteworthy irony in all this, as any of our aggrieved fireballers will be happy to tell you, is that the ITF never tests clay courts for degree of *slowness*. If the idea is to have a surface that doesn't unduly reward—or punish—a specific style of play, why don't they test some of the slow clay courts on which we have to play, to make sure they're not significantly slower than typical dirt courts?

I called Jay Berger shortly before I went to Baltimore and had him beat the bushes for a few talented, local juniors whom I could use to test the court. We hit on the unlined, netless court in a Premier warehouse in a bleak, industrial zone. I felt that the ball was still bouncing up too high. I told Rossi I needed something that allowed the ball to slide through the court even faster. He went back to work and I went home, to return three days later. But finally, I was satisfied.

The value of all this due diligence was apparent in the match stats for 2007. It was an exceptional year for our ace machine, Andy Roddick. To the best of my knowledge, Andy didn't lose his serve *once* in the entire year of home Davis Cup ties. I know it was true in his matches, but I believe it was also true in all of our practice sessions.

I felt that Andy was serving so well that he could pop them in at 75 percent speed and still hold comfortably on that fast court. Off the ground, Andy likes that little hack-slice, and when the ball stays low he can get away with pushing—getting less than ideal penetration. A court that produced a higher bounce would take speed and energy off that backhand, and allow the ball to sit up, begging for a spanking.

As for James, well, he's a mercurial player if not a great returner. I thought the court would help his serve, and allow him to play high-risk tennis. The Bryans would take a bit of a hit as returners, but they were so reliable, and so good in other aspects of doubles, that they would cope.

The Tarpischev Head Trip

Safin decided not to play for Russia. He was in one of his blue periods, playing listless, error-strewn tennis, so it was just as well for them. But Tarpischev surprised us when he left Davydenko out of the singles lineup and went with Tursunov and Youzhny instead.

Granted, Davydenko had some shoulder problems, the extent of which we couldn't know. What we did know was that James Blake owned Davydenko by way of a 6–0 head-to-head advantage. Davydenko doesn't serve big, and while both men hit pretty flat, James is even more prone to take the ball early; he's a little bigger and more physical than Nikolay as well, so he has success pushing him around.

Tursunov has a much bigger serve than Davydenko; if he could hold against Andy Roddick and get to the tiebreaker, anything could happen. But there was another dimension to Tarpischev's choice—one that reflected his crafty nature. Back in 2006, we'd traveled to Moscow to play Russia in the semis, and the last guy we expected to see in their lineup was Tursunov. For the Russians had Marat Safin, Davydenko, and Youzhny at their beck and call. It seemed a lock that Safin and Davydenko would lead the charge, because playing on clay boosted Davydenko's chances considerably.

Safin got that tie off to a great start for Russia, taking out Andy in straight sets, after which Youzhny took care of James in four. The Bryans came through in the doubles, as they always do, which left us still alive—if barely—on the third and final day.

When Tarpischev named Tursunov for singles on Sunday, Andy looked at me, astonished, and said, "What? *Tursunov?*" Theirs was the first match on Sunday, and it became one for the Davis Cup highlight reel—and a tall feather in Tarpischev's captain's cap.

Andy played his heart out, but fell just short, losing 17–15 in the fifth, in one of the most bitterly fought Davis Cup battles in Open-era history. I was absolutely drained by the time it was over. John Roddick (Andy's brother and coach at that time) and I were walking back to the tiny little locker room we'd been assigned in Moscow's cavernous Olympic stadium when we saw Andy, still in his match clothes, sitting slumped against the wall in the distance down the empty hall.

Andy was covered in clay. There was clay everywhere, in fact. He was sitting there, a glistening trail of tears on either of his clay-dusted cheeks. I walked up to him and quietly said: "Hey, you gave it absolutely everything you had and then some. It's gonna hurt now, but it will be something you can remember with a lot of pride."

So in Portland, I thought maybe Tarpischev was playing a bit of mind games. Nothing illegal or unethical about that, either. Tursunov also has a much bigger serve than Davydenko so he could be dangerous on the court we chose. It takes consistent play over seven matches to win a Grand Slam, and Tursunov was the kind of guy who had trouble keeping his eyes on the prize. But he could certainly get hot for two Davis Cup matches, and the payoff was national hero status. If Tursunov could hold serve against Roddick and Blake and get into a few tiebreakers, anything could happen.

Suddenly, we also saw why the Russians had brought along the clay-court expert Igor Andreev. Tarpischev probably wanted to keep his two singles players fresh, so he was willing to concede the doubles—or at least rattle the Bryan brothers by making them play an utterly unfamiliar team, Andreev and Davydenko. It was a classic Tarpischev move.

You-Ess-A! You-Ess-A! You-Ess-A!

The atmosphere in the Portland Memorial Coliseum was vintage Davis Cup when Andy took the court to open the tie against Tursunov. Apparently, we weren't the only people who had built up a huge appetite to hug the Davis Cup for the first time since 1995.

Flags danced and shimmered everywhere, the guttural chant *You-Ess-A!, You-Ess-A!, You-Ess-A!* rolled down from the stands in wave after wave, and while the 12,000-seat arena wasn't by any means the largest one in which we've played (in fact, the ITF was miffed at us for choosing so small a city), but modest size of the place just intensified the atmosphere, made the lights focused on the court seem that much brighter. It increased our already significant home-court advantage.

My only worry was that Andy, with the adrenalin racing through his veins and the memory of that devastating loss to Tursunov in 2006 still in his mind, would lose it, mentally or emotionally. The pressure of playing before a huge, hopeful home crowd, with the odds in your favor, can be worse than playing on the road before a hostile crowd. You never worry about disappointing the partisans when you're on the road, and it's slightly less painful to absorb a beating far from the eyes of your countrymen.

But Andy was a thoroughly seasoned Davis Cup player. He'd experienced everything the competition had to offer, a few times over. He was jacked-up to the hilt. The real question was: Would he stay within himself? I liked the look in his eye and the set of his jaw. He was curiously quiet and still, the eye of the hurricane.

The court played just as I'd hoped and expected. Andy's serve was preemptive, and his slice troublesome enough to tease Tursunov and force him into making errors in his eagerness to attack the seemingly mild shot. Two errors, a great shot by Andy, and there's the break, first set over. As the second set started, I had a feeling that the cheap break Andy put together to get the set was dancing around in Tursunov's head. He had to be thinking: *There's no way I can break this guy, and all I do is make two lousy shots and that's the end of it.*

It was over quickly, with Tursunov getting just 10 games, 6–4, 6–4, 6–2. The crowd loved every moment of it. Some guy on stilts, in an Uncle Sam costume, was dancing in the aisles. I made eye contact with Melissa and she smiled; she'd done her job with the anthem, I'd done mine with the court, and Andy had done his—the toughest job of all. He had played a pitch-perfect match; he didn't go out there for payback, or to fire a hero shot. He went in thinking he was just going to serve, and let the other guy lose.

Andy and His Big Whupping Stick

Over time, Andy had emerged as the clear Davis Cup team leader. His willingness to drop everything when the captain calls is unusual in today's world. He fulfills every criteria of good leadership, including the toughest one for a big star and celebrity: He would never expect or ask his teammates to do something he wouldn't do himself. Andy is a team player to the core. He rides in the team van (even though he sometimes poaches my seat), puts up with Davis

Cup politics and the USTA's self-celebrating tendencies, and, most important, he gives everything he has, every time he sets foot on the court.

He's a good-time Charley and, well, a ballbuster, too. He shows up in the lobby of a hotel before the squad has to march off to some official dinner nicely dressed in a suit, but wearing a pair of worn, clay-stained tennis shoes and that cocky, crooked grin of his. He snaps a towel in the locker room with the best of them, but he watches everything around him like a hawk.

Most of all, though, and I want to say it again—Andy always gives his all and it matters to him, and not just when the cameras are rolling and 20,000 people are chanting, *You-Ess-A! You-Ess-A! You-Ess-A!*

Highly ranked singles players are often like high-performance race cars; they can be temperamental and in need of special fine-tuning. Not Andy. During Davis Cup weeks, he'll mix it up in practice. None of this showing up five minutes before his scheduled hit and leaving five minutes after. No special needs.

One morning a few days before our 2009 tie against Switzerland, he decided he wanted to practice with the Bryans and a new practice partner we brought along, Alex Domijan.

I described the Bryans' extraordinary practice routine earlier; they work fast and furiously. Andy, being Andy, gets totally into this. So he trotted out to warm up and soon the balls and jibes were flying around like tracer rounds until Andy said, "Okay, I'm ready to take my punishment."

Meaning, he was ready to play a bunch of those two-up, two-back drill games the Bryans love.

They did that for a solid hour, and I figured Andy's done. I told Ryan Sweeting, our other practice player, to lace them up—to get ready to sub for Andy as a doubles player. When Andy saw Sweeting getting ready, he yelled, "What're you doing, Captain? Me and Alex are playing."

"Fine with me," I said. I've enjoyed watching Andy work with the younger guys through the years. He enjoys that mentor role, and often he'll come to me after and we'll talk about the kid's game and nature, like two coaches.

Andy and Alex started playing, and Andy was giving Alex all kinds of advice—and this is a guy whose doubles record is as thin as Andre Agassi's hair. I stood in my usual position when the Bryans are practicing, right behind them, way back from the baseline. I couldn't resist yelling, "You found your calling, Andy, doubles coach!"

The men were playing under what we've come to call the "Roddick Rules." Because Andy can go for months—literally—without having his serve broken, he's not allowed to bust out his big whupping stick. The Bryans want a chance to get their return games grooved—not stand idly watching as one ball after another sizzles by. The Roddick rules enabled the Bryans to just cruise through the first set. Andy, while usually a realist, was not pleased.

In the second set, I noticed that Andy was serving a little bit bigger each time, enough to carry his young partner Domijan into a tiebreaker. But the Bryans lifted their games and went up, 6–2, with Andy to serve. I walked up behind the Bryans and whispered, "Watch out, Andy's going to unload a bomb here . . ."

Sure enough, Andy cracked a monster, a blistering ace that violated the Roddick rules but kept his team alive. We cracked up as Andy sheepishly protested, "Come on, I had to let one go—I've been holding back all day."

After the doubles, we had a little time left to play Andy's favorite game, Squares. This is an agility drill, really, in which each of four players stands in one of the four service boxes. Each player can tap the ball into any box but his own, and the player there has to return it before it bounces twice. They keep score, and the guy who loses has to go stand at the baseline, with his back to the net, while the other three try to drill his backside with serves (It's called "Butts Up.")

Andy is remarkably good at Squares. At times in the heat of a match, with the crowd going wild after he's made a particularly athletic shot, Andy will glance at me and silently mouth the word: "Squares."

A Wild and Crazy Guy

Andy called me from the July tournament in Washington, D.C., in the summer of 2007. "Can you help me at the (US) Open, Capt'n?"

That was after Andy parted ways with Jimmy Connors, the celebrated iconoclast who coached him for a while. John Roddick, Andy's brother, had filled in for a spell, during which time Andy coincidentally suffered a shoulder injury. It wasn't his only concern. Roger Federer was stronger than ever, and Rafael Nadal had emerged as a player for all surfaces. Novak Djokovic and a handful of other young bloods also were pressing in on Roddick.

Andy had trouble putting in good back-to-back matches all summer. He was stunned at Wimbledon by Janko Tipsarević, and Viktor Troicki took him out in Washington. Both were formerly Roddick strongholds. Having his brother John for a coach wasn't working out; they fought and severed the (coaching) relationship. Andy's ranking in August dipped to no. 9; he was in danger of falling out of the Top 10 for only the second time since 2002. (He'd dropped below 10 briefly in the summer of 2006, before hooking up with Connors.) With the US Open fast approaching, he had nowhere to turn.

"I'm desperate," he told me. "Can you at least help me at the Open?"

"Sure."

We practiced for a week. This wasn't the Andy Roddick I knew from Davis Cup; this wasn't the fresh-faced kid who stormed tennis in 2003 to win the US Open and assume the no. 1 ranking. He had zero confidence. He eventually averted disaster in New York, reaching the quarterfinals. But it was a telling episode and another testament to how fast things can change, and how unnerving life can be, for a guy who doesn't enjoy the same luxury as a Federer or a Nadal—a bulletproof game.

By the end of 2008, just a year later, Andy had found a new coach in Larry Stefanki; he dropped fifteen pounds, shored up that problematic backhand, and he was playing well enough to be a contender at the US Open again. It was an epic effort, but what did it net him—three, four places in the rankings? If you weren't paying attention, you might have thought it was business as usual for a guy in the middle of the top-10 pack. Andy has invested a massive amount of energy and effort to keep himself in the mix, when he might have coasted and only his peers would know he was no longer a man to be feared.

Andy has never stopped working on his game; he's probably out there on a court near his home in Austin right now, tinkering with his forehand volley or that flipperlike backhand. He has obvious limitations, but he's spent a career improving and working around them. Back in the day, a guy like Andy could bluff his way through matches, relying on that deadly combination of atomic serve and nuclear forehand. Now, if you have a weakness, the other guys will find it and make you pay like never before.

The effort Andy's put into improving his backhand, finding ways to make up for a habit of playing from too far behind the baseline, and compensating for his lack of nimbleness has made him a far, far better player—even if he's had to live with the curse of Federer. (Among other things, Federer pretty clearly denied Roddick a great shot at four Wimbledon titles, with wins over him in a semi and three finals.) Take Federer out of the picture and Andy might have three or four majors, yet still be a less accomplished player.

Roger may have denied Andy a measure of greatness he might have earned under more favorable conditions, but he helped him achieve a different kind of greatness—the kind that will never show up in the record books. I like to think Davis Cup also has played an important role in Andy's evolution.

I watched Andy grow up in Davis Cup. Oh, he still flies off the handle. He's still got the wiseguy gene, and that edge that compels him to wear his heart on his sleeve and stick his chin out, just to see if someone has the guts to take a poke at it. But he knows himself and he's developed an uncanny understanding of the game. The kid who showed up with a Fred Flintstone game has evolved into a genuine student of the art of winning tennis.

And a lot of the respect I have for Andy accrued when he was in situations, many situations, where the average sports fan isn't even paying attention. But he still put himself out there, in the hinterland far from the spotlight, to bleed red, white, and blue. That Tursunov match in Moscow is a good example. So was our relegation tie with Belgium in 2005, and our semifinal against France in 2002.

That year, we made our first deep run as a team. The French hosted us in the semi in September, at the home of the French Open, the storied Stade Roland Garros. It was a huge occasion in France. Andy opened up the tie, but he lost to Arnaud Clément. Sébastien Grosjean then took out James Blake. We salvaged the doubles in a brutal five-setter, thanks partly to James (he played with Todd Martin). But Grosjean came out in the reverse singles and hammered Andy in four, clinching for France.

After the loss, Andy sat in the shower, a cascade of hot water hiding the fact that he was weeping. The following morning Andy, Jim Courier (who was there helping me out), and I took a van to the airport together. We were all going to different destinations, so we said our good-byes standing outside in front of the departure lounges.

"Hey guys," Andy said. "I'm sorry."

"What are you sorry about?" I answered. "You don't have anything to be sorry about. You put it on the line. You were here, you played pretty well, you lost. End of story, and tomorrow we begin a new chapter."

As it turned out, we lost in the first round (to Croatia) the very next year, so we had to play a relegation tie just two weeks after the US Open. That was no ordinary Grand Slam for Andy; he won it and became an overnight star.

But just days after that, we were to convene in the Slovak Republic for our relegation match. It was sobering, how in 12 months we'd gone from being two wins from a final to having to fight for the right to remain in the World Group in a battle we'd have to wage on red clay in Bratislava.

Andy was drawn to open the tie against Dominik Hrbatý, a good all-around player who knew how to work the ball and take full advantage of the slow nature of clay. While Andy warmed up, a few hours before the match, his coach Brad Gilbert confidentially told me, "I don't know, Andy's not in a good mood today. He's . . . different."

Sure he was different. He was the new US Open champ, and he had to be here in Bratislava, playing a Davis Cup match that relatively few people back home in the U.S. would watch or care about. He had just hosted *Saturday Night Live*, now he was eating cabbage and looking at grinding it out on clay in front of people who would remind him of those SNL skits Steve Martin and Bull Murray used to do about goofy East European swingers in the U.S., the Wild and Crazy Guys. Success and celebrity were working like acid on his character.

As we prepared to go on the court, Andy somewhat curtly said, "Don't say anything to me. You don't need to say anything to me today."

I was like, "Okay." I glanced at Gilbert, he kind of shrugged.

I understood the deal. Andy had just won the US Open. He'd been on *Saturday Night Live*. He didn't need anyone telling him to mix up his serve, or try to get the guy pinned into his backhand corner. Maybe he decided that he doesn't need Davis Cup anymore either; it was all well and good to develop that gung ho, patriotic image when you were an up and comer. But now he was a big star.

Maybe, like some others in the past, he decided he'd outgrown this traditional, crazy, demanding Davis Cup deal.

Right off the bat, Hrbatý had Andy on the yo-yo, and he jerked him all over the court. Andy lost the first set, 6–3, and seemed no more effective in the second. I sat watching, biting my lip. I didn't say a word, as per Mr. Big Wig's request.

Meanwhile, the USTA faithful in the courtside box behind me were whispering and murmuring: *What is Patrick doing, what the hell is going on here? He's not saying a word to Roddick.*

I felt pressure to intervene, but I just sat there, thinking: *Okay, this is a long-term deal—this is the guy I want to build the team around for as long as I've got the job and he's got the legs. Let's see if he still wants to be part of that program.*

I let Andy flounder. I encouraged him, all right, but cheerleading was the extent of it. He went down a break in the second. On the changeover, he came and sat down beside me, as usual. I stared straight ahead as he hung his head. The atmosphere was icy. He finally said, "All right, what do I do?"

"Now can I talk?"

"Yeah," he said, "let's talk."

I shared what I'd been thinking, about Hrbatý's game and his own. It was too late to salvage the second set, but Andy won the third. He ultimately went down in four, but I put that down to the toll of his hectic September. And fortunately for us, Mardy Fish came through in a big way, beating Karol Kučera in four sets. The Bryans then did their thing, wiping out Slovakia's doubles team. We were alive at 2–1.

On Sunday, Andy was a different player. He went to town on Karol Beck, a substitute for Kučera, losing just 11 games to clinch the tie that kept us in the World Group.

To me, that match against Hrbatý will always be a turning point in the development and career of Andy Roddick. Maybe it was just an aberration, but I like to think the experience helped him become the man and player he is today. With 31 wins, all in singles, Andy ranks right behind my brother John and a heartbeat ahead of Andre Agassi as a Davis Cup stalwart. It may be some time before those statistics are challenged, and they form the cornerstone of his legacy.

The Buccaneer's Ship Comes In

I heaved a great sigh of relief when Andy won the first singles in Portland, because the match I worried about most was the matchup of Youzhny and Blake. Our no. 2 man's dedication, and the hard work he put into the Davis Cup effort, were exemplary. But he didn't always react well to the unique pressures of the competition.

Youzhny and Blake had never played before, but we knew Youzhny was solid. James is a buccaneer, scurrying around the court like a surefooted pirate on the deck of a listing ship, slashing with that big forehand. Youzhny is a more well-balanced player, but he's not a really big server. That helped, because James wasn't a great returner. Objectively, this was an intriguing matchup, but I wasn't in a position to experience it as a connoisseur.

James came out on fire. He always drew inspiration from having us, the team, there on the sideline, and a supportive crowd helped him considerably. He's one of those guys who automatically plays better at home than away, probably because he lacks Roddick's natural taste for confrontation. James blazed through the first two sets, But Youzhny patiently fought his way back into it in the third, and won it.

In the fourth set, I sensed Youzhny's tide still rising. It was lapping at the edges of James's confidence, as well as mine. Having paid close attention to Youzhny's serve all along, I felt he was getting too many free points, exactly the way Roddick had gotten them, with games that often featured two aces and an unreturnable.

But Youzhny is no Roddick, servewise. He was more of a spot server—a guy who could be very effective if he hit his favorite targets and you did nothing to take those places away. With Blake once again standing right on the baseline, to take the ball fast, hard, and on the rise, Youzhny was free to pick his spots, especially out wide.

James needed to make an adjustment, and I knew from experience that I had to be very careful about how I told him. But I wasn't about to sit there thinking I ought to do something while the championship slipped away. At 3–all I signaled James to come to my chair.

"Listen, James," I said. "He's really picking his spots and hitting that wide serve very well. Why don't you just take one step back to buy that extra split second and take his serve moving forward and into it."

There. For once, I laid it all on the table, plain as can be.

James marched back out and—he actually did it. On his next serve, Youzhny went to the well again, wide. And this time James unloaded one of the biggest forehands I've ever seen—he hit it absolutely clean and pure, and although the return sailed a few millimeters long, I stage-whispered, "That's it. That's great, James."

Although James didn't break, his modified return took away Youzhny's ticket to a free lunch. Like similar spot servers, Youzhny could be neutralized if you gave him a different look, or moved back and thereby denied him the ability to slip the ace by you. Unlike a Roddick, Youzhny couldn't just blow it by you unless you allowed it.

James went on to win the fourth set tiebreaker, and the match. It's his highlight Davis Cup match. I was deeply happy for him, and felt a little like the teacher who finally manages to get through to a problem student who's resisted him all the way. I was glad because for all of Blake's stubbornness, the guy has always been there. At times in the past I'd benched him. At times I made him play doubles. He always did whatever I asked, even when I could see in his eyes that he wasn't entirely happy about it.

Everyone on the team shared the feeling; like Andy, James had earned the right to his exquisite moment. And it was an added bonus that with a 2–0 lead, the Bryans would get a chance to do the honors—to clinch the Davis Cup for the U.S. for the first time in over a decade, on home soil.

Even at home, the Bryans often had to play on a court that wasn't best suited to their style; they preferred a slower court than our singles players did, but as important as the Bryans' contribution was, I always had to think of my singles guys first. But the twins' attitude was almost like that of comic book superheroes: *Whatever it takes, Captain, not to worry. We'll get it done.*

And get it done they did. The strange pairing of Andreev and Davydenko gave us some anxious moments in the first set, but the boys pulled out the tiebreaker. Then they steamrolled the Russians, like they had almost every other team that had the misfortune to find themselves across the net from these red, white, and blue doubles maniacs.

The moment Bob Bryan saw his cutoff volley land for a clean winner on match point, he whirled and leaped toward Mike. The two collided in a midair bear hug. Our bench erupted, and seconds later Andy, James Blake, Mardy Fish, and every other player who had taken part in Davis Cup that year (we flew them all in) flowed onto the floor of the arena to join Bob and Mike.

I was told later that I snapped to my feet, as if the captain's director chair in which I'd been sitting had suddenly been hit by a couple thousand volts of electricity. In the USTA box, the suits were clapping one another on the back and exchanging man hugs; the fans were screaming, whistling, and dancing around with their neighbors.

I'm not an overly demonstrative guy, and besides that I felt completely drained as I sought out my counterpart, Shamil Tarpischev, to shake his hand: "Bad luck, well played." Then I started looking around for my wife and daughter, Victoria. What I really remember is standing with them for photos and then holding a giddy Victoria up high to let her play with the confetti that had collected in the big silver bowl of the Davis Cup itself. It's a beautiful trophy; it looks like a giant birthday cake.

I'm not sure it can ever get any better than that for me. I know not everyone shares my passion for Davis Cup, and I know that I won't be Davis Cup captain forever. But I wasn't a tennis player forever, either. When some players are done with their careers, they fade out; tennis becomes a part of their past, something to look back on with nostalgia and pride, but there's also a hole there, permanently. It's like a part of you has died.

It's a great gift to feel as if you're still alive and kicking, and I confess that I never thought that being a "former" pro player can be this good. There are more roads winding away toward a future I can't see. More bridges to cross and, I hope, more moments to savor like that one I experienced in Portland, in the fall of 2007.

Acknowledgments

Mom, I know this won't rank up there with the day I got my driver's license (and you no longer had to ferry me to the ends of the earth, racket bag stuffed in the trunk), but in case you don't already know, you've been our rock and my main source of comfort from day one.

And John, thanks for believing in my ability, despite the bar you set so high for everyone, including yourself.

Mark, you put up with my pestering all those long summer days in Douglaston Manor, and always threw the baseball with me. Is there a better definition of a good older brother?

Dad, you were there at the very start, you sat through every Davis Cup match (usually wearing those goofy suspenders), and even peered over my shoulder while I wrote this, exercising your formidable copy-editing skills. Is "overbearing" too strong a word? But I'm sure you know by now that I wouldn't have it any other way. . . .

Some of my childhood friends became lifelong buddies, and played a significant role as I made my way on the pro tour. They include Paul Palandjian, John Schmitt, Scott Moody, and Alan Van Nostrand. Alan, while our friendship overshadows all else, you may be surprised (check that: "shocked") to hear that you were one heck of an unofficial coach, too.

I had numerous coaches through my junior, college, and pro

careers, many of whom I write about in this book. But I would be remiss not to single out two of them: Tony Palafox, who taught me the basics game, and Dick Gould at Stanford University, from whom I learned much about managing a team and used all of it in my Davis Cup efforts.

The USTA often takes it on the chin, from tennis nuts, coaches, the media, and parents of every stripe. But both as Davis Cup captain and head of player development, I deeply appreciate the good sense, support, enthusiasm, and responsiveness that the organization and its various leaders have always shown toward my desire, ideas, and needs. I owe a special thanks to Arlen Kantarian, former CEO of Pro Tennis at the USTA, for going to bat for me in a big way to help me land my job as Davis Cup captain.

I got my start in television at CBS, through the executive producer of the US Open broadcasts, Bob Monsbach (an assist to my brother John on that one, for suggesting CBS hire me shortly after the untimely and unexpected death of our good friend, Vitas Gerulaitis). And, after thirteen years at ESPN, I feel I've found a second home. I especially want to thank Dennis Denninger, who was my strong supporter early in my broadcasting career, as well as coordinating producer Jamie Reynolds and my longtime producer, Bobby Feller, who *always* has my back. What can I say about Cliff Drysdale, my broadcast booth teammate? I better not say much, because Cliffy will definitely find a way to use it to embarrass me. . . .

My agent at IMG, Sandy Montag, has worked tirelessly and effectively to keep my commentating career chugging along, despite all the other roles and obligations I've taken on.

Byrd Leavell of the Scott Waxman Literary Agency is a guy who knows his tennis. More importantly for me, he also knows books, and this book is the direct result of his vision and enthusiasm for stories that usually being with something like, "Did I ever tell you about the time that . . ."

Sarah Landis at Hyperion was both a guiding light and a joy to work with, despite the fairly tight deadlines we faced writing a book as substantial as this one. And the guy who helped me write it, Peter Bodo, is a true veteran of the tennis wars, and someone with whom I go back far enough to have felt utterly comfortable. I hear they're going to put up a little brass plaque at "our" table at NoHo Star, the Lafayette Street restaurant where Pete and I had so many of the taping sessions that became the essence of *Hardcourt Confidential.* And we never would have gotten this manuscript finished in time were it not for the flying fingers of our two favorite transcibers, Julie C. Rabe and Linda Christiensen.

And to all my friends and the tennis fans I've met along the way . . . thanks, and enjoy.